Making an Impact

by the same author

Mothering Through Domestic Violence
Lorraine Radford and Marianne Hester
ISBN 978 1 84310 473 5

of related interest

The Truth is Longer Than a Lie
Children's Experiences of Abuse and Professional Interventions
Neerosh Mudaly and Chris Goddard
ISBN 978 1 84310 317 2

Domestic Violence and Child Protection
Directions for Good Practice
Edited by Cathy Humphreys and Nicky Stanley
ISBN 978 1 84310 276 2

Talking about Domestic Abuse
A Photo Activity Workbook to Develop Communication
Between Mothers and Young People
Cathy Humphreys, Ravi K. Thiara, Agnes Skamballis and Audrey Mullender
ISBN 978 1 84310 423 0

Talking to My Mum
A Picture Workbook for Workers, Mothers and Children Affected by Domestic Abuse
Cathy Humphreys, Ravi K. Thiara, Agnes Skamballis and Audrey Mullender
ISBN 978 1 84310 422 3

Childhood Experiences of Domestic Violence
Caroline McGee
ISBN 978 1 85302 827 4

Domestic Violence
Guidelines for Research-Informed Practice
Edited by John P. Vincent and Ernest N. Jouriles
ISBN 978 1 85302 854 0

Enhancing the Well-being of Children and Families through Effective
Interventions
International Evidence for Practice
Edited by Colette McAuley, Peter J. Pecora and Wendy Rose
ISBN 978 1 84310 116 1

Making an Impact

Children and Domestic Violence

A Reader

Second Edition

Marianne Hester, Chris Pearson
and Nicola Harwin, with Hilary Abrahams

Jessica Kingsley Publishers
London and Philadelphia

First edition published in 2000

This edition published in 2007
by Jessica Kingsley Publishers
116 Pentonville Road
London N1 9JB, UK
and
400 Market Street, Suite 400
Philadelphia, PA 19106, USA

www.jkp.com

Library of Congress Cataloging in Publication Data
Making an impact : children and domestic violence : a reader / Marianne Hester... [et al.]. -- 2nd ed.
p. cm.
Previously published under the author, Marianne Hester.
Includes bibliographical references and index.
ISBN-13: 978-1-84310-157-4 (pbk.)
ISBN-10: 1-84310-157-2 (pbk.)
1. Family violence--Great Britain. 2. Children and violence--Great Britain. 3. Child welfare--Great Britain. I.
Hester, Marianne, 1955-
HV6626.23.G7H47 2007
362.76'80941--dc22

2006037401

British Library Cataloguing in Publication Data
A CIP catalogue record for this book is available from the British Library

ISBN 978 1 84310 157 4

Printed and bound in Great Britain by
Athenaeum Press, Gateshead, Tyne and Wear

CONTENTS

Chapter Three: The Impact of Domestic Violence on Children

Part Two: The Legal Context

Part Three: Practice Interventions

INTRODUCTION

There has been a growing awareness of the scale of domestic violence and its consequences for women and children, and with this has come increasing public, policy and political concern. Research, practice experience and children's and young people's own accounts all demonstrate that domestic violence has a significant impact on the lives of children and on their current and future wellbeing.

Traditionally, the abuse of women and the abuse of children were examined as separate issues, with services and policies being developed at different stages by different groups, often in isolation. We now have a much better understanding of the interrelationship between domestic violence and child abuse. We know that when a woman is being abused, not only is her parenting capacity likely to be affected, but also there is a heightened probability that her children may be abused. The Farmer and Owen (1995) study, *Child Protection Practice: Private Risks and Public Remedies*, found that in three of five cases where children had suffered physical abuse, neglect or emotional abuse, their mothers were also subject to violence from their male partners. Professionals were found to give little attention to children who were witnessing and living with high levels of violence. Domestic violence was a feature of most of the cases with the worst outcomes for children.

The Department of Health originally commissioned the development of this reader and the associated training resource in 1998 to increase awareness of the impact on children of domestic violence and to develop professional understanding of how best to help and support. The materials were developed by Barnardo's, the National Society for the Prevention of Cruelty to Children (NSPCC) and the Domestic Violence Research Group at the University of Bristol, with the help of a multidisciplinary advisory group. The reader was written for individual study and to provide the necessary underpinning knowledge for both trainers and individuals taking part in a programme of training concerning children and domestic violence.

Since the reader and training pack were first published, there have been major changes in legislation and policy, and our understanding has developed further as a result of significant research programmes. The policy and practice context within which services are delivered is changing dramatically in response to the Every Child Matters agenda, with an increased emphasis on improving outcomes for all children, on recognizing that safeguarding and promoting children's welfare is everybody's responsibility, and on developing integrated services built around the needs of children. A supplement to the training pack (Barnardo's, NSPCC and University of Bristol 2003), available from the NSPCC publications unit, was published in 2004 to take account of changes in policy and legislation, and now the reader has been substantially revised and updated.

This second edition of the reader provides an updated and comprehensive review of research into domestic violence and the consequences for children, as well as for practice, and an overview of the relevant legislation. Research and practice originating in the UK are emphasized, with reference to research and practice from other countries where especially relevant. This new edition also addresses work with women who have experienced domestic violence. When the first edition was published, insufficient data were available on this important subject.

The first part of the reader is intended to show the links that exist between living in a context of domestic violence and the abuse of children. It begins with an overview of domestic violence, what it is and whom it involves. This provides an insight into the dynamics of this form of abuse and lays the basis for understanding its consequent impacts. Statistical data have been included from the British Crime Survey 2001 (Walby and Allen 2004).

The second part deals with key pieces of legislation, both criminal and civil, which have a bearing on children and their carers who experience domestic violence. There is a focus on the relevant aspects of the legislation and discussion of the implications for practice. Since the first edition, there has been a significant programme of legislation with implications for those experiencing domestic violence and in relation to safeguarding and promoting children's welfare, including the Domestic Violence, Crimes and Victims Act 2004, the Children Act 2004, and the Adoption and Fostering Act 2002, and these are discussed in Part Two.

The third and final part provides detailed overviews and discussion of practice issues in relation to children, male perpetrators, women and multi-agency working.

It is hoped that the material in the reader and in the training resource together will enable professionals working with children and their families to develop informed and appropriately sophisticated responses that safeguard and promote the welfare of children living in circumstances of domestic violence.

Language

Throughout the training pack and the reader, the term 'black and minority ethnic' is used to describe African, Caribbean and Asian people. There are more specific references in some case studies.

The term 'victim' is not generally used, as it is seen to have negative connotations, although we also recognize that women experiencing domestic violence are being victimized by their violent partners. The term 'survivor of domestic violence' conveys a more positive outcome for women and children, and this is used alongside 'victim/survivor' as the preferred terminology.

PART ONE

Children and Domestic Violence

CHAPTER ONE

DOMESTIC VIOLENCE: WHAT IS IT?

Having knowledge and understanding of what domestic violence is about and the effect it has on those involved is crucial for practitioners to be able to work with 'children and domestic violence'. Without knowledge about the dynamics of domestic violence, the actions of those concerned can be difficult to understand, and the behaviour of mothers may appear contradictory or unreasonable.

1.1 Terminology

A variety of terms have been used to talk about domestic violence, such as 'family violence', 'domestic abuse', 'violence from men to known women' and 'domestic violence'. Increasingly, the term 'domestic abuse' is being adopted by agencies, local authorities and domestic violence forums. To different degrees, all of these terms have their limitations. We have decided to use the term 'domestic violence', not because it reflects most accurately the phenomenon we are discussing but because it is still the most commonly used. Consequently, a number of issues need to be considered in relation to the term:

- The word 'domestic' might appear to limit the context for the violence to those who live together, whereas violence from male partners often continues after women leave (Binney, Harkell and Nixon [1981] 1988; Hester and Radford 1996; Walby and Allen 2004).

- The word 'violence' may indicate exclusively physical abuse, whereas individuals subject to domestic violence experience a range of different forms of abuse from their partners, not all of which are, in themselves, inherently 'violent' (Barron, Harwin and Singh 1992; Hague and Malos 1993). When we talk about violence in this reader, we include both directly violent and more indirectly abusive behaviours such as physical, sexual, emotional and verbal abuse.

- 'Domestic violence' masks the issue of gender, the fact that perpetrators tend to be men and their victims usually women (Dobash and Dobash 2000; Mirrlees-Black 1999; Walby and Allen 2004).

- 'Domestic violence' is violence or abuse from one adult to another that takes place within the context of a close relationship, as intimate partner or family member (Inter-Ministerial Group 2005). It masks the interrelationship between such abuse and abuse experienced by children (see Chapter Two).

1.2 What is domestic violence?

A common definition has been adopted for use across government departments in England, which sees domestic violence as 'Any incident of threatening behaviour, violence or abuse (psychological, physical, sexual, financial or emotional) between adults who are or have been intimate partners or family members, regardless of gender or sexuality' (Home Office 2006). This definition recognizes the range of behaviours involved in domestic violence and incorporates both same-sex and heterosexual relationships as well as wider family relationships. However, it does not stress the coercive control elements that are an important characteristic of domestic violence. In this reader, we take domestic violence to mean any violent or abusive behaviour (whether physical, sexual, psychological, emotional, verbal, financial, etc.) that is used by one person to control and dominate another with whom they have or have had a relationship.

Most studies have focused on domestic violence in heterosexual relationships, where it has been found that the vast majority of cases involve violence from men to women (Dobash and Dobash 2000; Mirrlees-Black 1999; Walby and Allen 2004). For instance, the National Children's Home (NCH) Action for Children study suggested that 90–97 per cent of domestic violence is from men to women (Abrahams 1994, p.6), and a national 24-hour snapshot of domestic violence incidents reported to the police found that 81 per cent of callers were women (Stanko 2000). Where it is women who are violent to male partners, it is often as a means of self-defence and in response to long-term violence and abuse from their partners (Dobash and Dobash 2000; Hague and Malos 1993).

Domestic violence can also take place in same-sex relationships, although the limited research in this area suggests that there may be differences in comparison with the way in which domestic violence manifests heterosexual relationships, at least where help-seeking is concerned (Lobel 1986; Radford, Kelly and Hester 1996; Taylor and Chandler 1995). Moreover, domestic violence may involve the wider family network, for instance abuse by in-laws (Batsleer *et al.* 2002; Bhatti-Sinclair 1994).

In this reader, the main focus is on violence in relationships between men and women and the abuse of children in this context. We largely talk about men as perpetrators and women on the receiving end of the violence and abuse.

1.3 Is domestic violence 'mutual'?

It is sometimes argued that domestic violence is *mutual* between male and female partners or even a phenomenon directed mainly by women towards their male partners. Many practitioners are probably aware of this perspective but do not know its origins. Straus, Gelles and Steinmetz (1980) in the USA carried out research into domestic violence using an instrument called the Conflict Tactics Scale (CTS) and involving self-report questionnaires. Their research led to results that suggested that men and women were equally violent in heterosexual relationships and that a 'battered husband syndrome' existed with at least a similar extent to domestic violence against women. However, the original CTS relied on a hierarchy of behaviours that omitted the context and anticipated effect of a particular violent act, ignoring that in reality a threat to use physical violence may be more controlling than the physical act itself and failing to distinguish whether an act of violence is used to control or as a means of self-defence (Dobash and Dobash 1992; Nazroo 1995; Saunders 1988). The CTS, without examining the context of the replies, therefore provided an inaccurate picture of the main direction and impact of the violence. Straus and Gelles now acknowledge that there are problems with the instrument, and some modifications have been made (Gelles and Loseke 1993; Hyden 1994). However, the instrument continues to be used quite widely, especially in the USA.

In the UK, the CTS approach has also been used in the British Crime Survey to assess frequency of domestic violence, although with increasing recognition that 'the CTS concentrates on the perpetrator's actions to the exclusion of the impact and consequences' and 'tends to generate a spurious gender symmetry that vanishes if and when the impact of the act is brought into focus' (Walby and Allen 2004, p.37).

1.4 How much?

Although there are no national data in the UK concerning the general incidence of domestic violence, the most robust source of data for England and Wales is that provided by the 2001 British Crime Survey self-completion module on interpersonal violence (Walby and Allen 2004). The survey explores non-sexual domestic violence, sexual assault and stalking and includes aspects of domestic violence that are frequently hidden, such as financial and emotional abuse, isolation, threats and intimidation. In an attempt to rectify the inherent bias involved in the use of the CTS approach (see Section 1.3), the 2001 British Crime Survey collected data both within the CTS framework and on a separate scale of impact. It was estimated that while one in five women and one in ten men were likely to experience some form of non-sexual domestic threat or force after the age of 16 years, women were much more likely to be severely impacted and 'women are the overwhelming majority of the most heavily abused group' (Walby and Allen 2004, p.vii). We do not know how many women with children separate from male partners because of domestic violence, but a study based on the British Crime Survey findings suggests that at least 29 per cent of divorces are due to domestic violence (Walby 2004), and crime statistics show that domestic violence is the most common context for the homicide of women (Povey 2004).

Despite the detrimental effects on the individuals experiencing domestic violence, which the studies highlight, the behaviours involved may not necessarily be deemed to amount to the commission of a criminal offence. Physical assault and rape may in some instances be deemed to constitute 'common assault', 'actual bodily harm' or 'grievous bodily harm', and ongoing harassment after a woman is no longer with her violent partner may be considered under the Protection from Harassment Act 1997 (see Chapter Five for legislation details):

- Of 427 women completing surveys in general practitioners' (GPs) surgeries in Gateshead and South Tyneside, over a quarter (27%) indicated that they had experienced violent behaviour at home (Westmarland, Hester and Reid 2004).

- In 2001–02, 47 per cent of female homicide victims in England and Wales – two women per week – were killed by their present or former partner, compared with 5 per cent of male victims (Povey 2004).

- The Exeter Family Study (Cockett and Tripp 1994) found that one in four separated women with children had separated from their partners because of domestic violence. Earlier research suggested that one in three marriages may have broken down partly as a result of domestic violence (Borkowski, Murch and Walker 1983). Between 40 and 60 per cent of separated or divorced women have experienced violence in their relationships (Hughes 1992).

- In a random-sample survey in London of 1000 men and women, 30 per cent of women reported having been subject at some time to physical violence more severe than being grabbed, pushed or shaken from a (current or former) boyfriend or male partner, 27 per cent had been injured, 27 per cent had been threatened with violence, 23 per cent had been raped, and 37 per cent had suffered mental cruelty (Mooney 1994, 2000).

- Figures extrapolated from the 1991 British Crime Survey (which excluded both sexual and emotional abuse) suggest that one in ten women who have lived with a male partner have experienced domestic violence from their partners at some time in their lives. The 2001 British Crime Survey reported that 45 per cent of women and 26 per cent of men aged between 16 and 59 years could recall being subjected to domestic violence (abuse, threats or force, sexual victimization or stalking) at least once during their lifetime. For 37 per cent of women, abuse continued in one form or another, including stalking, after leaving the relationship (Walby and Allen 2004).

- In 2003–04, 18,569 women and 23,084 children were accommodated in refuges in England. In a census taken in English refuges on 2 November 2004, 2914 women and 3555 children were living in refuges; 45 per cent of the children were under five years of age.

- Twenty-five per cent of the assaults recorded by the police are cases of domestic violence (Mirrlees-Black, Mayhew and Percy 1996).

- A survey of 484 women in Surrey's shopping centres found that one in four women defined themselves as having experienced domestic violence from a male partner/ex-partner after the age of 18 years (Dominy and Radford 1996).

- A study of domestic violence and the impact on costs in Hackney, London, estimated that one in nine women in the borough in 1996 had experienced domestic violence (Stanko et al. 1998).

1.5 Accounts of survivors, abusers and witnesses

Our knowledge about domestic violence comes from the accounts of survivors and to a lesser extent from the accounts of perpetrators of domestic violence and witnesses (e.g. Dobash and Dobash 1980, 1992; Dobash et al. 2000; Hanmer and Saunders 1993; Hearn 1996a, 1996b; Hoff 1990; Homer, Leonard and Taylor 1984; Kelly 1988; Pahl 1985; Thurston and Beynon 1995; Women's Aid Federation of England 1989). We know from these accounts that the perception of the perpetrator and the perception of the woman he has abused often differ: perpetrators may not see their behaviour as abusive or controlling, in the way the individual on the receiving end does (Dobash et al. 2000; Hearn 1996a, 1996b). Hearn points out, based on his interviews with men who have been violent to women they know: 'Men generally define violence in much narrower terms than do women. The paradigm form of violence for men is physical violence. But even here certain kinds of physical violence are often excluded or referred to in passing' (Hearn 1996a, pp.27–28).

Perpetrators are likely to deny and cover up their abusive behaviour and may, therefore, appear as quite different people in public than at home. Many women have described their violent partners as appearing very 'charming' at work, to the police, in court and so on, but generally aggressive and abusive at home. An Asian woman, whose marriage had been arranged, describes how her husband appeared 'charming' to others but was 'violent and cruel' to her:

My family and the people who arranged the marriage did not know that he was violent and cruel. We were led to believe that the family he belonged to, including him, were all good respectable people, which is why I married him. We married very quickly once introduced, and I was not able to get to know him beforehand, but he was a 'charmer' able to convince people into believing he was nice.

(Bowstead, Lall and Rashid 1995, p.11)

In the report of the Bridge Consultancy Service on the death of five-year-old Sukina Hammond by her father, who was also a domestic violence perpetrator, it is pointed out that many apparently conflicting descriptions were attributed to the father by the professionals involved:

In meeting with professionals at the centre of the case, we were struck by the very wide range of descriptions given of Sukina's father. For example we heard him described as 'gentle, vicious, flamboyant, withdrawn, aggressive, deferential, caring, cold'. It is quite an extraordinary range of descriptions in respect of one individual.

(Quoted in Harris Hendriks, Black and Kaplan 1993, p.31)

The accounts of survivors provide the nearest we will get to the truth about what domestic violence involves, how it feels and what the implications are (Hague, Mullender, Aris and Dear 2002; Kelly 1988; Kelly and Radford 1996). It is therefore important to take the experiences of survivors of domestic violence as the starting point for definition, understanding and the development of realistic practice, bearing in mind that 'experience' is a complex phenomenon, perhaps remembered selectively or in stages and perhaps presented as various versions. This means including in any definition of domestic violence the wide range of behaviours that women have described as abusive and controlling (what Kelly (1988) has described as a 'continuum' of violence). It also means taking into account the impact of such violence on the individuals concerned and how that impact may be influenced by, for example, social, cultural or religious contexts (Batsleer *et al.* 2002; Bhatti-Sinclair 1994; Mama 1996).

Domestic violence includes physical assault, sexual abuse, rape, threats and intimidation, humiliating and controlling behaviour, withholding of finances, deprivation, isolation, belittling and constantly criticizing (see also Department of Health 2000). Perpetrators may use any one of these behaviours, and usually use a mixture of these, to achieve control. Kirkwood (1993, p.58) describes this as a 'web of abuse' in which differing types of behaviours act to reinforce each other to provide the perpetrator with total coercive control of every aspect of the victim's life. Perpetrators may also be aided in their abuse by other family members or friends or even agencies. As Amina Mama outlines, talking in this instance about black women: 'Many women are in fact multiply abused; at the hands of their partners and the police, or their partners and his relatives, or their partners and their employers' (Mama 1996, p.11).

Domestic violence is not limited to any particular class, ethnic or social group but is perpetrated by men against women across the social spectrum (Hague and Malos 2005; Smith 1989). However, the experience of domestic violence may differ as a result of these different contexts (Hester, Kelly and Radford 1996; Kelly 1994; Mama 1996). For instance:

> The economic and power relations are very different when one is considering domestic violence against a middle class but financially dependent wife, as compared to domestic violence against a single mother of three in a local authority flat, or violence against a professional working woman.

> *(Mama 1996, p.46)*

It can be particularly shocking to hear women describe the often gross physical and/or sexual abuse to which they have been subjected to by their male partners. It has to be recognized, however, that the less obvious behaviours – the emotional abuse, constant criticism, undermining, humiliation, isolation and living in fear – may have equally detrimental consequences upon the health and wellbeing of women. These more psychological forms of abuse may serve to destroy a woman's sense of self or can be used to allude to even worse abuses, often involving (verbal or non-verbal) threats to kill.

> ...mental torture can be just as bad. Not being able to have any friends or freedom or just being totally put down that you almost believe that you're such a bad person really.

> *(Hester and Radford, unpublished interview)*

> It was a look...and if he looked at me I knew, you know, it was just a look. [Previously] he had followed me up and threw me on the bed and had his hands round my throat, and he said: 'You know I can kill you.' And that was the look in his face...that's from where the look came...

> *(Hester and Radford, unpublished interview)*

The abusive behaviour usually escalates over time, and in particular escalates when women attempt to leave or in other ways assert their individuality and strength. As one woman survivor describes: 'I was becoming myself again... I had moved away from the kind of person he had all this control over. And as he was losing his control over me, his violence was getting worse' (Hester and Radford, unpublished interview).

1.6 When does it begin?

Although domestic violence can begin at any time during a relationship, many studies indicate that violence tends to start early on, in particular once the relationship has become 'formalized' through the couple living together or through marriage (Hester and Radford 1992; Kelly 1988; Pahl 1985). Walby and Allen (2004) suggest that if repeated acts of violence are a feature of the relationship, then for 49 per cent of women this will emerge within the first year of starting to live together, and for 19 per cent of women violence will begin within the first three months. This pattern may be explained in terms of the woman now being perceived to 'belong' to the man. It is exemplified by Kiranjit Ahluwalia's description of her own violent relationship, where her husband-to-be was charming until the moment they were married. As soon as the marriage had taken place, he started to be physically, psychologically and eventually also sexually violent towards her in his quest to control all aspects of her life (Ahluwalia and Gupta 1997).

For many women, violence from their husband or male partner is likely to begin or increase at the time of pregnancy or when the children are small (Hoff 1990; McGee 2000; Mezey and Bewley 1997; Mooney 2000; Pahl 1985). Abrahams (1994), for example, outlines how this was very much the case for the women in the NCH Action for Children survey and increased their vulnerability as a result:

> The majority of the respondents in this survey were…not only young women but young mothers when they first experienced violence from their partners. Being young themselves and having one or more small children of their own means that they were vulnerable emotionally…they were also vulnerable materially… A significant number of the mothers who were interviewed said that the violence had begun around the time of pregnancy or babyhood, and others claimed that it had started once their children had become toddlers.
>
> *(Abrahams 1994, p.23)*

1.7 Domestic violence is often ongoing

It is easy to assume that once a domestic violence perpetrator is no longer living with his wife or partner, then the violence will stop. However, that is unlikely to be the case. It has to be recognized that violent male partners are likely to continue to abuse and harass their ex-partners and will use any situation where both are present or in contact with each other (e.g. via contact arrangements for the children) to do so (Hester and Radford 1996; Humphreys and Thiara 2002; Johnston 1992; Kelly 1988; Radford and Hester 2006). As indicated earlier, the 2001 British Crime Survey found that for more than a third of women experiencing domestic violence (37%), the abuse continued in one form or another, including stalking, after leaving the relationship (Walby and Allen 2004). In Hester and Radford's (1996) study of child contact arrangements in circumstances of domestic violence, all but three of the

53 mothers interviewed had been assaulted or abused further during child contact negotiations and arrangements after separation. Malos and Hague (1993a) also provide instances of continued violence and abuse after families had been rehoused.

Violence may escalate and thus become especially apparent around the time of separation. As a result, it may appear that such 'separation violence' is a one-off. As Peter Jaffe points out: 'Men's violence may be minimised as only an emotional reaction to the separation' (Jaffe 1996, p.24). Instead, physical violence at the time of separation is likely to be an extension of abusive behaviour that the perpetrator was already using during the relationship. Professionals may want to emphasize 'separation violence' because that feels easier to deal with or to dismiss. As a family court welfare officer (now a family court adviser) pointed out in a national survey, there may be a comfort in thinking that the violence is 'merely' a product of the immediate separation and that as professionals they therefore do not have to cope with any history or further instances of violence (Hester, Pearson and Radford 1997).

1.8 Impact of domestic violence

Domestic violence may have a considerable impact on both women and children. The impact on children is discussed in Chapter Three.

Violence from male partners may leave women with severe and permanent physical damage and affect their mental health. There are large cost implications (both monetary and social), which are beginning to be recognized by the Department of Health and other areas of public health. Guidance has been produced aimed at encouraging health authorities and trusts to review existing practices and to put in place consistent practices towards domestic violence (Department of Health 2000); discussions are ongoing regarding the implementation of routine enquiry (Hester and Westmarland 2005). None the less, marked discrepancies continue to exist between policy and practice. Service users have acknowledged that there have been improvements but still feel that health professionals often fail to hear their voices and meet their needs (Abrahams 2004; Bossy and Coleman 2000; Hague, Mullender, Aris and Dear 2002; Humphreys and Thiara 2002). Studies that have been carried out in the UK indicate the following:

- Abused women are more likely than accident victims to have internal injuries (Burge 1989).

- Over half the women interviewed in Northern Ireland in a Department of Health and Social Services-sponsored study said they needed medical treatment for their injuries as a result of domestic violence; 39 per cent required hospital treatment at least once. A third were hit while they were pregnant (McWilliams and McKiernan 1993).

- In Mooney's (2000) survey in London, 8 per cent of women had to stay overnight in hospital as a result of violence, 20 per cent took time off work, 46 per cent suffered depression or a loss of self-confidence and 51 per cent said they felt worried, anxious or nervous.

- Individuals experiencing domestic violence are more likely to be injured than other victims of violence. Nearly a third of cases reported to the early 1990s British Crime Survey required medical attention; 69 per cent of incidents led to an injury, and 13 per cent resulted in broken bones (Mirrlees-Black *et al.* 1996). In the 2001 British Crime Survey, 75 per cent of women reported sustaining injuries following their worst incidence of domestic violence, of whom a quarter did not seek medical attention, 8 per cent suffered broken bones or teeth and 21 per cent suffered severe bruising. Only 30 per cent sought medical help (Walby and Allen 2004).

- Stanko *et al.* (1998), in a study of domestic violence in Hackney, London, found that the estimated costs of providing assistance, support and advice for domestic violence were £7.5 million. The real costs were social as much as economic and were borne by children as much as their mothers. Walby (2004), on the basis of the British Crime Survey, has estimated the overall cost of domestic violence, including the cost in human and emotional terms to those experiencing it, to be £23 billion a year in the UK.

The impact of domestic violence varies greatly for each woman and may depend on the form and frequency of the violence, although the impact can be similar regardless of whether there is physical violence or more emotional or psychological abuse. As outlined above, the range of impact from physical abuse can include injuries, disability and death (Dobash and Dobash 1992).

Apart from these direct physical forms of harm, many women also experience psychological effects, including loss of self-respect, low self-worth, feelings of hopelessness, depression, loss of confidence, dependence on the perpetrator, and minimization or even denial of the violence (Kirkwood 1993; Radford and Hester 2006; Walker 1984). The links between domestic violence and women's emotional wellbeing and mental health are now well established (Barron 2004; Coleman and Guildford 2001) and have been evident in a range of research. In Maynard's (1985) examination of social work case files, all the women who were experiencing domestic violence were referred to as lethargic and lacking in energy; for some of the women, a pattern emerged of depression, committal to mental hospital and sometimes attempted suicide. The possible impact of domestic violence on women's mental health was echoed by McGibbon, Cooper and Kelly's (1989) London study, in which some women indicated they were feeling depressed, isolated and not coping, especially as they were often deprived of any family support. Humphreys and Thiara (2003) found symptoms of emotional disturbance, including depression, panic attacks, suicide attempts, anorexia, obsessive behaviour patterns, high anxiety and hypervigilance. The British Crime Survey found that 37 per cent of women suffered emotional or mental problems as a consequence of domestic violence (Walby and Allen 2004). It has been found that women may be prescribed tranquillizers in order to live through the abuse, and concern has been expressed about the apparent readiness of doctors to prescribe these drugs without investigating fully the root cause of the problems (McGee 2000; Mullender 1996a).

There is a tendency by professionals to see incidents of domestic violence in relation to a hierarchy of severity, where physical violence is perceived as the most extreme and emotional or psychological abuse is rated as less severe. Clearly this echoes what the courts perceive as actual evidence (Hester 2006a; Hester and Radford 1996; Hester *et al.* 1997). This is similar to the development of knowledge over the past couple of decades concerning child protection, which started with the 'battered baby' and is now beginning to explore the impact of emotional abuse (Glaser and Prior 1997). It has to be recognized that where actual impact of the violence and abusive behaviour is concerned, it is often the emotional and psychological abuse that women talk about as having the greatest and longest lasting impact. (This may similarly be the case for children – see Chapters Three and Nine.) The psychological effects can be even more difficult to deal with than physical injury, partly because they are so hidden and therefore difficult to prove and have taken seriously:

> It was only bruises I could show... I can't show my insides and say like, I'm totally messed up, the children are messed up, I can't do that.
>
> *(Hester and Radford, unpublished interview)*

Although bruises and broken bones fade and mend, the emotional impacts, especially the sense of worthlessness and fear, can be very long-lasting and much more difficult to overcome (Dobash and Dobash 1992; Hague and Malos 1993; Hoff 1990). The implications for supporting the women concerned are discussed in Chapter Twelve.

The psychological impact of domestic violence has been found to have parallels with the impact of torture and imprisonment on hostages (Graham, Rawlings and Rimini 1988; Herman 2001). Graham and colleagues suggest that women's experiences in violent relationships can be understood through the model of the Stockholm syndrome, 'which has been developed to account for the paradoxical psychological responses of hostages to their captors' (Graham *et al.* 1988, p.218):

> The model shows how the psychological characteristics observed in battered women resemble those of hostages, suggesting that these characteristics are the *result* of being in a life-threatening relationship rather than the *cause* of being in the relationship. Second, the model uses a power analysis that shows

how extreme power imbalances between an abusive husband and battered wife, as between captor and hostage, can lead to strong emotional bonding.

(Graham et al. 1988, p.218)

The experience of captivity, which brings the hostage into extended contact with the captor, thus creates a relationship in which the perpetrator becomes the most powerful person in the life of the captive. The exercise of coercive control over every aspect of life, isolation from all other contacts and feelings of terror and helplessness lead to a loss of self-identity and dependence on the captor, who is also seen as the source of any slight privileges or amelioration in the conditions of captivity. The captor becomes the only permitted emotional contact, beliefs and attitudes change to reflect his beliefs, and an emotional bond of identification and attachment develops. Applying this approach specifically to contexts of domestic abuse, Herman argues that:

> The same traumatic bonding may occur between a battered woman and her abuser. The repeated experience of terror and reprieve, especially within the isolated context of a love relationship, may result in a feeling of intense, almost worshipful dependence on an all powerful, godlike authority. The victim may live in terror of his wrath, but she may also view him as the source of strength, guidance and life itself. The relationship may take on an extraordinary quality of specialness.

(Herman 2001, p.92)

Moreover, the pre-existence of an emotional bond on the part of the woman allows the situation to become particularly entrenched. Whereas hostage-taking is sudden and unexpected, a woman who experiences domestic violence is 'taken prisoner gradually, by courtship' (Herman 2001, p.82).

Seeing domestic violence in this way may help us to understand what is going on when women behave in a seemingly contradictory way, unable to leave violent relationships and often returning even after they have left – in particular, the way perpetrators often isolate and undermine women, thus rendering them dependent, the way perpetrators terrorize through unpredictable threats of violence and death, leading women to be ever watchful and appeasing, and the way perpetrators at times appear kind, thus creating the hope that it will be possible to rescue the relationship. Women attempting to survive and cope in such circumstances may feel that staying with the violent partner will appease him and thus lessen the violence, or the women might be optimistic about the future of their loving life together and thereby minimize the danger that they are in.

1.9 Impact of domestic violence on parenting

For mothers living with violent and abusive partners, protection of their children is often a prime concern, although their actions may not necessarily be perceived by professionals as protective. This can lead to inappropriate and punitive interventions. Milner (1996) provides an example of how a mother's attempt to keep her three-month-old son quiet in order to prevent violence to him led the mother, and not the abuser, to be prosecuted:

> One man with convictions for violence regularly beat his partner, including hitting her with a spade, and attacked his 3-month-old son when he was fretful. The mother gave the son a sleeping pill to keep him quiet and safe from assault before reporting matters to the police. Remarkably, the man was not prosecuted while the mother was charged with ill-treating her child. Her child was taken into care and she was sentenced to a 2-year probation order.

> *(Milner 1996, p.121)*

Both Hester and Radford's (1996) study of child contact arrangements and McGee's (2000) study of mothers and children living with domestic violence found that mothers generally wanted contact between children and their fathers to take place, but would attempt to stop contact if they felt this posed a danger to the children. Rather than seeing this as protective, however, the courts and child welfare professionals would tend to see the women as obstructive or manipulative (Radford and Hester 2006). Women may also contact social services in order to obtain help with protection of their children and yet might not disclose the domestic violence in the fear that their children will then be taken away. As Kelly (1994) points out, women will instead suggest that they are 'unable to cope', leading to them being seen as inadequate mothers.

For some women, the physical and emotional effects of the domestic violence can have a detrimental impact on their mothering and relationships with their children. Mothers may therefore appear to professionals as inadequate or unable to cope. It has to be recognized, however, that this is likely to be a direct effect of the domestic violence and that with support, and in particular help to be safe, mothers can resume parenting of their children (discussed further in Chapter Eight).

Holden and Ritchie (1991), in their US study, found that mothers might be inconsistent in their parenting due to the abuse they were experiencing from their partners. In some cases, the abuse prevented mothers from maintaining standards of care or led them to perceive childcare as more stressful compared with women not experiencing violence. Some mothers were also found to act in more punitive ways towards their children in the presence of a violent man; this finding was echoed by Brandon and Lewis (1996). A number of the mothers in the NCH study described the effects of domestic violence on them as mothers, including losing their self-confidence as mothers, being emotionally drained and with little to give their children, taking out their frustrations on their children, and experiencing an emotional distance between themselves and their children (Abrahams 1994). The mothers pointed out how these effects could be compounded by the difficult behaviour of the children at a time when they too could be trying to come to terms with the violence they were witnessing and experiencing. These effects were echoed by McGee's research, which found in addition that once they had left the violent man, 'most mothers felt that they had in fact become closer to their children because of everything they had been through together' (McGee 2000, p.48).

Kelly (1996) has suggested that the impact of domestic violence on mothering might include women being forced to make difficult choices, such as leaving without the children in order to protect themselves or their children. Violence against the children from mothers can at times be understood as a means of protecting the children from harsher treatment from their male partners or because of their own sense of frustration or distress. Kelly also points out that the abuse of the woman and her daily caring for the children might in some instances be connected so closely that the impact of the violence on her mothering could be especially powerful (Kelly 1996, p.130). This might include situations where:

- children are conceived through rape

- pregnancies are used as a means of control

- children are encouraged or choose to side with the man

- children join in the abuse or replicate the man's behaviour.

All of these can lead women to feel ambiguities and contradictions about their children. Kelly argues that it is therefore essential for women to be given time and space to explore these issues.

1.10 Parenting by violent and abusive fathers

Another aspect that needs to be taken into account is parenting by violent and abusive fathers. Holden and Ritchie (1991) found that children were more likely than other children to have to cope with negative fathering from the domestic violence perpetrator. In Holden and Ritchie's study of women and children in American refuges and a comparison group of women, the violent men were reported as being more irritable, less involved in child rearing, less physically affectionate and using more negative control techniques such as physical punishment than men in the comparison group. Harne (2004), in a study of violent fathers' own views and perceptions regarding their parenting, found that fathers who looked after their children while the relationship was still ongoing were often deliberately mentally or physically cruel to their children, rationalizing this by saying that the children were too demanding, 'annoyed' them or failed to live up to their expectations of how their children should be. They had a sense of ownership of the children, which also led them to insist on contact even when they knew that the children were terrified of them. They tended not to be prepared to consider or prioritize the children's own needs or wishes while living with them or post-separation. McGee's (2000) interviews with children indicated that fathers used a variety of controlling behaviours and emotional and physical abuse towards their children, and the children spoke of being scared, wary, embarrassed or ashamed of their fathers.

In Hester and Radford's (1996) study of child contact arrangements, fathers were often reported to lack parenting skills or interest in caring for children, leading in some instances to dangerous or even deadly situations for the children concerned. Yet they also found that professionals are often very optimistic about men's parenting skills, while scrutinizing women's parenting in much greater detail (see also Chapter Eight and Farmer and Owen 1995). McGee found similarly that 'these men [perpetrators] appear confident that their own parenting skills are above reproach and have no fear of the consequences of others learning about their violence' (McGee 2000, p.219).

1.11 Staying/leaving

Despite the impact of domestic violence as described above, some professionals still find it difficult to understand why women do not leave a violent partner or why they return to the violent relationship once they have left. The research points to two main ways of understanding the decision-making processes of women who are being abused by their male partners:

- learned helplessness and the cycle of battering

- use of active strategies for survival and coping.

LEARNED HELPLESSNESS

In a highly contentious approach, it has been argued by Lenora Walker (1984) that the reason women stay in violent relationships is because they become locked into a 'cycle of battering' through 'learned helplessness'. Walker describes this 'cycle of battering' as having three stages, which are repeated over and over again. There is the initial build-up of tension, which is released by a violent episode and followed by reconciliation and sweetness – until tension builds up again, and so on. Women end up responding to the different phases of the cycle, victimized into helplessness and ever hopeful that the reconciliation-and-sweetness phase will predominate. This model has led to the so-called 'battered women's syndrome', used as a defence in criminal and other proceedings in North America, the UK[1] and elsewhere (Dobash and Dobash 1992; Quaid and Itzin 2000).

Although Walker's model may seem to reflect the experience of some of the women abused by male partners, it misses out many of the aspects that women describe. 'Learned helplessness' presents a passive view of the victimized wife, and yet women in violent relationships are seldom passive:

Generally, they were always scheming about how to stop the battering, e.g.
by examining their own behaviour or ways of escaping the situation, by considering how they could get and keep some money. They took steps to please
their mates and to satisfy their demands; they protected and took care of their
children.

(Hoff 1990, p.64)

The women in this study were also found to be actively engaged in trying to deal
with violence and seeking outside assistance with these efforts. These women were
neither helpless nor hopeless. Although they did speak of the negative effects of
living with violence, most had considerable strengths and held many positive views
about themselves, despite the harm and degradation they had suffered (Dobash *et al.*
2000, pp.94–95).

Furthermore, the 'cycle of battering' presents the violence as part of a regular or
regularized pattern, and yet women describe their experiences of abuse from their
male partners as often unpredictable or irregular (and therefore even more controlling) and the outcome as neither reconciliation nor sweetness. As Lee Ann Hoff
found in her interviews with women who had experienced domestic violence:

Some beatings occurred in the middle of the night when totally unantici-
pated. After the first beating there were no routine pleas for forgiveness, but
rather diminishing remorse by the man. Also, some incidents were not remembered by the man because he was drunk, or they were denied outright.

(Hoff 1990, p.65)

Finally, 'learned helplessness' presents the women's situation as a form of individualized psychological trait, where it is the woman who ends up as the problem, rather
than her circumstances and the violence and abuse she faces. Consequently, professional intervention is likely to focus on enabling *her* to change, for instance by
offering her assertiveness training, rather than dealing with her need for real
material support in the form of housing, finance and stopping her partner from being
able to continue his violence and abuse against her. As the Dobashes point out: 'An
explanation of the behaviour of women trapped in violent relationships does not
require the specification of unique psychological traits associated with learned helplessness and a battered woman syndrome' (Dobash and Dobash 1992, p.233).
Instead:

Women's efforts to 'manage' violent men and their difficulty in escaping violence must be understood in the wider context of a moral climate that places
responsibility for family problems on women and their own ambivalence
about the man and their relationship with him and in a world of financial dependence and other factors that make it difficult for women to leave and live
an independent existence.

(Dobash et al. 2000, pp.94–95)

USE OF STRATEGIES FOR SURVIVAL AND COPING

Women are faced with complex choices when they are making decisions about leaving violent partners. For each woman, those decisions are dependent on the particular circumstances she faces, such as:

- perceived dangerousness (he will kill her if she leaves; or, he will kill her if she does not leave)
- her access to money, housing and other resources
- the (anticipated or actual) reaction of family and friends
- the (anticipated or actual) reaction of the agencies she approaches
- her emotional attachment to her partner.

The potential outcomes of some or all of these aspects are crucial to women's attempts to survive and cope in the immediate or longer term. At the same time, a particular event – a 'final straw' – may precipitate that she leaves, and she may realize that 'solutions to the man's violence do not reside in a change of [her] own behaviour' (Dobash and Dobash 1992, p.230). In relation to the women in Hoff's study, these 'final-straw' events included 'fear that he would kill her; that she would kill herself; fear for her children or family; recognition that there is no hope for change; the shock of a particular beating; the horror of being beaten while pregnant' (Hoff 1990, p.63).

In the NCH Action for Children survey (Abrahams 1994), mothers gave the reasons shown in Table 1.1 why they found it difficult to leave their violent partner permanently.

Table 1.1 Reasons given for women finding it difficult to leave a violent partner permanently (Abrahams 1994, reproduced with permission)

Reason (n = 102)	%
Thought he would change	72
Afraid of what he might do	63
Didn't want to leave the home	58
Didn't want to upset the children	54
Nowhere to go	49
Couldn't afford to leave	44
Too much in love with him	37
Didn't want to end the relationship	31
Thought the violence was a 'one-off'	23
Family pressure not to leave	22

For some women, the fear of being killed stops them attempting to leave, as one woman in a refuge explained, whose husband had put his hands round her neck until she passed out: 'I was too scared to leave' (Women's Aid Federation of England 1989, p.17). Almost two-thirds of the women in the NCH survey were discouraged from leaving their violent partner 'for fear of what he might do to them if they did' (Abrahams 1994, p.68) (see Table 1.1) and had experience of the threats being acted upon. As outlined earlier, it has to be recognized that violence continues post-separation; the period after a woman leaves a violent man is an extremely dangerous time for her, as the man is likely to attempt to find her. Homicide statistics show that most women are killed in the period after they leave (Dobash and Dobash 2001; Jones 1991; Povey 2004). As a result, some women might (realistically) feel it is actually safer, despite the terrible problems, to go back once more. They may also feel that going back will appease the man, thus making him less violent. For some black and, in particular, Asian women, the pressures to stay, or to go back if they have managed to leave, may be especially great if the family (his and/or hers) is hostile or takes part in the abuse or if 'bounty hunters' have been hired to find them (Bhatti-Sinclair 1994; Mama 1996). Moreover, immigrant women face particular problems leaving violent men due to their uncertain status and lack of access to public support (Batsleer *et al.* 2002; Humphreys and Thiara 2002) (see also Chapter Seven).

Women may also see staying in a refuge or with family and friends as a means of indicating to the perpetrator that his behaviour must change, in the hope that they can continue to live together as a couple or family in the future. As indicated in Table 1.1, nearly three-quarters of the women in the NCH survey thought that the man would change. Although research shows that this view tends to be unrealistic, the underlying sentiment is perhaps not surprising considering the public pressures to keep families together and the negative light in which single-parent families are seen. Moreover, Dobash *et al.* (2000) found that the woman leaving often had a temporarily salutary effect on the perpetrator, and other research on perpetrators indicates that this may be an important point of intervention with the men concerned (Hester *et al.* 2006).

Not having access to alternative accommodation, or having to stay with friends and family – in other words, having nowhere to go – is a fundamental reason for many women staying (Malos and Hague 1993a; Mama 1996). Some women are reluctant to uproot themselves and their children from home, school and friends when it is the man's violent and abusive behaviour that is at issue. In the NCH survey, 'not wanting to leave the home' (58%) ranked higher than 'nowhere to go' (49%) (see Table 1.1). This is echoed in a more recent survey of survivors: 'Why should we have to go into a refuge when they carry on living in our homes?' (Bossy and Coleman 2000, p.35). The Family Law Act 1996 now provides means for abusers to be ousted from the family home (see Chapter Six). The 2002 Homelessness Act also encourages a constructive approach to women and children made homeless through domestic violence (see Chapter Seven).

The children are another important part of the equation. Many women make decisions about staying or leaving on the basis of the children and leave a violent relationship only once they feel the children are affected or if the children disclose that they are also being abused by their father or the mother's partner (Hilton 1992; Kelly 1988; Radford and Hester 2006). Some women decide not to leave violent relationships because they feel the children would be materially worse off if they left; in the NCH survey, over half the mothers stayed because they did not want to upset their children (see Table 1.1). Violent and abusive men are also likely to use threats concerning the children in order to make women stay, such as threats that the woman will lose her children because she will be reported to social services as a bad mother (this is especially powerful when the man appears charming and capable) or that the children will be abducted (Hester and Radford 1996; McGee 2000; Radford and Hester 2006).

The added impact of racism on black children also needs to be recognized in relation to women's decisions. Imam, in an example where a woman decided to return to live with her violent husband, describes how the children's experience of racism in a refuge created greater pressures on their mother to return. The children said that they were frightened of their father and 'hated what he was doing to Mum', but they found the racism from other children and mothers in the refuge was worse (Imam 1994, p.190).

Disclosing domestic violence

The ease with which women are able to disclose violence and abuse they are experiencing is subject to the same coping and survival strategies as outlined above in relation to staying and leaving. Women are concerned that if they disclose, then the response they get might be hostile or indifferent or blame them for the violence. Moreover, they have no guarantee that disclosure will make them safe. Women also find sexual abuse and rape especially difficult to talk about. For practitioners to enable individuals who have experienced domestic violence to disclose the details of their experience, and to elicit information regarding the particular impacts for the individual, it is important to respond positively to the woman and to believe what is being said. It is also crucial to focus on how women themselves perceive their own and their children's safety. (The issue of disclosure is looked at again in relation to adults in Chapters Eight and Twelve and in relation to children in Chapter Nine.)

Agency support

Women often contact numerous agencies for help regarding the violence and abuse they face, including social services, GPs and the police. Research has found that women often need to contact several agencies before they obtain the help they need, and they may have experienced many incidents of domestic abuse before they do so (Hester and Westmarland 2005):

- In Homer *et al.*'s (1984) study of women leaving violent relationships in Cleveland, over half of the 80 women had contacted between six and eight agencies, and a sizeable proportion (13%) had contacted between 9 and 11 agencies (often a number of times, and not including the refuge where they ended up staying).

- Mama (1996), in her survey of 100 black women's experiences of domestic violence and support services, found a wide variation between ethnic minority groups in the access to and/or support provided by social services. Thirty-three per cent of the women had made contact with social services, with Asian women more likely than African or African Caribbean women to do so.

- Hanmer and Saunders (1993), in their West Yorkshire study, found that women on average contacted 11 agencies before they obtained the help they needed, with black women contacting an average of 17 agencies.

- Yearnshaw (1997), in a study of reporting of domestic violence incidents to the police, found that women had on average experienced 35 incidents of domestic violence before contacting the police.

Hague and colleagues, in a survey of survivors, found that 59 per cent of their sample believed that services had improved. Aspects of particular improvement noted included 'increases in the number of services available, more understanding or sympathetic officers and an agency emphasis on taking domestic violence seriously' (Hague, Mullender, Aris and Dear 2002, p.13). Nevertheless, they found that:

> ...the majority of the women interviewed felt that their views were overlooked to a considerable extent by service providers and that their needs were not adequately met. They felt silenced, regarded as not important and unable to achieve the type of service and policy responses which they sought. Many felt that they were powerless to influence the direction of policy or service development and related accounts of inadequate or potentially dangerous responses by agencies.

> *(Hague, Mullender, Aris and Dear 2002, p.13)*

Abrahams (2004) concludes that as a result of the approaches being used and inconsistencies in provision:

> ...women are in danger of being re-victimised by service providers who are unwilling to understand their individual needs and see them only as mothers,

partners or recipients who have failed to take responsibility for themselves or act in the way seen as 'correct' by the service provider.

(Abrahams 2004, p.77)

We have to understand the many complexities outlined above, as well as the inconsistent responses women receive, if we are also to understand the seemingly contradictory (but, in reality, safety-oriented) choices that women in violent relationships are seen to make with regard to their children and themselves in their attempts to optimize their own and their children's survival.

1.12 Summary

- Domestic violence is taken to mean any violent or abusive behaviour (e.g. physical assault, sexual abuse, rape, threats and intimidation, humiliating and controlling behaviour, withholding of finances, deprivation, isolation, belittling, constantly criticizing) that is used by one person to control and dominate another with whom they have or have had a relationship. The vast majority of cases involve violence from men to women. Perpetrators may also be aided in their abuse by other family members or friends or even agencies.

- Domestic violence is not limited to any particular class, ethnic or social group but is perpetrated by men against women across the social spectrum. The experience of domestic violence may differ as a result of these different contexts.

- Violence to women from male partners is widespread, is a feature in a significant proportion of divorces, and provides the most common context for homicide of women.

- The perpetrator and the perception of the woman he has abused often differ. Perpetrators may not see their behaviour as abusive or controlling, in the way the individual on the receiving end does. Perpetrators are likely to deny and cover up their abusive behaviour and may therefore appear as quite different people in public than at home.

- Although domestic violence can begin at any time during a relationship, many studies indicate that violence tends to start early on, in particular once the relationship has become 'formalized' through the couple living together or through marriage.

- The abusive behaviour usually escalates over time and, in particular, escalates when the woman attempts to leave or in other ways asserts her individuality and strength.

- Violence from male partners may leave women with severe and permanent physical damage and can affect their mental health. There are large cost implications, both monetary and social.

- The impact of domestic violence varies greatly with each woman and may depend on the form and frequency of the violence, although the impact can be similar regardless of whether there is physical violence or more emotional/psychological abuse.

- There is a tendency by professionals to see incidents of domestic violence in relation to a hierarchy of severity, where physical violence is perceived as the most extreme and emotional or psychological abuse is rated as less severe. Yet it is often the emotional and psychological abuse that women talk about as having the greatest and longest-lasting impact. The psychological impact of domestic violence has been found to have parallels with the impact of torture and imprisonment on hostages.

- For mothers living with violent and abusive partners, protection of their children is often a prime concern, although their actions may not necessarily be perceived as protective by professionals.

- For some women, the physical and emotional effects of the domestic violence can have a detrimental impact on their mothering and relationships with their children. Mothers may therefore appear to professionals as inadequate or unable to cope. It has to be recognized, however, that with support, and especially with help to be safe, mothers can usually resume parenting of their children.

- Some women may feel ambiguities and contradictions about their children as a result of the domestic violence, and it is therefore essential for women to be given time and space to explore these issues.

- Children are more likely than other children to experience negative fathering from domestic violence perpetrators.

- Women are faced with complex choices when making decisions about leaving violent partners. For each woman, those decisions are dependent on the particular circumstances she faces.

- The ease with which women are able to disclose violence and abuse they are experiencing is subject to coping and survival strategies. Women are concerned that if they disclose, the response they get might be hostile or indifferent or blame them for the violence. Moreover, they have no guarantee that disclosure will make them safe.

- Women often contact numerous agencies for help regarding the violence and abuse they face, including social services, GPs and the police. They are often not provided with the response or help that they need, although the response from many agencies is improving.

Note

1   Helena Kennedy explores the issues and problems of this legal approach in an interview with Sheila Quaid and Cathy Itzin (Quaid and Itzin 2000).

CHAPTER TWO

DOMESTIC VIOLENCE AND THE ABUSE OF CHILDREN

An increasing variety of research has highlighted that children are likely to be at risk of physical, sexual or emotional abuse in the context of domestic violence. From the research, it is apparent that *domestic violence is an important indicator of risk of harm to children*. Moreover, the risk of domestic violence for women is nearly doubled if there are children present in the household (Walby and Allen 2004).

Much of the initial research indicating links between domestic violence and abuse of children was carried out in the USA, Australia and Canada (Daro, Edleson and Pinderhughes 2004; Edleson 1999), with studies in the UK echoing the findings from elsewhere. The evidence in the UK concerning the abuse of children in circumstances of domestic violence has arisen both from research focusing on domestic violence and from that focusing on child abuse and protection. The studies have often included accounts of women survivors of domestic violence and examination of records from social services or health. Recently, there have been an increasing number of accounts from children who have lived in circumstance of domestic violence, and research focusing more explicitly on the co-occurence of domestic violence and child maltreatment has begun to emerge.

From the research, a number of aspects are apparent:

- The domestic violence perpetrator may also be directly – physically or sexually – abusive to the child.

- Witnessing violence to their mother may have an abusive and detrimental impact on the child.

- The perpetrator may abuse the child as part of their violence against women.

The studies regarding child protection and domestic violence often separate out, and focus on merely one aspect of, abusive behaviour to children, and also separate the experiences of mothers from those of children. Many of the studies have taken a somewhat narrow look at abuse of children in the context of domestic violence, perhaps focusing only or primarily on physical abuse of children and carers. There has been a more limited incorporation of the sexual abuse of children and only a small number of studies examining the emotional abuse associated with children living with or witnessing violence to their mothers.

Overall, however, the research indicates that in order to develop professional understanding of, and practice in relation to, child abuse, we need to recognize that children often experience a mixture of physical, sexual and emotional abuse and that focusing on only one aspect of these different forms of abuse can therefore be false (Saunders 2003). Similarly, where there is both domestic violence and child abuse, we need to examine the whole picture. Child abuse in the context of domestic violence also has to be understood as gendered – that is, not as 'family violence' carried out by family members or parents but specifically as violence and abuse primarily carried out by men against their children and female partners.

2.1 Domestic violence as an abusive context for children: 'direct' abuse

Research from the USA was some of the first to suggest that abuse of children was likely to take place in circumstances of domestic violence and that domestic violence might thus be an indicator of child abuse. The studies have been carried out in very different ways and using different types of samples, which makes it harder to make direct comparisons. Even so, the studies provide clear indications of a link between the direct abuse of children and living in a context where there is domestic violence to mothers.

A couple of American studies from the late 1960s and early 1970s indicated that men who sexually abused their children were, in many instances, also physically abusing their wives. For instance, Tormes (1972) found that 13 of 20 fathers who sexually abused their daughters were physically violent to their wives and other members of their families. Similarly, Browning and Boatman (1977) found that a majority of fathers who sexually abused their children were physically abusive to other family members.

Many of the studies in the USA examining links between child abuse and domestic violence have focused on physical abuse of both children and mothers. In an overview of American studies, Edleson (1995) indicates that in 32–53 per cent of all families where women are being physically beaten by their partner, the children are also the victims of direct abuse by the same perpetrator.

Generally it has been found that:

- Domestic violence is the most common context for child abuse.

- Male domestic violence perpetrators are more likely to be abusive to children, and more extremely so.

- The more severe the domestic violence, the more severe the abuse of children in the same context.

- Children may experience multiple forms of abuse.

Stark and Flitcraft (1988) examined a sample of 116 children who had been identified as subject to abuse or neglect in the records of a hospital. They also examined medical records in order to look for incidents of physical injury to the mother. It was found that 45 per cent of the children had mothers who were also being physically abused and another 5 per cent had mothers whose relationships were full of conflict. They conclude: '[wife] battering is the most common context for child abuse, [and] the battering male is the typical child abuser' (Stark and Flitcraft 1988, p.97). Truesdell, McNeil and Deschner (1986, p.140), who examined the incidence of domestic violence in child sexual abuse cases, concluded similarly that 'wife abuse is more common in families in which incest occurs than in the general population'.

In another US study, Bowker, Arbitell and McFerron (1988) found that there was a direct link between 'wife beating' and abuse of children. Their sample of 1000 battered women was not representative of the population generally. None the less, a clear link between abuse of children and the context of domestic violence emerges. From the 775 women in the sample who had children with their violent partners, it was reported that 70 per cent of their husbands also physically abused the children. The more frequent the violence to the wives, including physical violence and marital rape, the more extreme the physical abuse of the children. The authors conclude that 'the severity of the wife beating is predictive of the severity of the child abuse' (Bowker *et al.* 1988, p.165)

Yet another US study focusing on physical abuse concludes that 'marital violence is a statistically significant predictor of physical child abuse' (Ross 1996, p.589). The study, based on a representative sample of 3363 parents, examined violence by both men and women against their partner using the Conflict Tactics Scale (CTS) and is therefore likely to have overrepresented violence by women against their husbands and children (see Chapter One). Despite this methodological problem, the study showed that male perpetrators are more likely to be violent to both wife and children. Ross concludes: '…even women who are the most chronically violent have only a 38 per cent probability of physically abusing a male child, whereas the most chronically violent husbands are almost certain to physically abuse their children' (Ross 1996, p.595).

Goddard and Hiller (1993) in Australia examined different types of violence and abuse to children in order to examine wider implications. They surveyed 206 cases of child abuse presenting at the child protection unit of a hospital. Domestic violence was a feature in over half of the cases of physical child abuse (55%) and in slightly fewer cases of sexual child abuse (40%). The physical abuse involved mainly boys (63%), while the sexual abuse involved primarily girls (82%). Moreover, in almost all of the cases involving both child sexual abuse and domestic violence, the siblings were also being emotionally, sexually or physically abused.

A US study examining exposure to multiple forms of abuse involved a longitudinal sample of US Navy families reported for allegations of domestic violence, physical abuse or sexual abuse (Saunders *et al.* 2002). Of the children reporting living with domestic violence, 39 per cent reported experiencing sexual assault, 42 per cent physical assault and more than half (55%) physical abuse; more than three-quarters (79%) had witnessed community violence. One of the authors concludes: '…among clinical or reported samples of children, the proportion of victims having only one violent episode in their histories is small. Most have experienced multiple types of violence and multiple victimisations' (Saunders 2003, p.362).

2.2 Domestic violence as an abusive context for children: living with and witnessing violence

Alongside the work examining direct physical and sexual abuse of children in the context of domestic violence, attention has also been focused on the experiences of children living in such contexts but who might not be directly abused. In a sense, this development parallels the studies concerning women's experiences of domestic violence, where the initial focus was on physical violence from male partners but with an increasing recognition that the psychological effects of living with the fear and threat of possible violence often had a greater impact on the women concerned (see Chapter One).

In recognition of the potential impact on children of witnessing domestic violence, a number of local authorities in the UK have at various times defined witnessing domestic violence as abuse of children, for instance Strathclyde Regional Council Social Services Department (Hague, Kelly *et al.* 1996). The impact on children of witnessing domestic violence to a carer has also been recognized in legislation (Section 120 of the 2002 Adoption and Fostering Act – see Chapter Four).[1]

A wide range of research has found that witnessing violence to their mothers can have a detrimental impact on children, tantamount to emotional abuse or psychological maltreatment (Abrahams 1994; Carroll 1994; Christensen 1990; Jaffe, Wolfe and Wilson 1990; McGee 2000; Radford and Hester 2006; Saunders *et al.* 1995). Kolbo, Blakely and Engleman (1996) concluded, in their mid-1990s review of the research literature concerning children who witness domestic violence: 'Two decades of empirical research indicates that children who witness domestic violence are at increased risk for maladaptation' (Kolbo *et al.* 1996, p.289).

A more recent meta-evaluation of 118 (mainly US) quantitative studies of psychosocial outcomes of children exposed to domestic violence echoes this, showing a significant correlation between exposure to domestic violence and occurrence of child problems (Kitzmann *et al.* 2003). Children who had witnessed domestic violence had significantly worse outcomes than comparison groups of children who had not witnessed domestic violence: it was found that 62 per cent of child witnesses were not faring as well as the average child.

The term 'witnessing' of domestic violence may suggest that the child is present in the room or location when an incident takes place. However, children can witness domestic violence in a number of ways, which extend beyond direct observation of violent and abusive acts to their mothers or other carers. Even if children do not directly witness the violence or abuse, they might overhear incidents or in other ways be aware that violence or abuse has occurred. The British Crime Survey has echoed these findings, suggesting that many children are aware of domestic violence, even if they are not involved directly:

> Every day thousands of children witness cruelty and violence behind closed doors. More than a third of children of domestic violence survivors are aware of what is going on and this rises to a half if the women have suffered repeat violence.

> *(McCarry 2003, pp.42–43)*

Hughes (1992) found that in 90 per cent of cases, children are in the same room or the next room when domestic violence takes place. In the NCH Action for Children study (Abrahams 1994), 73 per cent of the children had directly witnessed violent assaults on their mothers, including 10 per cent of the children whose mothers had been sexually abused or assaulted by violent partners in front of the children; 62 per cent had overheard violent incidents; and 52 per cent saw the injuries resulting from domestic violence. Children interviewed in the study recounted some of these incidents:

> He would come in and rip my mother's clothes off. He tried to strangle her, just to beat her up like… We were always watching it… He used to tell us to get back to bed…

> *(Child quoted in Abrahams 1994, p.31)*

> A lot of times I just heard it from the bedroom, and once [my sister] and I heard it, and we were just crying our eyes out for my mum, you know, she just sounded so desperate downstairs…crying and screaming.

> *(Child quoted in Abrahams 1994, pp.31–32)*

> It was depressing. My mother was always on edge, scurrying around… And I was frightened as well, every time he was there, thinking, 'Oh, what's he going to do today? Is he going to knife her or what?'

> *(Child quoted in Abrahams 1994, p.33)*

Humphreys and Thiara (2002, p.31), in interviews with 14 children from domestic violence outreach projects, report how 'children spoke graphically of their experience of watching and hearing their mothers being abused' and that it 'was clearly something that they found very distressing'. At the same time, the children did not overemphasize distinctions between the emotional abuse associated with witnessing violence to their mothers and experiencing physical abuse themselves:

> He hurt me, my mum, Billy and my little, little brother, but he never hurt Mary. But Mary did go through a lot; she never got hurt but she saw my mum hurt…and she used to help my mum get cleaned up.

> *(11-year-old boy, quoted in Humphreys and Thiara 2002, p.31)*

Although much of the research has focused on the witnessing by children of physical violence to mothers, McGee (1996, 2000) points out that witnessing other ongoing abusive behaviour is at least as important: although children may not directly witness physical assaults to their mothers, they will be exposed to other forms of violence and abuse directed at her. A 12-year-old girl told McGee:

> I've never seen Dad hit her, but I've seen him get very angry and like once when Mum was really ill, she had to be taken to hospital in fact, he said 'No, just leave her, leave her.' And then I was the one who had to phone the doctor.

> *(McGee 1996, p.16)*

2.3 Domestic violence as a context for child deaths

During the 1970s and 1980s, cases involving child deaths began to highlight the importance of domestic violence as a context for child abuse. Domestic violence was found to be an important feature in the highly publicized death of Maria Colwell at the hands of her father in 1974. In the background to the fatal abuse of five-year-old Sukina Hammond by her father and of three-year-old Toni Dales by her stepfather, both in the late 1980s, was the ongoing violence and abuse from these men to the children's mothers (Bridge Child Care Consultancy Service 1991; National Children's Bureau 1993; O'Hara 1994) (see also London Borough of Greenwich 1987). Yet in these and many other cases where children have been killed, the significance of violence to the mothers as an indicator of potential risk to the children has tended not to be understood nor acknowledged (James 1994; O'Hara 1994; Saunders 2004).

Despite the earlier research findings and the child deaths that had been found to have occurred in the context of domestic violence, and despite knowledge from refuges about links between domestic violence and abuse of children, it was only during the 1990s that these links began to emerge in the public and social work debates in the UK.[2] Even so, the indicator of domestic violence as a serious risk factor for children has continued to be ignored, as evidenced by the appallingly high number of child homicides in such circumstances. In a study of serious case reviews,[3] it was found that 22 of the 40 instances examined involved previously violent behaviour by the father, stepfather or mother's cohabitee (Sinclair and Bullock 2002).

Saunders (2004) examined the homicides of 29 children from 13 families who were killed in the decade between 1994 and 2004 in the context of post-separation contact or residence. She found that domestic violence was involved in at least 11 of the 13 families, and that in one of the other families 'the mother has spoken of her ex-partner's obsessively controlling behaviour (a characteristic feature of domestic violence) and in the other case there were concerns about the child's safety' (Saunders 2004, p.4). In five of the cases, contact had been ordered by the courts. Saunders points out the apparent lack of understanding by the professionals of domestic violence and controlling behaviour by perpetrators and of risks to children living in such circumstances. She concludes:

- In several cases where statutory agencies knew that the mother was experiencing domestic violence, the children were not viewed as being at risk of significant harm, even when she was facing potentially lethal violence.

- Some professionals clearly did not have any understanding of the power and control dynamics of domestic violence, and did not recognize the increased risks following separation or the mother's starting a new relationship.

- In several cases professionals did not talk to the children and this meant that, in effect, there was no assessment of their needs. Sometimes this was because the perpetrator prevented any meaningful contact with the child.

(Saunders 2004, p.5)

2.4 UK research on child abuse and protection

Child protection studies have provided probably the largest body of research in the UK to indicate that domestic violence is an important feature in the background of children who have been subject to abuse or risk of harm. There are certain limitations to the use of child protection data, in particular that they provide a narrow clinical sample that is unlikely to be representative of the population as a whole. Only a small proportion of incidents of child abuse come to the attention of agencies, with underreporting in relation to middle-class sectors of the population and over-representation of ethnic minorities (Hooper 1995; Kelly, Regan and Burton 1991).

None the less, from the child protection studies it is apparent that domestic violence is often a significant and consistent feature, regardless of the form of abuse (physical, sexual or emotional) a child is deemed to have suffered (see also Section 2.1). Although most of this research did not set out to examine domestic violence, it indicates that in instances of child abuse, between one-fifth and nearly two-thirds of the children were also living in circumstances of domestic violence. The more detailed the studies, the more likely they were to find that domestic violence was also an issue:

- Moore (1975), in an in-depth study of 23 'violent matrimonial cases' referred to the NSPCC, found that children had been adversely affected by this context.

- Hyman (1978) found in relation to 85 cases of non-accidental injury to children that social workers described 41 per cent of mothers and 19 per cent of fathers as having been 'violently treated' by the other partner.

- Maynard's (1985) examination of 103 social services case files found that one in three of these mentioned domestic violence.

- A study by the social services department of the London Borough of Hackney (1994) indicated that the mothers of at least one-third of children on the child protection register were experiencing domestic violence.

- A study of allocated social services cases in the London Borough of Hackney (1994) found that one in five involved domestic violence.

- Cleaver and Freeman (1995), in a detailed study of 30 families undergoing the early stages of child abuse enquiries, found that 12 of the cases also involved domestic violence.

- Gibbons, Conroy and Bell (1995) found that in 27 per cent of 1888 referrals with child protection concerns, across a number of authorities, domestic violence was also recorded.

- Farmer and Owen (1995), in their study of outcomes of child protection practice, found that 52 per cent of 44 sample cases involved domestic violence.

- Brandon and Lewis (1996), examining significant harm of children (i.e. maltreatment, neglect), found that 21 of 54 children in the background sample and 28 of 51 children in the intensive interview sample had witnessed domestic violence.

- Humphreys (1997a), in a study of Coventry social services child protection cases, found that in 11 of 32 cases, women were also reported to have severe injuries as a result of incidents of domestic violence.

- Examination by Hester and Pearson (1998) of NSPCC case files revealed that in at least a third of 111 cases accepted for service, domestic violence was also an issue. This rose to nearly two-thirds (62%) after the team included a more detailed focus on domestic violence in their work.

- In Farmer and Pollock's (1998) study of substitute care for sexually abused and abusing children, two in five children (39%) in a case-file sample of 250 newly looked after children had lived in families where there was violence between their parents – mainly violence by the man to the mother. This rose to over half (55%) in the more detailed follow-up sample of 40 sexually abused and/or abusing young people in care.

- Cawson (2002), in a national retrospective prevalence survey of child maltreatment involving a random probability sample of 2869 young people aged 18–24 years, found that domestic violence was reported by most (80%) of the victims of serious physical abuse, by more than half those deemed to have experienced intermediate physical abuse, and by 44 per cent of those who were smacked regularly and suffered physical effects lasting a day or longer. Of the young people sexually abused by parents, almost two-thirds came from families in which violence was constant or frequent. Moreover, an even greater proportion (88%) of the young adults neglected in childhood reported they had experienced violence between their carers.

- Farmer and Moyers (2005), in a further study of looked after children (in this case looked after by kin or unrelated foster carers), found that over half (52%) of the children in both types of placement had backgrounds of domestic violence.

During the 1970s, a small number of child protection oriented studies in the UK began to examine the effect on children of domestic violence. Two studies were carried out under the auspices of the NSPCC, one examining the impact on children living in a context of 'violent marital conflict' (Moore 1975) and the other drawing on social workers' perceptions of families where children had been injured non-accidentally (Hyman 1978). Both studies indicated the existence of links between some form of abuse of children and a context of marital violence. The studies are problematic, however, because they present the mothers in a very negative light and hint that they are the central cause of both the child abuse and the marital violence, despite the examples given in the studies that indicate that it is men who are being violent and abusive to children and their mothers.

Farmer and Owen provide one of the more detailed studies linking child protection work and domestic violence. In their study of the outcomes for children of child protection practice, they found that domestic violence (mainly involving violence from the male to the female partner) was a feature 'across the full range of households and categories of abuse in the study' (Farmer and Owen 1995, p.138), with abuse of children including physical, sexual and emotional abuse and neglect. In cases of child sexual abuse, they found that 'some form of family violence had been evident at the time of the abuse in two-fifths' of the cases (Farmer and Owen 1995, p.223). With regard to cases of physical abuse, neglect and emotional abuse, 29 cases in all, 'there were 17 instances (59%) in which there was also other current violence in the family apart from the child abuse which had brought the case to conference. This was usually a man's violence to a woman…' (Farmer and Owen 1995, p.224). They concluded that the children with the worst outcomes were especially likely to have mothers who were being abused by their male partners, although the domestic violence tended to be ignored by the professionals involved.

Glaser and Prior (1997) examined the cases of 94 children registered with local authorities solely or partly for emotional abuse. They looked at minutes from child protection conferences and carried out interviews with social work managers. They found that over 60 per cent of the emotional abuse of children was taking place in contexts where there was domestic violence and parental mental ill-health and/or alcohol or drug abuse. Domestic violence was the main feature in relation to 28 per cent of the children. It should also be recognized that for many women, mental ill-health or alcoholism is often a *result* of ongoing violence from male partners (Cleaver, Unell and Aldgate 1999; Humphreys 1997a; Stark and Flitcraft 1988) (see also Chapter One).

A number of UK studies have focused more specifically on domestic violence in child abuse cases. Brandon and Lewis (1996), for example, examined significant harm in relation to children who had witnessed domestic violence; 54 children were in a background sample and 51 in an intensive interview sample that included information from parents, teachers and some of the children themselves. Overall, 49 per cent of the children from each sample group had witnessed violence. About half (28 of 51) of the intensive interview sample 'warranted inclusion as cases of harm or potential harm from domestic violence' (Brandon and Lewis 1996, p.36). The authors conclude that the abusive consequences of witnessing domestic violence generally need to be recognized by social workers and other professionals:

> ...the evidence points to the possibility that the cumulative harm from witnessing violence will affect the child's emotional and mental health in future relationships... Until professions recognize that when the child sees violence at home there is a likelihood of significant harm, it will not be possible to act to prevent long-term damage.
>
> *(Brandon and Lewis 1996, p.41)*

Humphreys (1997a) examined the cases of 32 families, with 93 children, who were the subject of case conferences in Coventry. There was a deliberate over-sampling of (12) Asian families. Nearly half (11 of 32) of the women were reported to have sustained severe injuries from their male partners, with a further three women apparently experiencing other, more psychological forms of domestic violence. The research echoes the findings of Maynard (1985) that women who have experienced domestic violence are at particularly high risk of having their children accommodated. Two-thirds (24 of 32) of the women 'were either "threatened" with the accommodation of their children or did in fact have their children accommodated in situations where they were also the subject of abuse from violent men' (Maynard 1985, p.13); see Chapter Eight for further discussion of this issue. Humphreys also found that issues of mental ill-health and alcohol abuse were important features in the domestic violence cases. In particular, mental health issues were of relevance for women in 13 of the 32 cases, and for five of the 12 Asian women. Generally, however, connections were not made by the professionals involved between depression or psychosis and the domestic violence that the women experienced. In 18 of the 32 cases, alcohol abuse was seen to be a problem for the woman's partner. Child protection conferences appeared to find it easier to name as a problem alcohol rather than the men's violence to their partners, and the issue of domestic violence was consequently lost.

Hester and Pearson's (1998) practice-related study looked specifically at domestic violence in child abuse cases referred to the NSPCC. The study highlighted the direct links between sexual abuse of children and living in a context of domestic violence. Moreover, mothers and children were found to be most likely to be abused by the same perpetrator, who was usually the children's natural father. The study used a multi-method approach, which included analysis of case records over a two-year period. Most of the 111 cases accepted for service by the NSPCC team during this period involved sexual abuse as the main concern (77%), with the children also experiencing a range of other abusive behaviours, including physical and emotional abuse. Social services were involved in some way in 61 per cent of the cases. Over half the cases of sexual abuse involved domestic violence (almost exclusively male-to-female violence). With regard to the perpetrator, in over half (53%) of the cases of child sexual abuse, the abuser was the child's father or father figure. This rose to over two-thirds (69%) in instances where domestic violence was also identified. In other words, fathers and father figures were even more likely than other men to be sexually abusive to their children when these same men were also violent and abusive to the mothers.

Cawson (2002), on the basis of a national and randomized retrospective prevalence survey of child maltreatment, argues that there is a strong relationship between domestic violence and maltreatment of children: 'A quarter (26%) of respondents said that physical violence sometimes took place between those caring for them', with 5 per cent experiencing this constantly or frequently (Cawson 2002, p.37). The young people themselves did not necessarily see the domestic violence as the direct cause of their own maltreatment, and this differed by type of abuse:

> [T]hose who said they were emotionally or sexually abused [were] least likely to do so: 13% of emotionally abused and 7% of sexually abused, compared to 44% of neglected and 23% of physically abused, gave 'the carer's (person who did it) own relationship was violent' as a reason for their actions towards the respondent.
>
> *(Cawson 2002, pp.37–38)*

There was some indication from the survey of differences by social status, with those young people considered to be in semiskilled or unskilled occupations being three times more likely to report constant or frequent violence between their carers (11%) compared with those from professional or managerial and skilled manual or skilled non-manual occupations (3%). However, this may be an inaccurate picture of possible links between social status and domestic violence, as it focuses merely on physical violence rather than a wider range of domestic abuse behaviours.

Research on looked after children has also consistently identified a link between domestic violence and child abuse, with Farmer and Pollock (1998) and Farmer and Moyers (2005) showing an apparent rise in the prevalence of domestic violence. Farmer points out that this increase is more likely to have resulted from increasing awareness of the issues than from an actual increase in domestic violence:

> Since the prevalence of such violence is unlikely to have changed from our earlier studies, this rise in the proportion of looked after children known to have experienced domestic violence may suggest an increased awareness and more screening of violence by practitioners.
>
> *(Farmer 2006, p.130)*

2.5 UK research on women's experiences of domestic violence and the link with child abuse

Research in the UK focusing on domestic violence, in particular women's experiences, has consistently revealed a link between domestic violence and physical and/or sexual abuse of children. It has also shown that the majority of children living in circumstances of domestic violence witness the violence and abusive behaviour to their mothers:

- Levine (1975), in a study of 50 families with 117 children seen in a general medical practice, found that the 'children who observed their parents in violent conflict' were in danger of physical harm or were detrimentally affected by observing the violence.

- Dobash and Dobash (1984) interviewed 109 mothers from refuges and found that over half (58%) of their children had been present when there was violence to the women from male partners.

- A representative study of 286 married working-class mothers and single mothers from all social classes in Islington, London, found that many women experiencing domestic violence reported more severe violence when they were pregnant than at other times, and women experiencing violence were twice as likely to experience miscarriage (Andrews and Brown 1988).

- Women's Aid statistics estimate that between 22 and 33 per cent of the children of women coming to refuges are physically and/or sexually abused by the mother's husband or cohabitee (Hanmer 1989).

- In the NCH Action for Children study (Abrahams 1994) involving a questionnaire survey of 108 mothers who had experienced domestic violence, via NCH's family centres, at least 27 per cent of the children were said to be physically abused by the domestic violence perpetrator (usually the father). Almost three-quarters (73%) of the children witnessed violent assaults on their mothers, and almost two-thirds (62%) overheard violent incidents.

- In Hester and Radford's (1996) study of contact arrangements in circumstances of domestic violence, 21 of the 53 women interviewed in England reported that their children had been physically and/or sexually abused by fathers. In 11 instances, there was involvement of social services with regard to abuse of the children by the fathers. In six instances, all involving child abuse, no contact was formally ordered between fathers and children, and in a further two cases social services demanded that there be no contact, in order to protect the children. The majority of children were also reported to be affected adversely by witnessing violence to their mothers.

- Mezey and Bewley (1997) examined domestic violence in relation to pregnancy. They found that the risk of moderate to severe violence appeared to be greatest in the period after women have given birth.

- In Humphreys and Thiara's (2002) interviews with 14 children as part of wider research on domestic violence outreach projects, most of the children spoke about having been physically abused; several also mentioned verbal abuse.

2.6 UK research on children's experiences of domestic violence

Children's experiences of living with domestic violence have been examined in a number of ways, incorporating clinical samples and children who have decided to call helplines. However, only a few studies have been carried out in the UK that look specifically at how children make sense of their experiences of living with domestic violence and their coping strategies (McGee 2000; Mullender *et al.* 2002).

- Epstein and Keep (1995) examined a random sample of 126 of ChildLine's callers who talked about living with domestic violence. Over a third (38%) said their mother's partner (mostly the child's biological father) also physically abused them or their siblings.

- In Harris Hendriks and colleagues' (1993) clinical sample involving 160 children from 62 families where (mostly) mothers had been murdered by violent partners, one in ten of the children had experienced physical

abuse from a parent and 'very many' had witnessed violence from their
father to their mother.

- McGee (2000), in interviews with mothers and children who had
  experienced domestic violence, found a direct link between domestic
  violence of mothers and abuse of children.

- Mullender *et al.* (2002) interviewed 45 children from 25 families living
  with domestic violence, where two-thirds of the perpetrators were fathers
  and a third were the mother's partners. Although four of the children
  said that they were not aware of the violence, the majority had overheard
  arguments or witnessed violence. Over a third of the children had both
  overheard and witnessed violence. This group was also most likely to
  talk of threats to and abuse of themselves and their siblings.

2.7 UK research on mothers of sexually abused children

In the UK, there have been only a few studies focusing on mothers of sexually
abused children where domestic violence was also looked at as a potential issue.
These studies found that nearly all the mothers had also experienced violence from
the same abuser as their children.

- In her study of 15 mothers of sexually abused children, Hooper (1992)
  found that in 9 of 11 instances involving the father or father figure as the
  abuser, the woman had also experienced physical, verbal or sexual abuse
  from the same perpetrator.

- Forman's (1995) interviews with a self-selected sample of 20 mothers of
  sexually abused children with social services involvement revealed that
  all the mothers had also experienced violence or abuse from the same
  men. Of the alleged abusers, most (17) were the natural fathers, one the
  stepfather, one the adoptive father and one the mother's cohabitee.

2.8 Child abuse as part of the perpetrator's violence against the mother, and vice versa

Men's abuse of their children and partners may be difficult to separate into discrete
categories of 'child abuse' and 'domestic violence', because in some instances the
intention of the abuser is that the violence or abuse of a child will have a directly
abusive impact on the woman. Kelly (1996) explains this as a 'double level of
intentionality': 'That an act directed against one individual is at the same time
intended to affect another/others' (Kelly 1996, p.123).

Hester and Pearson's (1998) study of NSPCC child abuse cases involving domestic violence provides examples where abuse of the woman and of the child(ren)

by the same man were so closely interconnected that they were simultaneous expressions of both domestic violence and child abuse. This included an example where the father held a six-week-old baby over a first-floor balcony in order to prevent the mother from leaving after he had hit her. In another example, the mother was unable to intervene to protect her children from the man's physical abuse of them because she was too frightened of the repercussions of this for herself. In their earlier study concerning child contact arrangements, Hester and Radford (1996) found instances where the children had become implicated in the violence against their mothers through being forced to further the father's abuse. One father made his seven-year-old son kick and punch his mother despite the child's protestations and crying:

> He made them kick and punch me and they did because they were so frightened of him. [My son] kicked me, he punched me in the face. But, when he had done it his father told him he hadn't done it hard enough, and he was to go and put his shoes on and do it harder.

> *(Hilary, quoted in Hester and Radford 1996, p.10)*

Some of the men used the children to force the women to stay within the relationship. One father ensured he always had one of the children with him so that the mother could not leave the relationship, as he knew she would not leave without them (Hester and Radford 1996). Similar incidences are discussed in studies by Malos and Hague (1993a), McGee (2000), and Bossy and Coleman (2000).

Mullender *et al.* (2002), in their study of children's perspectives on domestic violence, asked mothers whether their abusers had used the children against them or as part of the abuse. All 24 mothers interviewed thought that this had happened to some degree, from it happening 'all the time' to those 'whose abuser had begun threatening to harm the children, or not let women have them, when it had become clear that the relationship was over' (Mullender *et al.* 2002, p.161). The authors suggest that professionals need to be aware of two broad categories of ways in which men use children: '…implicating and involving children in their mother's abuse, and controlling women through threats towards, and mistreatment of, the children' (Mullender *et al.* 2002, p.161).

They indicate that these categories are crucial for professionals to understand in order to challenge men's behaviour and promote child protection, because:

> It is relevant to the roles of the abusing and non-abusing parent in child care cases to contact and residence disputes between parents where there has been violence, and to work in perpetrators' programmes and on men's parenting following domestic violence.

> *(Mullender* et al. *2002, pp.161–162)*

Both Hooper (1992) and Forman (1995) argue, on the basis of their studies concerning mothers of sexually abused children, that the sexual abuse of the children could be seen as constituting domestic violence or abuse in relation to the mothers. The violence to the mothers also served to distance them as a source of support for the children, so that the men could more easily continue their sexual abuse. Hooper, for instance, found that the violence to mothers often preceded the sexual abuse of the children and usually continued alongside it, such that the man's abuse of the children was also directly intended to be abusive of his partner:

> Children were used by violent men both to extend means of control over their mothers (for example by battering or verbally undermining women in the presence of children as well as by sexually abusive behaviour) and to extend their domain of control to someone with less power to resist.

> *(Hooper 1992, p.355)*

Men may also threaten to, or actually, murder children as part of their ongoing abuse of women (see also Section 2.3). In a book documenting the killing of women and children in domestic homicides, the Women's Coalition Against Family Violence (1994) provides examples of fathers abusing children in order to control, abuse and torture the mothers. For instance, one woman was threatened with the death of both her and then her children when she tried to leave her violent partner. She had to leave without the children:

> He grabbed me and ran the blade around the front of my neck and then the back of my neck. As he was doing this he was saying that he was going to kill me. He ran the knife around my throat but not heavily enough to cut. He then said he wasn't going to kill me but would go upstairs and get [the children] and cut their throats in front of me and let me live to suffer knowing that I would have caused it... I agreed with him that I would not ring or talk to him any more and that I would leave the kids with him and get out of his life. I think that is why he let me go.

> *(Kay, quoted in Women's Coalition Against Family Violence 1994, p.31)*

The interconnectedness of men's abuse of both children and women is an important consideration with regard to the conflicts and problems women may face as mothers (outlined in Chapter One) and has direct implications for the ability of children to disclose to their mothers that they are being abused (see Chapter Three).

2.9 Children and post-separation violence: child contact

There is often an expectation in child protection work that women should leave violent partners in order to protect children (see also Chapter Four). This not only places undue responsibility on mothers for men's violence and abuse but also ignores the reality that the violence may not cease, despite the separation of the spouses or partners. In his attempt to continue to control 'his' wife and children, a violent man may continue to abuse and harass his ex-partner. Child contact is often the major flashpoint for the post-separation violence and provides a context in which the man may continue to abuse and harass both the woman and the child(ren) (Abrahams 1994; Anderson 1997; Debbonaire 1997; Hester and Pearson 1998; Hester and Radford 1996; Mullender *et al.* 2002; Radford and Hester 2006; Smart 1995).

Contact may also be used as the ultimate context for control by violent men – that is, to murder their children, the mothers or themselves (see also Section 2.3) (Radford and Hester 2006; Saunders 2001, 2004). Hilary Saunders lists some of the homicides that took place in relation to contact between 1994 and 2000. As can be seen from the instances below, they raise many questions regarding the safety of contact where men are domestic violence perpetrators (Saunders 2001, p.11):

- Daniella Hurst (aged two years) was killed by her father during a contact visit in Lincolnshire on 10 October 2000.

- Saba and Zeeshan Zaidi (aged seven and six years, respectively) were killed by their father when he came to Bracknell to collect them for a contact visit on 18 March 2000. Their mother Shazia was also stabbed to death.

- Christopher and Oliver Fairless (aged six and nine years, respectively) were hanged by their father on 17 April 2000 in the village of Scotter, North Lincolnshire. Their father had been allowed to have unsupervised contact, even though he was facing charges of rape and of assaulting his wife.

- Daniel and Jordan Philpott (aged seven and three years, respectively) were killed by their father during a contact visit on 2 August 1999 near Pontypridd in Wales. Unsupervised contact had been granted to Julian Philpott, even though he was due to appear in Cardiff Crown Court on charges of threatening to kill his ex-partner and causing her actual bodily harm.

- Daniel Brinnen (aged two years) was found dead with his father after a contact visit on 13 March 1999 in Mablethorpe, Lincolnshire.

- Imtiaz Begum was stabbed to death in Birmingham on 20 January 1996 when she was collecting her son after a contact visit. Her son was found strangled in her husband's car and her three daughters (who had been living with him in Bristol) were found dead in their beds with their throats cut.

- Nina and Jack Sandhu (aged four and three years, respectively) were killed by their father during a contact visit on 6 February 1994 in Derbyshire. Their mother, Sarah Heatley, had been persuaded by court professionals to agree to contact informally, although she was very worried about her husband's mental health.

Family court advisers have indicated that domestic violence is a regular feature in contested contact cases. A report from HM Inspectorate of Court Administration (HMICA) (2005), *Domestic Violence, Safety and Family Proceedings*, points out that, anecdotally, Children and Family Court Advisory and Support Service (CAFCASS) practitioners place the incidence of domestic violence in the region of 90 per cent or more of cases they deal with. Even so, the judicial statistics for England and Wales across 1999–2001 do not indicate that this is taken into account, with almost all (more than 99%) cases resulting in contact being granted. Moreover, the figures show that there has been a general increase in the number of contact orders granted and a year-on-year decrease in the number of cases where contact is refused (Saunders 2003, p.2):

- 1999: contact orders granted 41,862, contact orders refused 1,752.

- 2000: contact orders granted 46,070, contact orders refused 1,276.

- 2001: contact orders granted 55,030, contact orders refused 713.

It appears that things have not changed significantly for the better since Hester and Radford's (1996) study identified contact as a particular problem for the mothers and children concerned (see also Radford and Hester 2006). They found that of 53 post-separation families in England where women had left male partners, the men continued to be violent to their wives/partners in 50 of the 53 instances, and the possibility of further violence to the children remained. Failure to address the risks or to make provision for safety meant that for a substantial proportion of children in the study, contact with fathers was reported to have an adverse effect upon their welfare. It was apparent that many of the fathers were merely using parental responsibility and contact as a means of continuing their violence towards, and control over, their ex-partner. Parenting and caring for children was not the main objective. In only 7 of 53 cases did contact arrangements 'work'; that is, there was no further abuse or harassment of the women or children involved. Mothers reported that children had been physically or sexually abused or neglected on contact visits with fathers, and children were also being used to collude in ongoing abuse of the mother. Children were used by ex-partners to convey threats and abusive messages to their mothers, were pressurized into carrying out acts of violence against their mothers and were involved in plans to kill their mothers.

One of the children interviewed described being physically abused during contact with her father and how the abuse appeared to be escalating: 'He [father] was in a really bad mood…and he just grabbed me and started throwing me around and that…he'd hit me before but not like that, 'cos he got me and threw me into the door …' (Annie, aged 13 years, quoted in Hester and Pearson 1997a, p.286). She was also concerned that her father would try to persuade her to let him into the refuge where she and her mother were staying. This she found particularly worrying in view of her father's repeated threats to kill her mother: '…sometimes, because my dad like threatened to kill her...when I'd go over there and see him, he would be, like, you've got to let me in the refuge...'

Fifteen of the women who participated in the Hester and Radford study were black or Asian, and two of the white women had black children. The research showed parallels with Mama's (1996) findings, showing that black women may experience greater difficulties than white women in gaining protection for child contact arrangements. Asian mothers in particular experienced significantly less support from professionals because certain assumptions were made about Asian communities: 'Police and social workers were noticeably reluctant to lend support either due to beliefs that the support would be provided from within the community or because of fear of upsetting community leaders' (Hester and Radford 1996, p.33).

In their study of domestic violence and NSPCC practice, Hester and Pearson (1998) again found an overlap between domestic violence to mothers and the abuse of children during contact visits with fathers. In 18 instances where children were suspected of being abused or had been found to have been abused in relation to contact, 15 also involved domestic violence. The NSPCC was carrying out work with the children with regard to sexual abuse in nine instances, physical abuse in one instance and emotional abuse in eight instances. In two of the cases, the grandfather had sexually abused the children during the father's contact time.

Forman (1995) also indicates the difficulties mothers and their children may experience in relation to contact, including further abuse. In one example, the mother, although reluctant to send her children on contact visits to the father, thought they would be safe because the contact took place at the paternal grandparents' home. However, the children were abused by both father and grandfather. As Forman concludes, in such circumstances children may 'think their mother is "sending" them to be abused' (1995, p.15).

In Mullender et al.'s (2002) study on children's perspectives on domestic violence, both informally and court-ordered arrangements for contact were the reality for many of the children no longer living with their violent fathers. As found in previous studies (Hester and Radford 1996; McGee 2000), mothers often tried hard to enable contact to take place despite being concerned about the men's behaviour, and children often had mixed and confused feelings regarding their fathers involving fear, hatred and distress as well as love. Contact often provided opportunities for some of the fathers to continue their violence, including a number of instances of life-threatening violence. The authors provide an example of a child witnessing a potentially life-threatening attack on her mother after the father 'used contact arrangements to insinuate himself back into the home as a visitor' (Mullender et al. 2002, p.202). The father grabbed the mother by the throat, pushed her over the sink and held a knife against her throat. The daughter ran to a neighbour and the police were called, resulting in charges against the father. However, 'the father convinced [the daughter] that he had only accidentally picked up the knife and persuaded her not to give evidence against him', leading to a reduction in the charge (Mullender et al. 2002, p.202).

Contact may also be brought up as an issue in domestic violence-related criminal justice cases in order to obtain more lenient outcomes for the men concerned. In a study examining the progress of domestic violence cases through the criminal justice system, a number of such impacts were identified (Hester 2006a). Analysis of police data related to 291 incidents indicated that women who had children living with them were more likely to refuse to give statements, leading to some cases not proceeding further. Court observation and analysis of Crown Prosecution Service (CPS) case files revealed that reference to contact between children and alleged offenders was also likely to lead to more lenient outcomes, whether bail conditions or sentences:

> In one case, a CPS barrister indicated that a custodial sentence following a conviction for actual bodily harm and harassment was unlikely because the offender had almost daily contact with his three children. Yet...it was not questioned whether contact should be allowed to continue in such circumstances. Defence solicitors also explained that contact between the children and offender was an obvious area for the defence to exploit.

> *(Hester 2006a, p.88)*

The arrangements made for contact with violent fathers need to be considered in relation to the protection of children from abuse and harm. It is in the arena of contact that the ongoing abuse of children, both directly and indirectly, is likely to continue and yet may be ignored. The HMICA (2005, p.8) report *Domestic Violence, Safety and Family Proceedings* echoes this concern, finding 'unacceptably wide variations in quality and consistency' by family court advisory staff and that 'the nature of domestic abuse is not sufficiently understood by most CAFCASS practitioners'.

2.10 Summary

- Domestic violence is an important indicator of risk of harm to children.

- A wide range of studies have indicated that children are likely to be at risk of actual physical, sexual and emotional abuse from perpetrators of domestic violence.

- Domestic violence is often a significant and consistent feature, regardless of the form of abuse (physical, sexual or emotional) a child is deemed to have suffered.

- Witnessing violence to their mothers can have a detrimental impact on children, tantamount to emotional abuse or psychological maltreatment. Children can 'witness' domestic violence in a number of ways, which extend beyond direct observation of violent and abusive acts. They might overhear incidents or in other ways be aware that violence or abuse has occurred. Most children are in the same room or the next room when domestic violence takes place.

- Seeing or hearing ill-treatment of another (as in witnessing violence to one's carer) has been identified in legislation as constituting a potential risk of harm of children.

- Domestic violence has been an important feature in some instances of child death. In many cases where children have been killed, the significance of violence to the mothers as an indicator of potential risk to the children has often not been understood or acknowledged by childcare professionals.

- Men's abuse of their children and partners may be difficult to separate into discrete categories of 'child abuse' and 'domestic violence', because in some instances the intention of the abuser is that the violence or abuse of a child will have a directly abusive impact on the woman (or vice versa). Violent men may use the children to force the woman to stay within the relationship. They may also threaten to, or actually, murder children as part of their ongoing abuse of the woman.

- The interconnectedness of men's abuse of both children and women is an important consideration with regard to the conflicts and problems women may face as mothers and has direct implications for the ability of children to disclose to their mothers that they are being abused.

- In order to develop professional understanding of, and practice in relation to, child abuse, we need to recognize that children often experience a mixture of physical, sexual and emotional abuse, and that focusing on only one aspect of these different forms of abuse can therefore be false. Similarly, where there is both domestic violence and child abuse, we need to examine the whole picture.

Notes

1 Concerns have been raised that unless there is in practice a focus on the perpetrators of violence, then this legislation may merely lead to mothers being blamed for failing to protect their children from the abuse they are themselves experiencing (Radford and Hester 2006, pp.60–61).

2 The Dartington overview of the research into child protection, *Messages from Research* (Home Office 1995a), was particularly important in this respect.

3 The reviews of agency involvement carried out under Section 8 of *Working Together to Safeguard Children* (Department of Health 1998) when a child on the child protection register dies.

CHAPTER THREE

THE IMPACT OF DOMESTIC VIOLENCE ON CHILDREN

3.1 How does domestic violence affect children?

Studies outlined in Chapters One and Two have found generally that children who have lived in the context of domestic violence may have more 'adjustment difficulties' than children from non-violent homes. At the same time, it has to be recognized that there is no uniform response to living with domestic violence. Children's responses vary enormously, with some children being affected far more than others; children within the same family can be affected differently. Each child and each child's experiences and reactions are unique.

It is, therefore, important to find out exactly what each child has experienced in order to gain some understanding of what the possible impact of these experiences might be, rather than to think in terms of a simple checklist of indicators. Even so, it can be hard to discern the specific impact on a child of living with domestic violence, especially as some of the resulting behaviours also occur in children experiencing other forms of abuse or neglect (Holden and Ritchie 1991). For many children, the impact of living with domestic violence is compounded by, and interwoven with, the impacts of the direct sexual and/or physical abuse they are also experiencing from the same, usually male, abuser.

The wide range of effects children might experience in circumstances of domestic violence can include any of the following behavioural, physical and psychological effects, which may be short- and/or long-term and which may be influenced by factors such as age, race, economic status, gender, disability, sexuality and the child's resilience:

- physical injuries, including bruises and broken bones
- being protective of the mother and/or siblings by physically intervening, withholding information, getting help etc.
- advanced in maturity and in sense of responsibility

- aggression/anger to mother and/or others, including other adults and siblings

- introversion and withdrawal

- feeling guilty and to blame

- secretive, silent, unable to tell anybody

- self-blame and bitterness

- fear, insecurity and tension

- truanting and running away

- difficulties at school

- disruptions in schooling and living arrangements

- emotional confusion in relation to parents

- bedwetting, nightmares and sleep disturbances

- eating difficulties and weight loss

- self-harm

- developmental delays (in young children)

- sadness and depression

- social isolation

- difficulties with trusting others

- low self-esteem

- poor social skills

- highly developed social skills

- ability to negotiate difficult situations.

It should be noted that until the mid-1980s, many professionals within the field of psychiatry took the view that children of all ages react only to a mild or transient degree to situations of overwhelming stress, such as that created by living in a context of domestic violence (see Harris Hendriks *et al.* 1993). This view has been superseded by the findings from research into domestic violence and children.

3.2 How do we know about the impact of domestic violence on children?

There is clear evidence from various kinds of research that domestic violence can have a detrimental impact on children. However, knowledge about how factors such as age, race, economic status, gender, disability, sexuality and resilience influence children's perceptions and reactions, in both the short and the longer term, is still developing. We need studies that look at a wider range of the population, especially non-clinical samples, and there continue to be gaps in knowledge about black and minority ethnic women and children who are experiencing domestic violence.

Research studies in the UK have often been conducted with samples taken from refuges or child protection or child support services. This creates certain limitations. For instance, in refuge samples, there may be some confusion between the effects of the domestic violence and the effects of living in a refuge (Kelly 1994; Levendosky *et al.* 2002). Refuge samples in the UK are not generally representative, as they tend to overrepresent children from lower-income families. Those studies that have tended to draw their samples from child protection or child support services also lead to problems of generality, as most children living with domestic violence do not come to the attention of any services. Such samples, therefore, will be skewed towards lower-income families (Hallett 1995). It is also possible that such studies focus on situations where the violence is likely to have been more prolonged, has escalated over time and involves physical violence (Davis and Carlson 1987; Hester and Westmarland 2005; Pagelow 1982).

The source of the data about children in many studies is the child's mother. This may ignore differences between children's and adults' perceptions of the impact of living with domestic violence. In this respect, it is important, as far as is possible and age-appropriate, that the children themselves should be allowed to define the impact of their experiences.

This need to understand children's experiences from themselves is beginning to be addressed in research in Britain. McGee (2000), for instance, interviewed 54 children about their experiences of domestic violence and of the support they received from the child protection services, as well as 48 mothers. Mullender *et al.* (2002) carried out a study involving children and young people aged 8–16 years that included a survey of 1395 children's perceptions and understandings of domestic violence, and individual or group interviews with a further sample of 54 children about their experiences of living and coping with domestic violence. Although most other research has not incorporated children's voices in this way, some has included the views of small numbers of children (e.g. Abrahams 1994; Hague, Kelly *et al.* 1996; Hester and Radford 1996; Saunders *et al.* 1995).

3.3 UK research indicating the impact of domestic violence on children

Various studies in the UK have indicated the extent of the impact of domestic violence on children from the perspective of child professionals, refuge workers and mothers:

- Moore's (1975) study of 23 'violent matrimonial cases' on the NSPCC's caseload found that in 80 per cent of the cases, children had been

'adversely affected' by living in circumstances of matrimonial violence.
These effects included children being 'anxious', having difficulties at
school and being silent and withdrawn.

- In a study in Northern Ireland (Evason 1982), 72 per cent of the women
  interviewed felt that the domestic violence they had experienced had
  adversely affected their children. This included children suffering
  'mentally', such as being very nervous and having nightmares.

- In the survey by NCH Action for Children of 108 women who had
  experienced domestic violence (who between them had 246 children),
  91 per cent believed the violence had some sort of detrimental impact on
  their children in the short term. Most (86%) of the mothers considered
  that these effects had continued in the longer term as their children were
  growing up and into adolescence. The 9 per cent of mothers who
  thought there had been no impact on their children consisted mainly of
  women whose children were still babies at the time of the violence
  (Abrahams 1994).

- In a study of refuge provision for children (Hague, Kelly *et al.* 1996), 98
  per cent of the child refuge workers felt that children experienced
  problems and difficulties as a direct result of living with domestic
  violence. Only one of the children's workers thought that children were
  not affected, and a further two workers were unsure of the impact.

- All of the one hundred women in Mama's (1996) study of black women
  experiencing domestic violence reported being aware that their partner's
  violence was having a negative impact on their children.

- Mullender *et al.* (2002) interviewed 45 children (24 girls, 21 boys) from
  25 families. Half were under the age of 11 years and the other half were
  between the ages of 12 and 16 years. More than half were from black
  and minority ethnic groups, mostly South Asian. Nearly one in six had a
  disability, including Down syndrome, hearing impairment or asthma.
  The children who coped least well experienced frequent violence over a
  long period, severe depletion of the mother's physical and emotional
  resources, and having to move multiple times.

3.4 Impact of both 'direct' abuse and the 'indirect' abuse of witnessing domestic violence

As Chapter Two indicated, many children may both experience direct abuse and witness violence to their mother. Where children do not experience direct abuse, they
are still likely to witness or be aware of the violence to their mothers. Although those
cases involving direct abuse of children are more likely to come to the attention of

child protection services, there is a growing recognition that living with or growing up in an atmosphere of violence can have detrimental effects on the children concerned. Despite differences in research methods and in the measurement instruments used, in their review of the literature on children witnessing domestic violence, Kolbo *et al.* (1996) concluded that there is clear evidence from all these studies to suggest that witnessing violence can have a negative effect on children's emotional and behavioural development. Kitzmann *et al.* (2003), in a meta-analytical review of quantitative studies on children witnessing domestic violence, concluded that there is a significant association between exposure to domestic violence and child problems. Moreover, outcomes from witnessing domestic violence are similar to those of children who have been physically abused.

Some earlier research suggested that children who were abused physically and/or sexually and had witnessed domestic violence showed most distress (Davis and Carlson 1987; Hughes 1988; Hughes, Parkinson and Vargo 1989). Hughes *et al.* (1989) refer to this as children being 'doubly abused'. Others have suggested that children react more to the stress experienced by their mothers than to the violence itself (Hershorn and Rosenbaum 1985; Thoburn, Lewis and Shemmings 1995; Wolfe *et al.* 1985). Other research, however, such as the NCH study (Abrahams 1994), found from the mothers' perceptions that there were no great differences in effects between children who had experienced violence and abuse themselves and those who were witnesses to their mothers being abused. Abrahams concludes that professionals have probably minimized the impact on children of witnessing violence: 'This in turn suggests that living in a home where there is domestic violence may have a much more adverse impact on children…than might otherwise have been supposed' (Abrahams 1994, p.41). A similar minimization by social workers of the effects on children of witnessing domestic violence was found by Farmer and Owen (1995) in their child protection study.

The majority of children in Hester and Radford's (1996) study of child contact arrangements were also reported to be adversely affected by witnessing violence to their mothers. Mothers described the many ways in which the children were affected, including having nightmares and their development being delayed:

> …she had nightmares and everything after [witnessing violent assault on mother]… My eldest daughter is affected very, very badly and, I mean, she's tried to settle into senior school this year and her teacher's been really worried because of the effect this is having on her.

> (Laura, quoted in Hester and Radford 1996, p.9)

> …he saw a lot of violence and his speech is very delayed.

> (Davina, quoted in Hester and Radford 1996, p.9)

Similarly, in a study looking at the practice issues raised by focusing on domestic violence in relation to NSPCC child abuse cases, the case files were found to contain several examples of children having witnessed attacks of physical violence towards their mothers (Hester and Pearson 1998). This included instances of children witnessing their mothers being stabbed in the head and being attacked with a knife and attempts at strangulation. In one example, the father locked the children in the room with him while he physically attacked their mother, thus forcing the children to witness the violence. Some children remembered the violence, even though their mothers did not realize that they had been aware of it. In another instance, an older child recounted the violence she had witnessed as a much younger child (aged two or three years), while in yet another case a five-year-old daughter recounted 'unprompted memories from the past of abuse…that she observed and which [mother] remembers but never thought [her daughter] had seen' (Hester and Pearson 1998, p.33).

This replicates the findings from Jaffe, Wolfe and Wilson (1990) that even very young children are aware of violence occurring around them and can be adversely affected, though they cannot necessarily make sense of it at the time.

Mothers may underestimate the impact of the violence on their children, believing that children are unaware of the violence, for instance if they are very young, if they are not present or if the violence occurs at night. Some mothers feel that they have managed to protect their children from the worst of the violence, when in fact the children are fully aware of what is happening (Mullender *et al.* 2002).

3.5 Factors influencing the impact of domestic violence on children

Although research has indicated clearly the adverse impact of domestic violence on children, it is also clear that different children react in different ways, and the relationship between the violence and the effect it has on a child can be both complex and multifaceted (Mullender *et al.* 2002; Peled and Davis 1995; Saunders *et al.* 1995). A range of personal and contextual factors can influence the extent of the impact (Kelly 1996). These 'mediating variables' have been referred to as 'protective' or 'vulnerability' factors, as they can improve or accentuate the child's response to the violence (Moore *et al.* 1990). The factors might include any of the following:

- age
- race
- socioeconomic status
- gender
- culture
- religion
- emotional and physical development of the child

- issues concerning disability
- issues concerning sexuality
- child's role and position in the family
- child's relationship with parent(s)
- child's relationship with siblings
- child's relationships outside the immediate family, including with peers, other adults and other family members
- degree of maternal stress
- frequency and form of violence
- length of exposure to violence.

There is still much to learn about the ways in which such factors might influence the way children react to living with domestic violence. The societal context, with different levels of public awareness and options for support changing over time, may also have an effect on children's reactions and strategies. Some key aspects of current knowledge regarding the impact of some of these variables are discussed below.

3.6 Age as a factor influencing the impact of domestic violence on children

At the most fundamental level, age has an influence in terms of the ways that children are able to make sense of their experiences and the range of options they have to express their distress or anxiety. There are difficulties, however, in assessing and measuring the complexity of the impact of age, and there is still much to learn.

Generally, *pre-school children* are more likely to have physical symptoms of their anxiety, such as stomach aches, bedwetting and sleep disturbances, while *primary-school children* are able to present their fears in broader ways, including behaviourally and emotionally. *Adolescents* may attempt to gain relief through drugs, early marriage or pregnancy, leaving or running away from home (Mullender 1996b; Mullender *et al.* 2002) or involvement in criminal activity (Jaffe, Wolfe and Wilson 1990).

Age and other factors related to positioning in the family mean that siblings are likely to respond differently to living with domestic violence. As Mullender and colleagues point out:

> In terms of differences between siblings, being older meant that children had more experience of abuse, but also had more knowledge and resources to draw on both to make sense of what was happening and to protect themselves physically and emotionally. Being younger meant the reverse.

(Mullender et al. *2002, p.93)*

IMPACT OF DOMESTIC VIOLENCE ON PRE-SCHOOL CHILDREN

Echoing the indications from Mullender *et al.* (2002), a number of studies and pro-
fessional/clinical observations, mainly from the USA, have suggested that younger
children in particular may be most affected by living with domestic violence (Alessi
and Hearn 1984; Pfouts, Schopler and Henley 1982). Hughes and Barad's (1983)
study found that mothers identified their pre-school children as having more behaviour problems than their older children, although school-aged boys also displayed
some aggressive behaviour. Moreover, pre-school children recorded lower levels of
self-esteem on a self-concept scoring instrument compared with school-age
children. Hughes' study (1988), again based on mothers' reports, also suggested that
pre-school children displayed more behavioural problems than school-aged
children.

Younger children may also experience delayed development as a result of living
with domestic violence, as noted by one of the refuge workers in Hague and colleagues' survey of refuge provision: 'Our worst case was a child who hadn't developed physically – a 6-year-old in nappies and not talking, unable to communicate.
But in the refuge that child developed well eventually' (Hague, Kelly *et al.* 1996,
p.32).

Levendosky *et al.* (2002), examining symptoms of post-traumatic stress disorder
(PTSD) in a sample of 62 pre-school children, found that 'preschool children who
witness domestic violence or live in domestic violence families without directly witnessing it suffer from symptoms of PTSD' (p.159). Compared with other age groups,
'preschool children appeared to be most vulnerable to symptoms of re-experiencing
the trauma and hyperarousal' (p.159).

IMPACT OF DOMESTIC VIOLENCE ON YOUNGER SCHOOL-AGED CHILDREN

Hughes (1988) found that with regard to anxiety measures, the older age groups
(6–8 years and 9–12 years) had similar anxiety levels, and these were much higher
than the levels recorded by pre-school children. However, this was seen to possibly
be a result of less accurate self-reporting in the case of pre-school children.

In contrast, other studies have found that school-aged children were likely to
have more behavioural problems (Davis and Carlson 1987; Holden and Ritchie
1991; Hughes *et al.* 1989). According to children's refuge workers, younger children
generally displayed more behavioural difficulties but were more resilient, while
older children understood more, were angrier and found trusting others especially
problematic (Hague, Kelly *et al.* 1996).

IMPACT OF DOMESTIC VIOLENCE ON OLDER CHILDREN

Few studies have looked at the specific impact of domestic violence on older
(teenage) children or have been able to chart any possible changes in responses as
children develop from school age to young adulthood. Studies drawn from refuges

have been hampered in this by the fact that teenagers do not constitute a significant proportion of the refuge population: only 15 per cent of 2271 children in refuges in a 1994–95 survey were aged 11–17 years (Hague, Kelly et al. 1996). Research studies that have drawn samples from a variety of sources have also contained few older children (e.g. Hester and Radford 1996). Our knowledge about domestic violence dynamics suggests, moreover, that violence begins and is prevalent when children are young, thus rendering escape more difficult for the woman. Therefore, by the time the children are older, the woman may have left or given up hope of leaving and so come into contact with (and been documented by) agencies infrequently.

A small study focusing on teenagers involved interviews with 21 teenagers in Israel and looked primarily at coping strategies (Goldblatt 2003). It was found that for this group, the home became an unsafe space that needed to be concealed, while the outside was a safer and more predictable space. Mullender et al. (2002) also found that teenagers may choose to leave the house while the violence is taking place, so that they witness or experience less. Teenagers are more able to exert choice about where and who they live with and so some might remain at home rather than endure the disruptions of moving to a refuge or other short-term accommodation. This might be especially so given that teenagers are more likely to have established social networks (Malos and Hague 1993a).

A Swedish study has looked specifically at older children's experiences of, and reactions to, living with domestic violence (Weinehall 1997, 2005). The study involved in-depth interviews with 15 young people (ten females, five males) aged 15 or 16 years and carried out over a period of four years. All the teenagers lived in situations of domestic violence. According to these young people, they had all tended to adopt passive responses to the violence when they were younger, whereas when they were older they were able to react differently, either by staying away or running away from home, or by using drugs or alcohol. At other times, they had dealt with the violence by denying it, lying about it or creating a fantasized reality for themselves in which there was no violence. It was not unusual for them to experience difficulties at school, including irregular attendance, truancy and poor performance and concentration. Rather than using violence to solve problems, as anticipated by other research (e.g. Straus et al. 1980), at school they were more often subjected to bullying by others. Unlike younger children, none of the young people reported having physical signs of their distress, such as headaches or sleep disturbances, but some did appear to have eating disorders and mood swings, and some had attempted suicide. Having lived with domestic violence made the young people want their own future intimate relationships to be non-violent, although that did not always transpire.

Domestic violence can continue to have specific effects on older children, even after the woman has left the violent relationship. Malos and Hague (1993b) identified particular problems regarding housing. Under previous housing legislation, where councils had a responsibility to permanently rehouse women and their dependent children, 'dependent' was not defined clearly. In practice, children over 16 years of age tended to be excluded unless they were aged 16–18 years and in full-time education. Thus, children over 16 years and not at school, and young adults aged over 18 years, who had previously lived in the mother's household, were not considered for rehousing and were either forced to stay with the violent partner or to find alternative accommodation. This was particularly difficult at a time when they, in common with younger children, were experiencing uncertainty and emotional upheaval. Similarly, with larger families, where there was a shortage of adequately sized council accommodation, older children sometimes found themselves under pressure to live away from their families. For older children living with their mothers in refuges, there is evidence to suggest that refuge life can present particular difficulties, including having little space and privacy, a lack of facilities to do homework and a lack of activities separate from those for younger children (Hague, Kelly *et al.* 1996; Mullender *et al.* 2002).

3.7 Gender as a factor influencing the impact of domestic violence on children

Although domestic violence can clearly have adverse effects on both boys and girls, it would be wrong to assume that responses can be presumed to follow some given or predetermined gender pattern. The reality is affected further by other variables, especially age. There is no single common way in which boys and girls deal with their experiences of domestic violence. This does not, however, mean that gender is not important, but that there is a need for more sophisticated methods of looking at its impact:

> To say that simple models of gendered responses are unhelpful, however, is not to say that gender is irrelevant. Rather, what we need is a framework which takes gender into account as a critical factor, but which allows for differences within, as well as between, the responses of girls and boys.
>
> *(Kelly 1994, p.49)*

The earliest research concerning the impact of gender on children's ways of reacting to and dealing with domestic violence tended to be characterized by an assumption that girls and boys will respond in stereotypically gendered ways. According to this belief in the inter-generational transmission of violence, it was presumed that girls identify with their mothers and boys with their fathers. This implies that boys will copy their father's violent behaviour and adopt externalized responses, such as aggression, disobedience and bullying, while girls will become 'victims' and learn internalized responses, such as anxiety and depression. This has also been linked to a view that boys will automatically be affected more adversely by domestic violence than girls, perhaps explaining why some studies have chosen to focus exclusively on the impact on boys (e.g. Hershorn and Rosenbaum 1985; Rosenbaum and O'Leary 1981).

The earlier studies by Jaffe and colleagues (Jaffe, Wolfe, Wilson and Zak 1985, 1986a, 1986b; Wolfe *et al.* 1985) also tended to highlight the acting-out responses of boys and the passive or internalized responses of girls (although it is worth noting that the Jaffe *et al.* 1986b study focused only on boys). However, in their later overview of the research on domestic violence and children, Jaffe, Wolfe and Wilson (1990) suggest that such conclusions may be oversimplified. Jaffe and colleagues cite other research (Rosenberg 1984) that found that boys adopted aggressive responses and girls passive responses when exposed to low levels of domestic violence, but that higher levels of exposure to domestic violence led to more aggressive responses from girls and more passive responses from boys.

Closer examination of the findings from the earlier research shows that the reality is more complicated and that the stereotypical impact of gender has been overstated (Hughes 1992; Kitzmann *et al.* 2003). Some of the earlier studies did find a correlation between gender and the gender role stereotypes defined by society as aggression in males and passivity in females (e.g. Hilberman and Munson 1977; Hughes and Barad 1983; Porter and O'Leary 1980). Others, however, have not replicated this in such a clear-cut way. The difference between boys and girls that does appear to persist across a number of these studies is a greater propensity by boys and young men to condone or accept violence to women (Burton, Regan and Kelly 1998; Mullender *et al.* 2002).

A number of studies suggest that both boys and girls can react in externalizing and/or internalizing ways at different times:

- Christopoulos *et al.* (1987) had expected boys who had lived with domestic violence to show more externalized behaviour problems, but in fact this was true of both girls and boys in comparison with a matched group of children who had not been exposed to violence.

- Stagg, Wills and Howell's (1989) study on the effects of witnessing violence amongst younger children (aged four to six years) found indications that boys displayed both more externalizing and more internalizing problems than girls.

- Jouriles, Murphy and O'Leary (1989) found externalizing behaviour among the boys they studied, but they also found that both boys and girls expressed internalized problems, such as inadequacy and immaturity.

- McGee (2000) found that both girls and boys displayed aggressive behaviour as a result of living with domestic violence. Any differences appeared to be in relation to their targets, with boys more often aggressive to their mothers, other children and sometimes girls; and girls directing aggression more often at boys and men.

- Mullender *et al.* (2002) conclude that they did not 'encounter any single pattern or syndrome, or any obvious gender divisions in children's reactions' (p.114).

Thus, gender can be seen to be an influencing factor, but its impact varies considerably. As indicated earlier, the findings from some studies appear to link differences in gender to the age of the child, although again findings in this respect are not conclusive and can be contradictory (Peled and Davis 1995). Davis and Carlson (1987), for instance, found that in both the pre-school and the school-aged groups, girls responded to their experiences of domestic violence in stereotypically passive ways, but the school-age girls were more likely than the boys to exhibit aggressive behaviours. Overall, they concluded that pre-school boys and school-age girls were most affected by living with violence.

Some studies also indicate that differences in the responses of girls and boys may vary in adolescence. Hilberman and Munson (1977) reported that while adolescent boys tended to run away, adolescent girls might develop a distrust of men. This was echoed to some extent by McGee (2000), who found that young girls were more likely to feel vulnerable in relation to boys and fearful about the future. Carlson (1990) found that adolescent boys were more likely to run away from home and reported more suicidal thoughts than adolescent girls. Weinehall (2005) reported that the young women in her study felt more threatened by their fathers than did the young men; the young women worried about the possibility of their fathers killing them and the rest of the family.

3.8 Race and ethnicity as a factor influencing the impact of domestic violence on children

Very little of the research on children and domestic violence has examined the impact that race and racism might have on the reactions and coping mechanisms of black and minority ethnic children. This may be an important variable, however, in the impact of domestic violence, how families respond and how agencies respond to families (Fantuzzo and Lindquist 1989; Mullender *et al.* 2002). Two studies in the USA that attempted to measure this factor both found that white children had more externalizing (acting out) and internalizing (withdrawn and depressed) behavioural difficulties than African American children (Stagg *et al.* 1989; Westra and Martin 1981).

In the UK, the study by Mullender *et al.* (2002) attempted to incorporate ethnicity by over-sampling for black and minority ethnic children. Their resulting sample was none the less small, with 14 children of mainly South Asian descent being interviewed. The team found that coping with and surviving domestic violence were affected by barriers at the three (interacting) levels of society, family and community, and the individual:

On the wider, societal level, the clash of Western and South Asian cultures and values creates dilemmas and distress, as naturally, do institutional racism and racial harassment. At the intermediate level of family and community, it is religion, patriarchal cultural practices and the traditions of individual families that emerge as significant. At the individual level, a child may benefit from, or struggle with, the impact of his or her ethnicity.

(Mullender et al. *2002, p.135)*

One area where the South Asian children appeared to be especially affected was with regard to speech development, with more of these children experiencing developmental delay or stopping speaking for long periods. The authors suggest that the differences when compared with white children may lie in the South Asian children having to communicate in two languages and finding 'it all too much' (Mullender *et al.* 2002, p.151), or that the pressure of not bringing shame on the family through telling others about the abuse further silenced the children concerned.

Other literature has also pointed to the particular difficulties and experiences of black women and children living with domestic violence, especially when set against a racist and hostile society (Bowstead *et al.* 1995; Imam 1994; Mama 1996). Some of the impacts on children are likely to be exacerbated by the fact that some children may be subjected to the additional threat of abduction abroad or by being asked inappropriately to act as interpreters or translators if their mother's first language is not English (Bowstead *et al.* 1995).

Using the child as an interpreter is unsuitable in situations of domestic violence, whether this involves the child interpreting between their mother (or father) and professional agencies or for more informal networks. It might restrict the amount of information women feel able to disclose in the presence of their children or force women to give details that they believe they have protected their children from knowing; it may raise difficult issues with regard to confidentiality; and it could prove to be an onerous responsibility for children, thereby increasing any stress they may already be experiencing.

Imam (1994) points out that for many black and minority ethnic children, the family home is considered a refuge from the daily hostility and racism they experience. Thus, any violence inside the home can seriously undermine that sense of safety and can lead to particular feelings of vulnerability and insecurity for children. Imam also suggests that cultural and religious expectations for Asian girls might lead to them being ostracized by family and community if they try to leave with their mother to go to a refuge or other safe place (this might also apply to a lesser extent to Asian boys, and to children from other cultures). To prevent this ostracism, some mothers may choose to leave their (female) children behind when they escape the violence. This in turn may lead some young Asian women to run away from home (the reverse of some of the studies mentioned earlier, where (white) adolescent boys in particular were found to be more likely to run away from home).

The impact for children of living with domestic violence is probably influenced by how they make sense of what has happened, and race may have an impact on this. This will be influenced further by the institutional racism women and children encounter and by the probable lack of action by professionals to help them. For children from mixed-race relationships, trying to understand their experiences might be made more difficult by not knowing which parent to identify with; this might be complicated further by whether the violent man is black or white and by the age and gender of the child. Workers at a specialist refuge for black women and children in Hague and colleagues' study reported one such example, where the white father had been telling his children that it was 'wrong' or 'awful' to be black, with the result that the children were 'absolutely torn apart' (Hague, Kelly *et al.* 1996, p.51), unable to identify with their father because of what he had done, and unable to identify with their mother as a result of what their father had said.

Black children may also have difficulties with identification within black and minority ethnic families where abusive men might use racism as a further means of control. This might apply in relation to immigration, for instance, or as a reason to encourage women (and children) not to contact the police or have men excluded from the home (Mama 1996). Clearly, it is important to gain more knowledge about the impact of race and racism on children's reactions to domestic violence, especially as it involves a significant number of children. Most refuges, for example, at any given time will contain 'a significant population' of ethnic minority children (Hague, Kelly *et al.* 1996, p.19).

3.9 Socioeconomic status as a factor influencing the impact of domestic violence on children

Studies tend to be limited by their omission of economic status as a variable in terms of children's responses to domestic violence. There is usually no consideration, for instance, of how factors relating to poverty and poor housing – or affluence and adequate housing – may have a bearing on how children react to living with domestic violence. Data from the 2001 British Crime Survey (Walby and Allen 2004) show that women at risk of domestic violence are more likely to be living in social rented accommodation, thus also indicating that they are more likely to be poor. Regardless of whether this is an outcome or a cause of the violence, it suggests that children living with domestic violence may also be facing poverty. Economic status will undoubtedly have some impact on how agencies respond to families, as well as on how women are able to deal with, and find solutions to, the violence they are experiencing. This is especially so given that many research samples, as outlined earlier, are inevitably skewed towards lower-income families. This is an area where further research is needed.

3.10 Disability as a factor influencing the impact of domestic violence on children

Very little attention has been paid to how children's disability might influence the impact of domestic violence on children. This is despite the fact that attacks on women during pregnancy may mean that there is a higher proportion of children with disabilities living in domestic violence situations (Radford and Hester 2006) (see also Chapter One). Kelly (1992) has documented how both physical and learning disabilities can be caused by direct and indirect abuse within the context of domestic violence.

Confirmation of this possible link appears in Hague, Kelly *et al.*'s (1996) survey of refuges, which found that over a quarter of the refuge groups had at least one child resident who had a disability. The most commonly reported impairments (although not necessarily linked directly with domestic violence) were asthma and learning disabilities; there were also children with Down syndrome, cerebral palsy, spina bifida and hydrocephalus. Some refuges were attempting to address the needs of disabled children (and women) by employing specialist workers and improving the accessibility of buildings, but they were restricted to some extent by funding limitations. However, it is important that any developments in this area also recognize the fact that disability is a socially constructed concept. Thus, workers and refuge residents need to be aware of and challenge stereotypical attitudes and beliefs about disability if any long-term changes and improvements in service are to occur.

Mullender and colleagues interviewed seven children who had disabilities and were living with domestic violence. The authors state that this 'produced some very interesting and useful material about what had been witnessed and the impact it had had' (Mullender *et al.* 2002, p.27), although no details were provided. Again, this is an area where there is still much to learn, as there has been little consideration of the long-term implications of violence in pregnancy for children's physical and mental health.

3.11 Mother–child relationships as a factor influencing the impact of domestic violence on children

Some studies have suggested that the impact on children of living with domestic violence might be affected by the relationship between mother and child, and especially might be linked to the amount of stress experienced by the mother. As mentioned in Chapter One, some women experience depression as a result of being abused by their partners (Hughes 1992; Radford and Hester 2006), possibly exacerbated in some cases by other negative life events and by poor housing and poverty (Peled and Davis 1995). This may result in the care of children being particularly stressful for these women (Radford and Hester 2006; Holden and Ritchie 1991; Wolfe *et al.* 1985). Such maternal stress may at times compound the behavioural problems of their children (Wolfe *et al.* 1986, 1988). This is especially the case where the mother's experiences mean that she is emotionally distanced, unavailable or even sometimes abusive to the child, such that the consequent lack of support and attachment may increase the impact of the domestic violence for the child.

Mothers may find it difficult to talk to children about the violence, either believing this to be protective or because they are unsure how to talk about the violence (McGee 2000). Many mothers do their utmost to protect their children from witnessing the violence (Hoff 1990), although, as outlined earlier, the reality is that most children are aware of its occurrence and can describe episodes they have witnessed without their parents' knowledge (Hester and Pearson 1998; Jaffe, Wolfe and Wilson 1990). Thus, although children generally want to talk about their experiences of domestic violence, they are often unable to do so with their mothers (McGee 2000; Mullender *et al.* 2002). This may in turn have its own impact on children.

Some children might also have to deal with the confusing situation of their mothers being stricter and less affectionate in the presence of their violent partners (Radford and Hester 2006). This might be compounded by the father's negative and strict involvement with their children (Holden and Ritchie 1991).

3.12 Frequency and form of violence as factors influencing the impact of domestic violence on children

Both the amount and the forms of violence to which children are exposed may have an impact on how they are affected. In their meta-analysis of 118 studies relating to the effects on children of witnessing domestic violence, Kitzmann *et al.* (2003) found that there was a notably greater impact of witnessing physical violence between parents than in witnessing other forms of destructive behaviour between parents (e.g. verbal aggression). In a study that looked at the impact of different forms of violence, Fantuzzo *et al.* (1991) suggested that children who observed both physical and verbal violence displayed more behavioural difficulties than those children whose observations had been limited to verbal violence alone. Hughes (1992) also found that the difficulties experienced by children were greater when they were exposed to more forms of violence.

However, there has been almost no consideration in any of the studies that children may also witness or overhear the sexual abuse or rape of their mothers, and of whether the impact of this is different from the impact of other forms of abuse. Weinehall (1997) mentions that the five adolescent boys in her project often had to listen to their fathers raping their mothers and describes their sense of powerlessness at not being able to intervene to stop this. In the NCH study, one in ten of the mothers reported that they had been sexually abused or raped by their partners in front of their children. One of the mothers described the difficulties this presented for her children: 'I was raped once, in front of the children, with a knife at my throat. The children tried to pull him off, and it was just awful' (Abrahams 1994, p.31). On the whole, however, the issue of sexual violence and its impact on children remains secret and invisible, as tends to be the case with sexual violence to women generally.

In addition, there may be a correlation between the length and frequency of exposure to violence and an increase in the adversity of children's reactions (Christopoulos *et al.* 1987; Jouriles, Barling and O'Leary 1987; Kitzmann *et al.* 2003). Research is beginning to indicate that prolonged exposure to domestic violence may actually result in neurophysiological changes and impacts on the structure of the brain, making recovery more difficult and resulting in PTSD (see also Section 3.16). As Robbie Rossman points out:

> ...prolonged threat to survival may leave the individual in a dysregulated state, where perception, cognition, and emotional systems are functioning atypically (in part to compensate for dysregulation) and permanent changes to brain structure are possible...there could be major consequences for ongoing cognitive and emotional behaviour of traumatized children and perhaps for their developmental trajectories in these domains.
>
> *(Rossman 1998, pp.226–227)*

Hyperarousal and reduced ability to take on board new information might result, thus potentially resulting both in behaviour problems such as acting out and in difficulties with learning.

3.13 Children's coping and survival strategies as factors influencing the impact of domestic violence on them

Although living with domestic violence can undoubtedly have adverse effects on children, it is important to recognize that children are not merely passive bystanders to events around them but will act and make choices in highly individualized ways in order to cope with and improve their situation. Some of the choices made by children, especially older children, have been outlined above. Research evidence suggests that many children develop complex strategies of survival in order to deal with the stress and adversity they are experiencing (e.g. Hester and Radford 1996; Radford and Hester 2006). These strategies will depend to a certain extent on each child's behavioural and emotional development (Jaffe, Wolfe and Wilson 1990).

The survival strategies adopted by children living with domestic violence can be diverse and may appear contradictory. For instance, some children become protective of their mothers and/or siblings and choose various reactive and proactive methods to try to keep their mothers safe, including physical intervention, withholding information, and getting help from neighbours or formal organizations (Dobash and Dobash 1984; Hester and Pearson 1998; Hoff 1990; Jaffe, Wolfe and Wilson 1990; Mullender *et al.* 2002). Some children feel so concerned for their mother's safety that they want to protect her all the time; in such cases, children might refuse to go to school or feign illness so that they can stay at home with their mother (Jaffe, Wolfe and Wilson 1990; Jaffe *et al.* 1986c). Some children's coping strategies change over time. One 17-year-old woman who had lived with violence over a ten-year period explained how her initial protective way of coping had changed to staying away:

> At first…I wouldn't leave my mam. Wouldn't leave her anywhere. I was round her all the time. And then, when I was about 14, I used to just stay out all the time… I used to stay at my real dad's, at my sister's. At my boyfriend's. Anywhere. Anywhere I could just to get out of the house.

(Quoted in Hague, Kelly et al. 1996, p.98)

Even young children can show very complex patterns of protective intervention, such as trying to mediate between their parents or acting as a distraction to bring the violence to an end. These protective responses may become more frequent than distressed responses as the child gets older (Cummings, Zahn-Waxler and Radke-Yarrow 1984; Goldblatt 2003). Many of the children in the NCH survey were younger (average age 6.7 years), but almost a third (31%) were reported by mothers as being protective towards them, which for 22 per cent of the children included physically intervening to try to stop the violence:

> My mother sounded so desperate downstairs…crying and screaming…so we went downstairs with our tennis racquets and started hitting him.

(Abrahams 1994, p.37)

For some children, this desire to protect their mothers also includes fantasizing about killing the violent partner and plans for revenge (Weinehall 1997). For others, these fantasies might be a way of dealing with the guilt, shame and fear they feel concerning their own perceived inability or failure to protect their mothers.

Other children protect their mothers in less direct ways, for example by learning that their presence in the room will bring the violence to an end (Hester and Radford 1996; Radford and Hester 2006). Children may try to protect their mothers by gaining practical help and information for them. Many children contacting ChildLine about domestic violence, for instance, requested details of women's refuges to pass on to their mothers and said that they encouraged their mothers to leave their violent partners (Epstein and Keep 1995).

Some children protect their mothers by taking on responsibilities in the home, such as childcare for younger siblings and household chores, in the hope that this will help to keep the peace. If this fails, they may provide support for other members of the family after a violent episode or try to placate their fathers (Jaffe, Wolfe and Wilson 1990). This assumption of adult responsibilities can lead to children becoming 'parental children', which can be burdensome and may prevent the children from asking their mothers for help (Epstein and Keep 1995). After a woman has left a violent partner, this sense of responsibility to protect their mother might be expressed by some children wanting to live with their father. Though apparently contradictory, this might appear to the child to be the best strategy to adopt to keep their mother safe from further violence. It may also serve to allow children to act as caretakers for their fathers in those situations where the father has made threats to commit suicide if the mother and/or children leave (Hester and Radford 1996; Radford and Hester 2006). Others, especially older children, may adopt strategies aimed at self-protection, including presenting an external front of fearlessness in order to hide the fear and anxiety that lies beneath the surface (Grusznski, Brink and Edleson 1988) and appearing competent through opposing the violence (Goldblatt 2003).

Children are likely to believe that somehow they are responsible for the violence. Indeed, they are aware that violence can stem from arguments over childcare, children's behaviour or discipline, and resentment about the amount of time women devote to their children (Grusznski *et al.* 1988; Hilton 1992). This sense that they have in some way caused the violence can lead children to attempt to modify their behaviour (e.g. by being quiet or 'perfect' – the latter might include excelling at school) in the hope that this will prevent an episode of violence, thereby protecting their mothers (Saunders *et al.* 1995). Even babies are reported to sense that changing their behaviour can have an effect on what happens in their environment (Radford and Hester 2006). A children's worker in Hague and colleagues' refuge survey, for instance, noted how living with domestic violence could lead to babies being withdrawn and 'unnaturally' quiet: '…this baby just sits there and stays shtum, because it has learned that is the best coping tactic' (Hague, Kelly *et al.* 1996, p.43). Similarly, one of the mothers in the same survey reported that her two older children had immediately taken to sleeping all through the night, as though this was a way of ensuring that 'nothing bad would happen' (Hague, Kelly *et al.* 1996, p.43).

Other children decide that their optimum chance of survival might lie in siding with the father, including sometimes joining in with the abuse of the mother (Hilton 1992). This identification with the abuser might also provide some children with a sense of control in a frightening situation (Grusznski *et al.* 1988) and might include expressions of anger and aggression towards the mother, either for her (perceived) failure to protect them or because they mirror the process of the abuser blaming her for causing the violence (Abrahams 1994; Mullender *et al.* 2002; Saunders *et al.* 1995).

3.14 Children's secrecy as a coping strategy influencing the impact of domestic violence on them

The findings from a number of studies (Hester and Pearson 1998; Mullender *et al.* 2002) indicate that children living with domestic violence may keep silent about what they know or have observed and will disclose this information only when they are in some way given permission to do so. Mullender and colleagues point out that South Asian children are especially likely to keep silent because they 'bear a particular burden of upholding family honour and pride by not talking about the abuse' (Mullender *et al.* 2002, p.227).

Many children living with domestic violence learn from an early age that the violence must be kept secret at all costs. This may be because of the shame and social stigma attached to the violence, to protect the abuser, or because of fear of the mother being blamed or the children being removed (Abrahams 1994; Epstein and Keep 1995; Mullender *et al.* 2002). Children may not understand the reasons for the secrecy, but they learn to use a range of strategies to prevent disclosure and maintain the secret. These strategies might include lying about the violence, inventing stories to conceal the facts, limiting their contact with others and not bringing friends to the home (Abrahams 1994; Grusznski *et al.* 1988; Saunders *et al.* 1995). The pressure of secrecy makes disclosure difficult for children, who may go to great lengths to hide the reality of what is happening:

> My teacher tried to find out, but I just didn't let anything slip. I just said, 'No, everything's okay.' You just smile, don't you, and try to cover it…

> *(Quoted in Abrahams 1994, p.81)*

In addition, the presence of domestic violence and the dynamics created by it serve to silence children about their own or their siblings' physical and/or sexual abuse by the same perpetrator: 'The existence of other forms of violence, and the victimization of others by violence, will present a major obstacle to the disclosure of abuse. Resistance to disclosure can clearly be created by violence' (Goddard and Hiller 1993, p.27). In this way, domestic violence can be seen to be a factor in the continuation of abuse to children.

3.15 Children's resilience as a factor influencing the impact of domestic violence on them

Increasingly, studies suggest that resilience may be a factor in understanding why some children who live with domestic violence do not appear to be as adversely affected as others (Graham-Bermann 1998; Jaffe, Wolfe and Wilson 1990; Kitzmann *et al.* 2003; Radford and Hester 2006). In Wolfe *et al.*'s (1985) study, a significant number of children showed few negative reactions to domestic violence, and some were rated as having above-average social skills and social adjustment. Similarly, two of the studies in Fantuzzo and Lindquist's (1989) overview of the impact of witnessing domestic violence found no significant adverse emotional effects of this on the children involved.

The fact that children may cope very differently to similar stressful and adverse experiences has been explained partly by the notion of psychological resilience. Resilience does not necessarily act as a protection against adversity, but somehow it works to provide the ability to recover more readily from it, thereby preventing impacts in the longer term. An International Resilience Project, set up to study how

different cultures and countries promoted resilience, adopted the following definition of resilience:

> Resilience is a universal capacity which allows a person, group or community
> to prevent, minimize or overcome the damaging effects of adversity.

(Grotberg 1997, p.19)

Resilience as a concept has been explored for many years in attempts to develop an
understanding of which, if any, factors might contribute to the promotion of resil-
iency in children. According to Rutter (1985), these 'protective factors' against
adversity might include self-esteem, the timing of incidents, the child's ability to
attach meaning to and make sense of events, and the child's relationships with
others. As Mullender *et al.* (2002) point out, these are also the factors that are likely to
be undermined by experiencing domestic violence. Other studies (e.g. Fonagy *et al.*
1994; Garmezy 1985; Smith 1997; Thomas, Chess and Birch 1968) have identified
factors potentially leading to resilience in children, although little is known about
how these factors interact and how they work in different contexts (Grotberg 1997).
These factors include:

* even, adaptable temperament
* capacity for organized thinking and problem-solving
* physical attractiveness (in the sense that this enhances self-esteem and
  positive interactions with others)
* sense of humour
* good social skills and a supportive peer network
* sense of autonomy and purpose
* secure attachments to parent(s)
* connections to a wider community, such as religious groups, school or
  extended family members.

Resilience is often assumed to reside within the individual, and yet it is clear that the
above factors are also influenced by their interaction with environmental and social
contexts. The self-esteem of black children, children with impairments and econom-
ically disadvantaged children, for instance, may be affected by negative perceptions
of them being different or 'other'. Some research indicates that when parents (or
other adults) identify and acknowledge the adverse reaction a child will probably
encounter, then they are better able to cope. This was the case in relation to black
children in Rosenberg and Simmons' (1971) study and more generally in Mullender
et al.'s (2002) study.

Thus, it is possible for adults to deal with children in ways that can actually encourage resilient responses. From her work on the International Resilience project,
Grotberg (1997) suggests that adults can do this in various ways, including

encouraging children's autonomy and independence, teaching communication and problem-solving skills and showing children how to handle negative thoughts and behaviours. In turn, children themselves become active in developing their own resilience.

Clearly, there is a need for more detailed work to be undertaken to identify and understand what these protective or resilient factors for children living with domestic violence might be. This would help adults to promote resilience in such children, thereby reducing the potential for continued harm:

> Not all children are equally vulnerable; nor are they all equally resilient. But a combination of a resilient child who is also vulnerable means it is more likely they will find competent and functional ways of dealing with their vulnerability, reducing its potential negative impact.

(Smith 1997, p.52)

3.16 Witnessing domestic violence and post-traumatic stress disorder

Some clinicians and researchers have linked the trauma of experiencing and witnessing domestic violence with the impact exemplified by PTSD. This is seen as a type of enduring anxiety disorder following exposure to a traumatic event. Harris Hendriks *et al.* (1993, p.13) summarize some of the main manifestations of PTSD in children as:

- numbness and detachment with withdrawal

- disturbed sleep (possibly with recurrent dreams)

- impaired concentration and memory

- hyper-alertness and 'jumpiness'

- experiencing 'flashbacks'.

These effects may also be underpinned by neurophysiological changes, as indicated in Section 3.12.

In the context of domestic violence, it may be particularly difficult and stressful for children to deal with the fact that the trauma is occurring within the family, undermining the child's notions of safety and protection from harm. The child might react in ways consistent with the symptoms of PTSD. However, the reactions may become apparent much later than the traumatic event and may, therefore, be difficult to link to the original trauma: '...the notion of posttraumatic stress implies that children who chronically witness wife abuse in their homes may display emotional symptomatology at some point in time that may be quite far removed from the initial traumatic events' (Jaffe, Wolfe and Wilson 1990, p.72).

Silvern and Kaersvang (1989), for instance, proposed that children living with domestic violence perceived each episode of violence as a traumatic event. They concluded that this traumatic impact alone is enough to produce distress for children. Jaffe, Wolfe and Wilson (1990) suggested that some children's coping reactions to witnessing domestic violence can lead to behaviours that are similar to those of children suffering from PTSD.

In the UK, there has been some resistance to the notion of traumatic stress in childhood. Until 1985, some members of the psychiatric profession still considered that children reacted to even the most stressful experiences by displaying only very slight and short-lived emotional and/or behavioural changes (Harris Hendriks *et al.* 1993, p.9). There is now a growing body of research to suggest that children can experience PTSD in similar ways to adults and may react in such a way to witnessing violence (Rossman 1998) and to parental murder (Harris Hendriks et al. 1993). However, it is important to treat the concept with caution and not to apply it as some generalized pathology to all children living with domestic violence. As Finkelhor (1996) points out, it would be wrong to assume that all sexual abuse 'fits' into the PTSD model, because a whole range of individual and social factors affect each person's reactions to sexual abuse. The same complexities apply to the impact on children of living with domestic violence.

A number of studies of children witnessing domestic violence indicate that children aged six years and older may experience traumatic symptoms as a result of these experiences (Graham-Bermann and Levendosky 1998; Kilpatrick and Williams 1997; Lehmann 1997; Rossman 1998). For instance, Lehmann (1997) found that 56 per cent of a sample of 84 child witnesses of domestic violence met diagnostic criteria for PTSD. Levendosky *et al.* (2002) used maternal reports to examine the impact of domestic violence on a sample of 62 pre-school children. They found that pre-school children who witness domestic violence or who live in domestic violence families without directly witnessing it may also suffer from symptoms of PTSD[1] and appeared more vulnerable to symptoms of re-experiencing the trauma and hyperarousal.

The link between children witnessing violence and PTSD was also echoed by Brandon and Lewis (1996), who found that three of the six children over eight years old in their intensive sample could possibly be identified as suffering from PTSD. However, they add that 'the relationship between the behaviour and the violence is probable rather than proven' (Brandon and Lewis 1996, p.40) and acknowledge that their sample is very small.

3.17 Summary

- Domestic violence is likely to have a detrimental impact on children.

- In the context of domestic violence, many children experience direct sexual or physical abuse and witness violence to their mother.

- The witnessing by children of domestic violence has tended to be minimized by professionals, even though in some cases this might cause the child to react in ways consistent with the symptoms of PTSD.

- Children might experience a wide range of behavioural, physical and psychological effects, which may be short and/or long term.

- Children's perceptions and reactions to living with domestic violence will be influenced, both in the short and the longer term, by factors such as age, race, economic status, gender, disability, sexuality and their own resilience. Children's responses to living with domestic violence vary enormously, with some children being affected far more than others. Children within the same family may be affected differently.

- Generally, pre-school children are more likely to have physical symptoms of their anxiety, primary school children present their fears behaviourally and emotionally, and adolescents may try to gain relief through drugs, early marriage or pregnancy, running away or involvement in criminal activity.

- Gender can be an influencing factor in the impact of domestic violence on children, but this varies considerably and there is no single common response to the way in which boys and girls deal with their experiences of domestic violence.

- There may be particular difficulties for black and minority ethnic children living with domestic violence, especially when set against a racist and hostile society. Some of the impacts on black and minority ethnic children are likely to be exacerbated by additional threats of abduction abroad or by being asked inappropriately to act as interpreters or translators.

- The impact on children of living with domestic violence may be affected by the relationship between mother and child, especially linked to the amount of stress experienced by the mother and how this affects the mother's parenting role.

- Children are not merely passive bystanders to the domestic violence occurring around them. They act and make choices, and many children develop a wide range of complex strategies of coping and survival in order to deal with the stress and adversity they are experiencing.

- Children's resilience may be an influencing factor to explain why some children who live with domestic violence do not appear to be as adversely affected as others.

- There is a need for more detailed research in the UK, looking at a wider range of the population, in order to understand more about the complexities, similarities and differences between children's experiences of, and reactions to, living with domestic violence.

Note

1   They did not, however, meet the criteria for diagnosis of PTSD using the *Diagnostic and Statistical Manual of Mental Disorders*, 4th edition (DSM-IV) criteria.

PART TWO

The Legal Context

CHAPTER FOUR

MAKING SAFE ARRANGEMENTS FOR CHILDREN AFFECTED BY DOMESTIC VIOLENCE: PUBLIC AND PRIVATE LAW

The Children Act 1989 redefined childcare law and introduced new measures for working with children and families in both public and private family law. The Act was the first childcare legislation to take into account the child's religious, ethnic, cultural and linguistic background. It embodied a new approach to working with and for children, underpinned by the principle that the child's welfare is paramount.

In 2002, the Adoption and Children Act extended the definition of 'harm' as stated in the Children Act 1989 to include 'impairment suffered from seeing or hearing the ill treatment of another' (Section 120), and this came into effect in January 2005.

The Children Act 2004 provides a further legislative framework for the wider national programme aimed at improving children's lives and transforming children's services locally, set out in the publication *Every Child Matters* (Department for Education and Skills 2005).

The Domestic Violence Crime and Victims Act 2004 created a new offence of causing or allowing the death of a child or vulnerable adult, whereby a person is guilty of such an offence if a child or vulnerable adult dies as a result of an unlawful act and the defendant either was or should have been aware of the risk and failed to take steps to protect them. This clause was introduced in March 2005.

4.1 The Children Act 1989 and domestic violence

The Children Act 1989 does not overtly acknowledge the context of domestic violence in which many children live. Despite the fact that the Act is accompanied by ten volumes of guidance, none was issued on the issue of domestic violence; nor is there any recognition that domestic violence is a key factor in the breakup of many relationships. Until very recently, the concept of risk of violence to one parent from the other, or from another family member, and the possible impact of this on the first parent's ability to protect and care for children, was not identified as a factor requiring consideration.

The need to minimize the risk of violence during family proceedings was highlighted during the passage of the Family Law Act 1996 and was recognized as one of the key principles of Parts II and III of that Act (divorce, legal aid and mediation). The recognition by Parliament that this principle was needed was due, in part, to greater awareness following the Home Affairs select committee enquiry into domestic violence in 1992 and to subsequent publicity of the extent and nature of domestic violence, as well as growing concerns about the unfortunate effects of its absence within the Children Act 1989 itself, particularly in relation to Section 8 orders (private arrangements for children after relationship breakdown).

Although Parts I–V of the Children Act 1989 all contain implications for the welfare of children living with or witnessing domestic violence and the parent with care (usually the mother), there are a number of key sections that have specific relevance for individual and corporate strategies to improve protection and safety. The main features are set out below.

4.2 Part I of the Children Act 1989

Under this Act, proceedings can be heard in any court, concurrent with other proceedings, for example alongside proceedings for injunctions under the Family Law Act 1996 (see Chapter Six). Part I of the Act also introduced two new central features: the 'welfare checklist' and the concept of 'parental responsibility'. The welfare checklist determines the criteria that should be taken into account when decisions are being made relating to the upbringing of a child. These welfare considerations are paramount, and this is known as the 'paramountcy principle'.

The 'no order' principle should also be taken into account. This states that the court should make an order under Section 8 (which regulates contact and residence of children in private proceedings) only if it is first convinced that doing so would be better for the child than making no order at all.

The Act and these principles were designed to put the child and their welfare at the centre of all decisions.

THE WELFARE CHECKLIST [CHILDREN ACT 1989, SECTION 1(3)]

The court has to take into consideration the following factors in every case involving a child's upbringing where the making, variation or discharge of any order is opposed by any party, and in every case where the child may be at risk of harm. This applies both to orders in family proceedings under Section 8 and for applications by local authorities relating to care and supervision under Part IV:

- the ascertainable wishes and feelings of the child concerned, considered in the light of the child's age and understanding

- the child's physical, emotional and educational needs

- the likely effect on the child of any change in his or her circumstances

- the child's age, sex, background and any characteristics that the court considers relevant

- any harm that the child has suffered or is at risk of suffering

- the capability of the child's parents, and any other person in relation to whom the court considers the question to be relevant, in meeting the child's needs

- the range of proceedings available to the court under the Act in the proceedings in question.

From the perspective of those experiencing domestic violence, the implementation of the welfare checklist can be problematic in practice. For example, there is no formal requirement on the court to consider the effects of the decisions made under the Children Act 1989 on the safety of an adult (usually the woman) who may be at risk.

PARENTAL RESPONSIBILITY

'Parental responsibility' is defined in the Act as 'all the rights, duties, powers, responsibilities and authority which by law a parent of a child has in relation to the child and his property' [Children Act 1989, Section 3(1)] and is awarded according to birth status and residence arrangements.

The following provisions apply. The *natural mother* automatically has parental responsibility and never loses it until the child reaches age 16 years. The *natural father* can have parental responsibility if:

- he was married to the mother at the time of the child's birth

- he marries the mother subsequently

- (since 1 December 2003) he jointly registers the child's birth with the mother

- he and the mother make a parental responsibility agreement

- he applies to the court and the court grants it.

Anyone with a *residence order* (see below) in respect of a particular child also has parental responsibility for as long as that residence order lasts (unless the person is a parent of the child, in which case they keep parental responsibility even after the order ends).

The *local authority* has parental responsibility when a care order is in force, but it shares this with the natural parents.

Once parental responsibility has been given to a natural father (if he is not auto-matically entitled through marriage), he cannot have it removed from him, even if the child does not live with him. The natural father has precedence over others in rela-tion to guardianship of children after the death of the natural mother; however, if there is a residence order in force in someone else's name when the mother dies, then that person may be granted parental responsibility.

4.3 Making safe arrangements for children after relationship breakdown: private law proceedings under Part II of the Children Act 1989

Under Section 8 of the Children Act 1989, the court may make four types of order within family proceedings in respect of the child's welfare:

- *Contact order:* an order requiring the person with whom a child lives, or is to live, to allow the child to visit, stay or have contact with the person named in the order.

- *Residence order:* an order settling arrangements about with whom the child is to live.

- *Prohibited steps order:* an order prohibiting a person with parental responsibility from taking any steps contained in the order without the consent of the court.

- *Specific issue order:* an order giving direction regarding a specific question in relation to any aspect of parental responsibility for a child.

The court may also, within its powers under Section 10 of the Children Act 1989, make an order in any family proceedings where questions arise with respect to the welfare of the child (for example, with proceedings under the Family Law Act 1996; see below and Chapter Six).

WELFARE REPORTS AND THE ROLE OF CAFCASS

In Section 8 proceedings, a welfare report (ordered under Section 7 of the Children Act 1989) is often of vital importance in the court's decision-making in relation to the welfare of a child. The Children and Families Court Advisory Support Service (CAFCASS) was established in 2001 (from the former Family Court Welfare Service) to work with children and their families and to advise the family courts on what it considers to be in the children's best interests.

National Standards (1994) for the probation family court welfare service state clearly that if there is domestic violence, then the preparation of such reports should not require the woman to attend joint interviews with her abuser. CAFCASS intro-duced a new Domestic Violence Policy in 2005, which again states that women who have been subject to abuse should never be required to attend joint interviews with their abusers. Further guidance and training are being developed by CAFCASS in response to a 2005 report by HM Inspectorate of Court Administration (HMICA), which provides a detailed account of the numerous ways in which CAFCASS failed to ensure the safety of survivors of domestic violence and their children in family proceedings.

UNDERSTANDING THE DYNAMICS OF DOMESTIC VIOLENCE AND RISKS FOR SAFETY IN POST-SEPARATION ARRANGEMENTS FOR CHILDREN

When a woman leaves home because of her partner's violence, she will usually take the children with her and will probably wish to continue to care for them and make a home for them. Usually, this is in the children's own interests. The children and the absent parent may wish to see each other regularly, and sometimes this can be arranged without major problems. But in many cases, the mother will be reluctant for her children to see her abusive ex-partner because she is fearful for their or her own safety. These fears may, however, be ignored or minimized by professionals who believe, mistakenly, that if there is no clear evidence of substantial risk to the child, then contact with both parents is in the child's best interests (see Barron *et al.* 1992; Hester and Radford 1996; Hester *et al.* 1997; Saunders 2004).

This failure to recognize the risks of domestic violence to the safety of both the (usually) mother and the child has sometimes been compounded by the apparent lack of hard evidence of previous or present violence to the mother or the child. This itself results from a number of other problems, including lack of coordination of information and evidence across criminal justice and family proceedings; absence, until very recently, within statutory responses of full recognition of the impact of domestic violence on children living with it; court pressure to reach agreement over arrangements for children; inadequate legal representation leading to the full nature of the abuse being hidden or minimized; and the intrinsically private nature of the abusive behaviour itself.

The process of determining where the best interests of the children lie can be traumatic for many women. Where an application is made to the courts, in cases where there is no agreement between the parents on where a child should live or on how much contact (if any) the non-resident parent is to have, a CAFCASS officer will usually be appointed to prepare a report on the child's circumstances and to make recommendations to the court. Under the Children Act 1989, decisions about a child's welfare are taken by those with parental responsibility unless the family courts have become involved and the parents disagree. Applications are made to the courts about matters such as contact or residence, and outcomes are then determined by the courts rather than by those with parental responsibility. Those applying to the family courts for contact arrangements are, since 2005, required to complete a 'gateway application' form, which, among other questions, asks the applicant to identify whether domestic violence has been a factor in the breakdown of the relationship.

This is problematic in cases where the applicant is the violent parent and where the non-abusing parent/respondent who may be at risk is not aware of the need to complete the form herself.

In the past, professionals interpreted the need for joint decision-making by those with parental responsibility to mean that joint meetings should be held with both parents, and they have sometimes persuaded or pressured women into attending (see Hester et al. 1997). Meeting her abuser again face to face can be a frightening experience for the woman, and in many cases it has led to further threats and abuse against the woman and/or the children. Such practices are now less common, as a result of improved awareness, the critical report by HMICA and the development of a CAFCASS Domestic Violence Policy (see above). The new Domestic Violence Policy and recent nationwide training within CAFCASS should improve this situation further.

A number of problems have been identified with respect to Section 8 orders under the Children Act 1989 in cases where there is domestic violence. The lack of recognition within the Children Act in general, and within the welfare checklist in particular, of the risks and practical problems faced by women and children experiencing domestic violence in making safe arrangements after relationship breakdown has been acknowledged only recently. Some practitioners interpreting the 1989 Act have frequently assumed that, when parents do separate, the children will almost always benefit from continuing to have substantial and frequent contact with the non-resident parent (usually the father). (This has been enshrined in case law – see above.) However (as indicated in Chapters One and Two), it has been identified by the vice-chair of CAFCASS that almost 66 per cent of CAFCASS's caseload of applications to the family courts involve domestic violence, and we also know that almost 90 per cent of cases of domestic violence involve a male perpetrator and a female victim. Therefore, in many cases where contact arrangements are being decided, the absent parent (with whom contact may be ordered or arranged) may well be an abusive father who continues to pose a risk to the children and the mother.

CASE LAW AND JUDICIAL GUIDANCE IN SECTION 8 PROCEEDINGS

Despite provisions under the welfare checklist, the Children Act 1989 does not require the courts to ensure that orders for contact with violent parents are safe for children. The intent of the Act has been distorted by the following case-law precedents:

- In Re O (Contact: Imposition of Conditions) [1995], the appeal court set a very strong presumption of contact by ruling that it is 'almost always in the child's interest' for him or her to have contact with both parents.

- In Re H and R (Child Sexual Abuse) [1995], the House of Lords ruled that a higher standard of proof be required in family law cases involving more serious allegations than the simple balance of probabilities. This ruling makes it very hard to protect a child who has been physically or sexually abused, because it is notoriously difficult to prove child abuse, particularly child sexual abuse, in a court of law.

In a more recent case, involving domestic violence and child contact in the court of appeal, Re L, V, M, H (Contact: Domestic Violence) [2000], the UK's official solicitor commissioned Drs Sturge and Glaser to prepare a report for the court giving a child and adolescent psychiatric opinion on, among other matters, the implications of domestic violence for contact. Their report (Sturge and Glaser 2000) was accepted in its entirety by the court of appeal; the court reached its judgment informed by their report and decided that:

- family courts need to have a heightened awareness of the existence of and consequences to children of exposure to domestic violence between their parents or carers

- allegations of domestic violence should be heard and adjudicated upon before a final Section 8 order is made

- proven domestic violence is not a bar to contact but is an important factor in the exercise of discretion

- where violence is proved, the court will look to the ability and willingness of the perpetrator to recognize and change his behaviour as an important factor.

This judgment is now legally binding on all subsequent decisions in UK family courts, unless it is at any time overruled by the UK Court of Appeal, the UK House of Lords or the relevant European court.

MAKING A FINDING OF FACT

In private family proceedings under Section 8 where there are allegations of domestic violence, it is also open to the court to make a 'finding of fact'. The Lord Chancellor's 'Guidelines for Good Practice on Parental Contact' (Children Act Sub-Committee of the Lord Chancellor's Advisory Board on Family Law 2002) instructs courts to give early consideration to whether a finding of fact is appropriate. In most cases where a court feels it is appropriate, the finding of fact will occur early in proceedings, although a court can hold such a hearing at any point during the case. It is for the court to decide whether there should be a finding of fact hearing and for the court to give directions as to the practitioner's role at that point. However, if early screening by CAFCASS identifies domestic violence as a feature that could indicate a risk of abuse, the court should be alerted to the need for further enquiries.

In both public and private law, the welfare of the child is not treated as paramount in a finding-of-fact hearing. This is because it is a factual hearing, and so neither the welfare principle nor the welfare checklist applies.

The test that the court will apply to assess whether a finding-of-fact hearing is necessary when allegations are in dispute is 'whether the nature and effect of the violence alleged is such as to make it likely that the order of the court will be affected if the allegations are proved' (Children Act Sub-Committee of the Lord Chancellor's Advisory Board on Family Law 2002).

In making a finding of fact, the court will take the following steps:

1   Consider what evidence will be required to enable the court to make a finding of fact in relation to the allegations.

2   Ensure that appropriate directions under Section 11(1) of the Children Act 1989 are given at an early stage in the application to enable the matters in issue to be heard as quickly as possible, including consideration of whether it would be appropriate for there to be an initial hearing for the purpose of enabling findings of fact to be made. Section 11 of the Children Act refers to the requirement for a timetable of actions specified by the court that deals with the question of whether a Section 8 order is to be made.

3   Consider whether an order for interim contact pending the final hearing is in the interests of the child, and in particular that the safety of the child and the residential parent can be secured before, during and after any such contact.

4   Direct a report from a children and family reporter on the question of contact, unless satisfied that it is not necessary to do so in order to safeguard the child's interests.

5   Subject to the seriousness of the allegations made and the difficulty of the case, consider whether the children in question need to be represented separately in the proceedings; and, if the case is proceeding in the family proceedings court, whether it should be transferred to the county court; and, if in the county court, whether it should be transferred to the high court for hearing.

The private and confidential nature of the proceedings under Section 8 has also meant that abused parties and their children have been at risk of contempt of court when they have disclosed information to help services such as Women's Aid when trying to seek help to overturn court orders that they believed put their children at risk. However, from 31 October 2005, new rules were introduced to allow parties and other specified people to disclose to other specified people certain information from family proceedings heard in private and involving children, without needing the permission of the court and without being a contempt of court. Further consultation is now taking place on whether this should be widened to include public reporting of cases.

The combination of the lack of focus of the Children Act 1989 on domestic violence-related issues and insufficient awareness among many involved in operating within its tenets has produced many situations in which children and women have been left at continued risk of violence and abuse.

In Australia and New Zealand, growing awareness of these issues in recent years, highlighted by some particularly tragic cases, has resulted in changes to the equivalent legislation. In Australia, the Family Law Reform Act 1995 specifies that when determining the best interests of the children (when, for example, residence or contact is disputed), the court must be aware of the need to protect the children from physical or psychological harm and must look specifically at all the issues of family violence.

The New Zealand legislation goes further, stating that when a court is deciding custody or access, and is satisfied that a party to the marriage has used violence against a child or another party in the proceedings, then neither custody nor unsupervised access should be granted until the court is satisfied that the children will be safe. A list of criteria for assessing safety (a risk-assessment tool) is appended. Rather than the focus being on the mother's 'implacable hostility' to contact (as in the UK), the onus is on the abuser to convince the judge that he can be trusted with the children (Kaye 1996).

Numerous attempts have been made, without great success, to introduce amendments within recent legislation to put in place mandatory risk assessment where there is domestic violence in order to increase the safety of non-abusing parents and children. Further attempts are being made to improve risk assessment and management of safety within the current Children and Adoption Bill. These aim to provide safeguards to the Bill's provisions for introducing measures to enforce contact where orders have been breached, and to put in place mechanisms to ensure that contact orders are safe before they are enforced.

4.4 Care and protection of children under the Children Act 1989 Parts IV and V (public law)

The 1989 Act introduced a number of new measures in relation to the powers and duties of local authorities and others under public law:

- Under Section 47 of the Children Act 1989, local authorities have a duty to enquire into the welfare of any child suffering or likely to suffer 'significant harm' and to decide whether they should take action to safeguard the child's welfare.

- Under Section 44, an emergency protection order may be made, lasting up to eight days.

- Under Section 31, local authorities and the NSPCC may apply to the court for a care or supervision order, which may initially be granted on an interim basis. The applicant must be satisfied that the child is suffering or is likely to suffer significant harm because of a lack of reasonable parental care or because the child is beyond parental control.

- Under Section 20, local authorities must provide accommodation for children in need where the child is lost or has no parent or the parents are prevented (temporarily or permanently) from providing suitable accommodation or care.

- Under Section 46, the police (through police protection orders) have powers to remove children at risk of significant harm and to take steps to ensure that they are not removed from a safe place where they are being accommodated.

4.5 Removing a suspected child abuser from the family home

Under Children Act guidance (Vol. 1, para. 4.31), social workers are encouraged to remove the abuser rather than the child wherever possible. This guidance is soon to be updated in respect of removing the abuser but was not available at the time of writing. The principle will remain the same, as removal of the abuser is increasingly being acknowledged as the most effective way to reduce risk. Under Section 52 of, and Schedule 6 to, the Family Law Act 1996, an amendment has been made to Sections 38 and 44 of the Children Act 1989. The courts now have powers to exclude from the home someone who is suspected of abusing a child within the home. Where an emergency protection order or interim care order has been applied for or is in place, local authorities can now apply for an order to:

- remove a suspected abuser from the family home where the child lives

- prevent the relevant person from entering the property

- exclude that person from an area around the family home.

An order can be granted alongside an interim care order or emergency protection order in respect of the child only if the following conditions are satisfied:

(a) that there is reasonable cause to believe that if a person ('the relevant person') is excluded from a dwelling-house in which the child lives, the child will cease to suffer, or cease to be likely to suffer, significant harm; and (b) another person living in the dwelling-house (whether a parent of the child or some other person) (i) is able and willing to give the child the care which it would be reasonable to expect a parent to give him; and (ii) consents to the inclusion of the exclusion requirement.

(Children Act Section 38A(2))

There are several points to note about an exclusion requirement attached to an interim care order or an emergency protection order:

- The exclusion requirement may last for a shorter period than the interim care order or emergency protection order.

- The exclusion requirement may be granted ex parte (i.e. without all parties being present at the hearing or notified in advance).

- The exclusion requirement may have a power of arrest attached (although this can be for a shorter period than the order).

- The exclusion requirement can only be included within an interim order. (By the time the court considers making a final care order, a proposed carer, usually the woman, will be expected to have excluded the abuser either by her own legal remedies or through the intervention of criminal justice agencies.)

- The exclusion requirement will cease to have effect if the child is subsequently removed from the house by the local authority for a period of more than 24 hours.

- The local authority must notify all relevant parties, including the person who is excluded and the carer who consented, when an exclusion requirement ceases to have effect.

The court also has the power to accept undertakings (a promise made to the court to do or not do something) instead of making an order if the case is appropriate (see Chapter Six).

The Department of Health (1997) gives important guidance on the implementation of this new power to support the protection of children and its implications for practice in working with women at risk from domestic violence. First, court rules require the following:

- The mother's consent should be informed consent: it should not be elicited for reasons of convenience.

- The local authority should discuss the understanding of the carer giving consent to the exclusion order of the purpose and effect of the order, regardless of whether they are legally represented in the proceedings.

- If the person consents, then the local authority should ensure that this is available in writing for the court, signed and dated.

- Any application to renew or vary the order should be similarly agreed to by the person consenting to the exclusion requirement.

Second, the following points of guidance are also noted:

- The welfare of the child has to be seen alongside that of the child's carer. Where domestic violence may be an important element in the family, the safety of the parent with care (usually the mother) is also in the interests of the child's welfare.

- Local authority staff working in child protection should recognize the issues of conflict of interest in respect of responsibilities for the child and the need to give objective information and advice before, for example, the child's mother agrees to consent to an exclusion requirement.

- There may be a significant risk to the mother's safety if there has been a history of domestic violence, and an exclusion requirement might exacerbate this.

- Where possible, the local authority should ensure that the mother receives advice and information from a person within the authority independent of the caseworker with primary responsibility for the child.

- The mother could also be referred for specialist help to local Women's Aid services or by calling the 24-hour freephone National Domestic Violence Helpline (0808 2000 247) run in partnership between Women's Aid and Refuge.

- The mother may need considerable support throughout the duration of the order if there are threats against her or attempts to persuade her to agree that the order (and any attached power of arrest) be rescinded.

Under Schedule 2, Paragraph 5 of the Children Act 1989, social services can also offer financial assistance to enable the abuser to pay for alternative accommodation. This may be helpful in situations where there is domestic violence towards the proposed carer from the excluded abuser as it may decrease the risk to her.

4.6 Providing support for children in need: Section 17 of the Children Act 1989

Following the publication of *Child Protection: Messages from Research* (Department of Health 1995) and, more recently, the Every Child Matters national programme, local authorities and other agencies have been encouraged to place child protection work within the context of wider services for children in need. This was initially introduced to redress the concern that children were being routed inappropriately into the child protection system as a means of gaining access to services. The government is aware that enquiries into suspicions of child abuse can have traumatic effects on children and families and, therefore, it is important that professionals work in partnership with parents and their children while at the same time ensuring that the child's welfare is safeguarded. This refocusing by local authorities and others has been characterized by a shift from emphasizing Part IV of the Children Act 1989 (in particular, Section 47 investigations or enquiries) towards Part III of the Act (in particular, providing services for children in need under Section 17). The Every Child Matters agenda has taken this shift further to restructure local children's services with the aim of improving outcomes for children at risk of social exclusion.

Under Section 17.1(a) of the Children Act 1989, local authorities have a duty to 'safeguard and promote the welfare of children within their area who are in need'. Local authorities can provide a range of services for children who are 'in need'. Such services are intended to provide support and help to families, including families of children with disabilities and other special needs.

Financial assistance under Section 17 exists to promote the welfare of 'children in need' and can be applied to address the needs of children living with or leaving domestic violence in the following ways:

- Section 17(1)(b) to promote children's upbringing in their own families, provided that this is consistent with the child's welfare. There are a number of ways that social workers can give direct support to abused women to enable them to support their children's welfare, for example help and support in getting rehoused in safe accommodation.

- Section 17(5)(a) to facilitate the provision of services to children through voluntary organizations. Financial support for Women's Aid work with children living in refuges and children's resettlement can be provided under this section.

- Section 17(6) for giving assistance in kind and, in exceptional circumstances, cash payments to help children in need. These can be made to help women and their children leave abusive situations or survive within them. Such assistance might include:

  o cash for new clothes for children

  o cash for travel to get away from a violent man

  o assistance with fitting new locks, getting a telephone or installing an alarm system

  o transport to a refuge.

Amendments that came into effect under the Children and Adoption Act 2002 and that affect the implementation of Section 17 of the Children Act 1989 state that children and families in need can be assisted by local authorities in respect of their accommodation. Local Authority Circular (2003)13: Guidance on accommodating children in need and their families details these changes (Department of Health 2003b).

Assistance might also be given to help a family where children are in need because of immigration rules that mean their abused mother has no recourse to public funds.

4.7 Every Child Matters and the Children Act 2004

This national programme takes this approach a stage further (e.g. Department for Education and Skills 2005) to introduce a new long-term approach to promoting and safeguarding the wellbeing of children and young people from birth to age 19 years. The government's aim is for every child, regardless of background and circumstances, to have the support they need to:

- be healthy
- stay safe
- enjoy and achieve
- make a positive contribution
- achieve economic wellbeing.

Over the next few years, every local authority will work with partner agencies through children's trusts (developed between 2006 and 2008 in all areas) to find out what works best for children and young people in its area, and then to act on these findings. Key developments include:

- the appointment in March 2005 of the first children's commissioner for England to give children and young people a voice in government and in public life

- the introduction of a common assessment framework from April 2006 (to be embedded fully by 2008) to be used by services working with children with a view to improving interagency working and identifying any additional needs for the child and any additional services available to meet their needs

- a duty on local authorities to have established local safeguarding children boards by April 2006; these will build on and replace local-area child protection committees (ACPCs) in order to improve measures for safeguarding children

- developing and publishing a regular children and young people's plan to set out how local areas will provide services for all children and young people to meet the aims of Every Child Matters.

Further information on this programme is available at www.everychildmatters.gov.uk.

4.8 The Children Act 2004

The Children Act 2004 provides the legal underpinning for Every Child Matters: Change for Children. A series of documents have been published that provide guidance under the Act to support local authorities and their partners in implementing new statutory duties. Further information is available at www.everychildmatters.gov.uk.

New multi-agency guidance on *Working Together to Safeguard Children* (HM Government 2006) was published in spring 2006 to support these developments.

4.9 Domestic Violence Crime and Victims Act 2004

This Act created a new offence of causing or allowing the death of a child or vulnerable adult, whereby a person is guilty of such an offence if a child or vulnerable adult dies as a result of an unlawful act and the defendant either was or should have been aware of the risk and failed to take steps to protect them. All members of the household (subject to age and mental capacity) will be liable for the offence (which has a maximum penalty of 14 years) where:

- the death occurred as a result of unlawful conduct in anticipated circumstances

- a member of the household caused the death

- the defendant was or should have been aware that the victim was at risk but either caused the death or did not take reasonable steps to prevent it. It will not be necessary to show who caused the death and who failed to prevent it.

The victim in this new offence must have been at risk of serious physical harm, demonstrated by a history of violence towards them or another person in the household. Only people aged over 16 years may be guilty of this offence, unless they are the parent of the victim.

4.10 Summary

- The Children Act 1989 redefined childcare law and introduced new measures for working with children and families in both public and private family law. It does not contain guidance on the implications for the welfare of children living with or witnessing domestic violence or on ensuring the safety of adults who may be at risk. *Working Together to Safeguard Children* (HM Government 2006) provides more detail for practitioners when dealing with children who have been exposed to domestic violence. The issue is mentioned on occasions throughout the document under specific agency headings but also has a small section in Part II, which is devoted to non-statutory practice guidance.

- Part I of the Act introduced two new central features: the welfare checklist and the concept of parental responsibility. The lack of recognition within the Children Act 1989 in general, and within the welfare checklist in particular, of the risks and practical problems faced by women and children experiencing domestic violence in making safe arrangements after relationship breakdown has been acknowledged only recently.

- Section 120 of the Children and Adoption Act 2002 added to the original definition of 'harm' so that it now includes impairment suffered from seeing or hearing the ill-treatment of another person.

- Under Section 8 of the Children Act 1989, the court may make four types of order within family proceedings in respect of the child's welfare: contact orders, residence orders, prohibited steps orders and specific issue orders.

- Welfare reports are often of vital importance in the court's decision-making in relation to the welfare of a child. National Standards (Home Office 1994) for probation service family court welfare state clearly that where there is domestic violence, then the preparation of such reports should not require women to attend joint interviews with their abusers. This division was renamed Children and Families Court Advisory and Support Service (CAFCASS) in 2001 and set up as a national agency; their Domestic Violence Policy, developed in 2005, should improve practice further.

- A number of problems have been identified with respect to Section 8 orders under the Children Act 1989 in cases where there is domestic violence, in particular the impact of case law.

- Under Section 47 of the Children Act 1989, local authorities have a duty to enquire into the welfare of any child suffering or likely to suffer 'significant harm' and to decide whether they should take action to safeguard the child's welfare.

- Under an amendment made to the Children Act 1989 by the Family Law Act 1996, the courts now have powers to exclude someone from the home who is suspected of abusing a child within the home, where an emergency protection order or interim care order has been applied for or is in place. Guidance has been given by the Department of Health on the implementation of this new power to support the protection of children as well as women at risk from domestic violence.

- Under Section 17.1(a) of the Children Act 1989, local authorities have a duty to 'safeguard and promote the welfare of children within their area who are in need' and can provide a range of services.

- The Children Act 2004 and Every Child Matters build on previous legislation to introduce a new long-term approach to promoting and safeguarding the wellbeing of children and young people from birth to age 19 years.

- The Every Child Matters agenda incorporated legislatively in the Children Act 2004 focused on improving outcomes for children at risk of social exclusion and mainly dictated a new local framework for local children's services to promote integrated working between services, improved risk assessment and information sharing.

- More recently, the Domestic Violence Crime and Victims Act 2004 has focused on adult survivors of domestic violence but created a new offence in respect of child deaths.

- The combination of the Children Act 1989 and subsequent legislation and guidance lacks a focus on domestic violence-related issues, and insufficient awareness among many involved in operating within its tenets has produced many situations in which children and women have been left at continued risk of violence and abuse. Growing awareness of these problems has led to recent changes in policy and practice that may lead to improved responses.

CHAPTER FIVE

PROTECTION UNDER CRIMINAL LAW

Although under criminal law there is no specific offence of 'domestic violence', many offences may be used to apply to domestic violence, such as assault, false imprisonment, harassment, rape, criminal damage and attempted murder. Not all forms of domestic violence are illegal, for example some forms of emotional violence. However, these types of violence can have a serious and lasting impact on a woman's or child's sense of wellbeing and autonomy. Whether the criminal law can protect victims is therefore dependent on the circumstances of the violence and the responses of criminal justice agencies such as the police, probation and courts.

5.1 Police responses

Police responses to domestic violence have traditionally been variable, depending on the attitudes and approach of the individual officer. Until the late 1980s, the criminal justice system paid little attention to the needs of women and children experiencing domestic violence. A number of early studies documented the dismissive and derogatory way in which police officers tended to handle 'domestic disputes' (e.g. Bourlet 1990; Dobash and Dobash 1980; Edwards 1989; Hanmer and Saunders 1984). Domestic violence was frequently seen as a private matter and not 'real' violence, and the sympathies of a predominantly male police force were often with the violent man/partner. Women seeking refuge and help from Women's Aid complained frequently about the lack of protection, effective action or information about other sources of help from the police, although there were some individual police officers who did as much as they could to help, despite the overall approach.

Much domestic violence still goes unreported to the police. Many women have sought help from the police in an emergency, but for other women calling the police is not the first option and often is only a last resort after repeated attacks. Every minute in the UK, the police receive a call from the public for assistance for domestic violence. This leads to police receiving an estimated 1300 calls each day, or over

570,000 each year (Stanko 2000). However, according to the British Crime Survey, only 40.2 per cent of domestic violence crime is reported to the police (Dodd *et al.* 2004).

Many abused women have been ambivalent about calling the police: they fear they will not be believed or taken seriously; they may believe that the police can only respond to actual physical assault; they may fear it will provoke further or greater violence by challenging the man; and they may not want their partner or ex-partner to be taken to court.

Mama (1996) found that black women in particular are less likely to call the police if they fear racism against themselves or their partner and, consequently, are unsure whether the police will act or overreact. Racist stereotypes, lack of interest in the needs of black women and racist immigration laws mean that black women are often reluctant to call the police. Research shows that for some black women who have called the police, more problems resulted and they were assaulted or threatened with arrest.

From 1986, the need for changes in police practice to both domestic violence and rape was accepted by the Home Office, which led to a substantial Circular to Chief Constables in 1990 (updated in 2000). This circular signalled clearly that domestic violence is now viewed as a crime both by practitioners in the criminal justice system and by government. The circular urged the police to develop explicit force policies on domestic violence and to establish dedicated units with specially trained officers to deal with domestic violence 'where practicable and cost effective'. The circular also specified the central features that should be included in any force policy statements:

- the overriding duty to protect victims and any children from further abuse

- the need to treat domestic violence at least as seriously as other forms of violence

- the use and value of powers of arrest

- the dangers of conciliation between victim and offender

- the need to establish effective recording and monitoring systems.

The circular reminded officers that the primary duty was to protect the victim and any children involved and then to consider what action should be taken against the offender. Immediate protection could include referring or taking the woman to a refuge and liaising with statutory and voluntary agencies for long-term support. Chief constables were urged to liaise on the development and implementation of these policies with a wide range of agencies, and particular consideration was given to the need for good liaison with the Crown Prosecution Service (CPS), for the discussion of evidential and other matters to ensure consistency of aims and approach in the prosecution of domestic violence.

By its nature, however, domestic violence cannot be dealt with effectively under the criminal law alone. Many aspects of domestic violence are difficult to define as crimes, and they do not fit readily into common categories of assault under criminal law. The criminal law and the courts perceive harm in terms of physical abuse and, in the absence of independent witnesses, usually require some evidence of physical injury or harm as proof that a crime has been perpetrated. This incident-focused system does not address adequately many aspects of ongoing coercive, abusive and threatening behaviour and the psychological effects and harm that this can cause.

Nevertheless, the criminal justice system has an important role to play in preventing and challenging domestic violence, both symbolically and practically. Local and national attention within the past decade has focused on encouraging more women to seek help from the police and the criminal justice system and on encouraging this system to provide a better response for such women and their children.

During the past 10–15 years, there has been a significant change in police response to domestic violence, which has led to improvements in policy and practice. Significantly, in 2002 an inspection occurred into the investigation and prosecution of cases involving allegations of rape, which highlighted the link between rape and domestic violence: 45 per cent of rape is committed by current partners, and such cases are less likely to come to the attention of the police than those committed by strangers. This was followed in 2003 by HM Inspectorates of Constabulary and the Crown Prosecution Service conducting a joint inspection into police and CPS responses to domestic violence; the recommendations focused on improving working between the police and the CPS.

Now all 43 forces in England and Wales have domestic violence officers. In 2004 the National Centre for Policing Excellence, on behalf of the Association of Chief Police Officers (ACPO), produced national guidance for investigating domestic violence for all police forces, which is accompanied by a national modular domestic violence training pack. At the same time, the CPS has revised its national policy, guidance and training on domestic violence and rape.

The ACPO has also produced guidance for police officers who are perpetrators to ensure that police forces use screening mechanisms to identify police applicants with a proven history of domestic violence, such as evidence of domestic violence-related criminal cautions/convictions, civil orders/child contact orders with imposed restrictions and any breaches under the Children Act 1989.

5.2 Police powers under the law

The police are a key 24-hour agency for women experiencing domestic violence and perhaps the first port of call in an emergency. Each police officer has the discretion to use his or her powers to intervene in the situation and to arrest, caution or charge an abusive man. Arrests can be made to prevent further injury or to protect a vulnerable person or child. The police can also arrest someone who has broken bail conditions or an injunction.

Actual bodily harm has been defined by case law to include shock and nervous conditions, suggesting that more recognition is now being given to the psychological effects of abuse, both directly and indirectly on the survivor and victim. These changes are echoed in the widening of definitions of harm for protection orders under the civil law (see Chapter Six).

The police have strictly limited powers over the length of time they can keep a suspected criminal at the police station (usually 24 hours), and they cannot impose conditions when forced to release him or her on police bail. The police have the power to impose bail conditions on an arrested person only following charge. It is important to note that conditional bail may be imposed only if a custody officer would have otherwise detained the defendant in custody following charge. Requirements may include a condition of residence, not to go within a specified distance of a person or location, to sign on at a police station, and the imposition of a curfew. However, the custody officer cannot require the arrested person to reside at a bail hostel, to be available to assist the court or to undergo a medical examination.

From January 2006, the Serious Organised Crime and Police Act 2005 introduced a new single power of arrest for police officers, with the aim of simplifying arrest powers but also requiring police officers to apply a test of 'necessity' before they make an arrest. This repeals the clause in the Domestic Violence Crime and Victims Act 2004 to make common assault an arrestable offence (see below regarding implementation).

5.3 The Crime and Disorder Act 1997

This act placed a duty on local authorities and the police to work together with other agencies to tackle crime at local level through the provision of a community safety strategy, which should include domestic violence.

The police are key partners in multi-agency domestic violence groups that have been established in most areas to develop interagency responses to domestic violence and to improve service provision across agencies such as health services, specialist domestic violence services (refuges and outreach services), housing authorities and many other statutory and voluntary sector agencies (see also Chapter Eleven). This was updated in 2004 to place a responsibility on health services to participate through primary care trusts.

5.4 The Protection from Harassment Act 1997

In 1997 legislation was introduced to tackle stalkers. This Act also provides more effective protection for abused women, in particular those who no longer live with their abusers, than had been available previously. Although much of the publicity in the run-up to the legislation focused on obsessive stalking of strangers and celebrities, an ACPO survey of the worst cases found that nearly 40 per cent of these cases involved harassment of (usually) a woman by her ex-partner or a person with whom she had had a close relationship – in other words, post-separation domestic violence (Wallis 1996).

The Protection from Harassment Act 1997 introduced measures for protection under both criminal and civil law and also provides a link between criminal and civil law. The provisions include two criminal offences: the offence of criminal harassment (under Section 2, a summary offence, tried in the magistrates' court) and a more serious offence involving fear of violence (under Section 4, triable either as a summary offence or as an indictable offence in the crown court). If a person is convicted of either of these offences, there is an additional measure for protection: a restraining order can also be granted by the court, prohibiting the offender from further similar conduct. Under civil law, there is also an injunction for prevention of harassment for those people who are not eligible under the Family Law Act 1996 (see Chapter Six for further discussion of the usefulness of this).

Under Section 2 (the offence of criminal harassment), a person must not pursue a course of conduct that amounts to harassment of another and that he or she knows, or ought to know, amounts to harassment of the other; that is, if any 'reasonable person' in possession of the same information would regard such conduct as harassment. The term 'reasonable person' may be problematic in practice, but the aim of the legislation is to shift the emphasis from the subjective harmful intent of the alleged offender, which is often difficult to prove, to what actually happens and its effect on the victim.

Under Section 4 (the offence involving fear of violence), anyone whose course of conduct causes another to fear, on at least two occasions, that violence will be used against her is guilty of an offence 'if he knows, or ought to know, that his course of conduct will cause the other so to fear on each of those occasions'. Although there exist powers under existing criminal law to deal with fear of physical violence, this new offence may be useful as it will allow the courts to deal with serious stalking without having to wait until psychological or bodily harm is caused.

The police can arrest without warrant anyone whom they suspect of committing either of these offences, and the separate incidents do not have to be of the same kind each time. For example, shouting obscenities outside a woman's house on a Saturday followed by a broken window the next Friday could constitute a related 'course of conduct', even though the conduct is different each time. Both incidents could be prosecuted under existing legislation, for example as public order or criminal damage offences, but would also constitute an offence under Section 2 of the Protection from Harassment Act 1997. The police and the CPS would have to decide whether to take forward one or both offences. The advantage of going for the single offence of harassment is that it allows the court to hear the entire catalogue of incidents, the evidence for which may be weak individually but strong collectively.

A number of potential advantages include strengthening the options for police to protect women and to use the criminal law against men who continue to threaten, pester and harass women after the relationship has ended. A woman who does not live with her abuser and who cannot use the Family Law Act 1996 can gain protection under the Protection from Harassment Act 1997. In particular, criminal proceedings resulting in a conviction will mean that a restraining order can be attached. Restraining orders can provide the same protection as injunctions under civil law but may be more effective, as they carry stronger penalties. Lastly, action under criminal law coupled with restraining orders may avoid the problem of the costs of legal aid for civil remedies, in those cases where women do not need to apply for injunctions to exclude their abuser from the property (see Chapter Six for further discussion of civil law remedies).

5.5 Domestic Violence Crime and Victims Act 2004

This Act includes a range of measures (not introduced at the time of writing) that aim to increase the safety of survivors of domestic violence and to link some criminal and civil remedies. It is anticipated that most measures will be implemented during 2006 (see www.womensaid.org.uk). The Act includes the following:

- making common assault an arrestable offence (although this has since been repealed by the Serious Organised Crime and Police Act 2005 – see above)

- extension of restraining orders to any offence, on conviction or acquittal if there is a continued risk

- extension of availability of injunctions to same-sex couples and couples who have never cohabited

- breach of non-molestation order will be a criminal offence

- new offence of causing death of a child or vulnerable adult

- statutory domestic violence homicide reviews for adults

- victims' code of practice and commissioner for victims and witnesses; the code should ensure that domestic violence survivors are given clear information about the whole criminal justice process, from the reporting of an incident through to prosecution and sentencing, and regarding the support that is available.

The effectiveness of proposed measures in the Domestic Violence Crime and Victims Act 2004 is not yet known.[1] Although the proposals are welcomed by domestic violence services, issues such as resources for implementation remain a concern.

5.6 Prosecution process: key issues for women survivors of domestic violence

The CPS will, when considering whether to proceed with or discontinue a charge, consult with the police or ask them to clarify or obtain more evidence. Decisions about whether to proceed are informed by two key criteria:

- whether there is sufficient evidence to continue

- whether it is in the public interest to do so.

In cases of domestic violence, the likelihood of there being sufficient evidence will depend on there being independent evidence of the crime, such as other witnesses or forensic evidence. The police are now being trained to gather as much evidence as soon as possible, although there is inconsistent implementation of this across police forces (Hester 2006a; Hester and Westmarland 2005).

The CPS domestic violence policy and guidance is based on the knowledge that domestic violence can have a devastating effect not only on the victim but also on the victim's family and especially on children who witness or are aware of the violence. Each of the 42 CPS regions has a domestic violence coordinator with extensive experience in prosecuting domestic violence and other cases.

The CPS policy includes continuing with a prosecution against the victim's wishes or requiring a witness to go to court against the witness's wishes. This is because in some cases the violence is so serious, or the previous history shows such a real and continuing danger to the victim or the children or other person, that the public interest in going ahead with a prosecution has to outweigh the victim's wishes. Section 23 of the Criminal Justice Act 1988 allows the CPS, in very limited circumstances, to use the victim's statement as evidence without calling the victim to court. The CPS has to prove beyond reasonable doubt that the person who made the statement is afraid to give evidence or is being kept out of the way. The victim does not have to give evidence to prove that he or she is afraid. This proof can come from someone else, for example a police officer or doctor, or sometimes can be seen from the victim's behaviour in court. If the court decides that the statement can be used under Section 23, the court must then decide whether, in the interests of justice, the statement should be used in this way.

The Youth Justice and Criminal Evidence Act 1999 introduced special measures for vulnerable or intimidated witnesses from 2002. A victim can request that the measures are made available and may include the following:

- physically screening the witness (whether vulnerable or intimidated) from the accused in crown court

- evidence from the witness by live link (whether vulnerable or intimidated) in crown court and magistrates' courts and for child witnesses in cases involving sexual offences or violence (including threats and cruelty) in magistrates' courts

- evidence (whether a vulnerable or intimidated witness) given in private in crown court and magistrates' courts

- removal of wigs and gowns in court (not applicable for magistrates' courts)

- use of video-recorded evidence in chief for vulnerable witnesses in crown court and for child witnesses in cases involving sexual offences or violence (including threats and cruelty) in magistrates' courts.

Although the immediate arrest and removal of the abuser by police will often be helpful in providing many women and children with much-needed 'breathing space' and time to consider what they should do, proceeding with prosecution may not always be in the woman's and children's best interests. The difficulties include the following:

- Women may be extremely reluctant to give evidence against someone whom they love or have loved, and with whom they share or have shared a home, and who may be the father of their children.

- Women may feel under pressure to protect the family reputation.

- Black and minority ethnic women may be unwilling to risk community ostracism and allegations of disloyalty or collusion with police racism.

- Women are often at risk of further violence: waiting times in criminal proceedings are too long, and women will frequently be left without adequate legal protection while waiting for the case to come to court.

- Going to court can be an ordeal, and outcomes at court can vary.

- Effective action under criminal law may be undermined by civil proceedings, which can force women to have contact with violent men via the children, and by an uncoordinated approach across the criminal and civil courts.

Another major deterrent to effective prosecution in the UK has been the time it takes to get to court. In some groundbreaking US jurisdictions of, for example, Duluth and San Diego, offenders are taken back to court within 24 hours and the case is dealt with immediately. The case has to be prepared in the intervening period, and the survivor and offender are made aware of the options and choices. At court, the judge offers the offender the choice of custody or attendance at a specific perpetrators' re-education programme (subject to suitability), and ancillary orders are made. The court will grant protection orders, which may include both non-molestation and occupation orders, as well as interim child contact orders, which may either suspend a child's contact with the violent man for a limited period, subject to review, or order contact to be made through specialized child contact centres. (The problems of crossover between criminal, civil and family courts are discussed further in Chapter Four.)

New initiatives are being developed in a number of police forces in order to improve responses to domestic violence and to enhance evidence gathering (for example, increasing use of instant cameras at the scene) to enable the CPS to increase the chances of a successful prosecution.

The Government National Action Plan (Home Office 2005) includes the provision of more specialist domestic violence courts to be rolled out over several years in an attempt to improve case outcomes and bring more offenders to justice. Two types of specialist court system are being set up across England and Wales: *cluster courts*, where all cases are grouped into one court session in order to deal with pre-trial hearings – bail variation, pleas, pre-trial reviews, pre-sentence reports and sentencing – and *integrated courts*, which bring together criminal and civil proceedings (yet to be established[2]).

The provision of independent domestic violence advisers (IDVAs) to offer individual and institutional advocacy is key. Many IDVAs will be drawn from existing specialist domestic violence services. However, a wide range of local specialist domestic violence services will continue to play a key role in advocating for women and children survivors of domestic violence through the criminal justice system and providing the holistic support to enable them to take control of their lives and move on from an abusive relationship.

5.7 Summary

- Until very recently, the criminal justice system paid little attention to the needs of women and children experiencing domestic violence. While many women have sought help from the police in emergencies, often unsuccessfully, for other women calling the police is not the first option and is often only a last resort after repeated attacks.

- Many abused women are still ambivalent about calling the police: they fear they will not be believed or taken seriously. Black women in particular are less likely to call the police if they fear racism against themselves or their partner.

- The recognition of the need for changes in police practice to both domestic violence and rape led to the first Home Office Circular in 1986, followed in 1990 by the much more substantial Circular to Chief Constables. Now all 43 police forces have explicit force policies on domestic violence and domestic violence units. The police now have national policy and procedures including training on domestic violence, and all forces are expected to comply.

- The Protection from Harassment Act 1997 introduced new measures for protection under both criminal and civil law and also provides a new link between criminal and civil law. The provisions include two new criminal offences: the offence of criminal harassment and a more serious offence involving fear of violence. If a person is convicted of either of these offences, there is an additional measure for protection: a restraining order can also be granted by the court, prohibiting the offender from further similar conduct.

- The Domestic Violence Crime and Victims Act 2004 includes a range of measures (not introduced at the time of writing) that aim to increase the safety of survivors of domestic violence and link some criminal and civil remedies. It is anticipated that most measures will be implemented during 2006 (see www.womensaid.org.uk).[3]

- The effectiveness of proposed measures in the Domestic Violence Crime and Victims Act 2004 is not known. Although the proposals are welcomed by domestic violence services, issues such as resources for implementation remain a concern.

- The immediate arrest and removal of the abuser by police will often be helpful in providing women and children with much-needed 'breathing space' and time to consider what they should do. Proceeding with prosecution may not, however, always be in the woman's or child's best interests. There are a number of practical and emotional difficulties, and prosecution does not always guarantee protection or safety in the long term, as there may be increased danger of reprisals from a vengeful partner or ex-partner.

- The CPS has developed significant new policy, procedures, guidance and training in the management of cases of domestic violence, with new CPS domestic violence coordinators in the 43 police force areas.

- The Youth Justice and Criminal Evidence Act 1999 introduced special measures for vulnerable or intimidated witnesses from 2002.

- Effective action under criminal law may be undermined by civil proceedings, which can force women to have contact with violent men via the children and by an uncoordinated approach across the criminal and civil courts.

- Nevertheless, recourse to the criminal law and the protection of the police and courts must be developed in order to provide more effective protection and redress than is the case at present; examples from the USA have influenced new initiatives in the UK.

- The Government National Action Plan (March 2005) includes the provision of more specialist domestic violence courts to be rolled out over several years, in an attempt to improve case outcomes and bring more offenders to justice.

Notes

1   An evaluation is being carried out by Hester and colleagues for the Department of Constitutional Affairs, with findings due late 2007.

2   An integrated court is due to be established in Croydon during 2006.

3   It is not clear whether the implementation of the Civil Partnership Act 2004 will already have changed the situation with regard to same sex partners and ex-partners.

CHAPTER SIX

PROTECTION FROM VIOLENCE UNDER CIVIL LAW

Protection from domestic violence under civil law is provided by means of an injunction or court order requiring the abuser to do, or not to do, something.

Between 1976 and 1997, injunctions and protection orders could be obtained under three different statutes:

- Domestic Violence and Matrimonial Proceedings Act (DVMPA) 1976

- Domestic Proceedings and Magistrates' Courts Act (DPMCA) 1978

- Matrimonial Homes Act (MHA) 1983.

In the early 1990s, the need for better protection from domestic violence under civil law was highlighted through a number of reports and enquiries. One response to this was Part IV of the Family Law Act 1996 (which came into effect from October 1997), which consolidated these remedies and superseded the previous legislation (see below). The Domestic Violence Crime and Victims Act (DVCVA) 2004, when implemented fully, should provide further improved protection for sufferers of domestic violence.

6.1 Background to current legislation

Under the earlier legislation, as well as granting injunctions (under the DVMPA 1976 and the MHA 1983) and protection orders (under the DPMCA 1978), courts had powers to grant orders ancillary to other matters, such as linked to divorce or to an action for assault and trespass. In practice, the legislation that was used depended on a number of factors, in particular marital status, whether the woman lived with her abuser, whether the action was taken in the county or magistrates' court, and the preferences of local solicitors. Some orders had a power of arrest attached, which made them somewhat more effective. However, research has shown that injunctions and protection orders were more often breached than not and that enforcement was virtually impossible (Barron 1990; Women's Aid Federation, unpublished national surveys of refuge services in 1992 and 1994).

Abused women faced a number of problems within the legal process. For example, under the previous legislation, gaining access to legal representation was often stressful and confusing. Lack of specialist services or interpreters meant that black and minority ethnic women, including women whose immigration status made them ineligible for help with legal aid, were denied effective access to the law. The process of going to court was itself traumatic and frightening, due partly to the lack of separate waiting areas. Equally, Women's Aid research at the time highlighted the inadequacy of any legislation without effective implementation and training for court staff on the impact of domestic violence on women and children (Barron 1990). The courts, like many other agencies, have often failed to understand the whole range of emotional, psychological and practical reasons why many women stay with or return to a violent partner. This can and still does often have the effect of the women not being taken seriously.

Growing awareness of these problems led to the recommendations made in the Law Commission's report *Domestic Violence and the Occupation of the Matrimonial Home* published in May 1992 (Law Commission 1992). The report took account of evidence from lawyers and lay advocates, including Barron's (1990) findings about the ineffectiveness of injunctions. The National Interagency Working Party (1992) report and evidence from a wide range of statutory and voluntary agencies to the 1992 Home Affairs Select Committee Inquiry into Domestic Violence confirmed the inadequacy of protective remedies for abused women under civil law. The reforms to civil remedies for protection from violence in the home introduced by the Family Law Act 1996 (Sections 30–63) were, therefore, long overdue.

6.2 Remedies under the Family Law Act 1996 Part IV

Part IV of the Family Law Act 1996, in force since October 1997, rationalizes and consolidates the previous mishmash of legislation governing injunctions and protection orders. It is a comprehensive piece of legislation intended both to remove anomalies and to make civil protection against domestic violence more effective. The previous legislation in this area – DVMPA 1976, MHA 1983 and relevant parts of DPMCA 1978 – were all repealed and replaced by the new provisions.

Part IV of the Family Law Act 1996 provides a single set of remedies available in all family courts, including the high court, county court and family proceedings (magistrates') court. It extends eligibility to a wider range of people in family or similar relationships, although it gives weaker rights to protection from violence to some cohabitants.

There are two main types of order under the Family Law Act:

- *occupation orders*, which regulate the occupation of the family home

- *non-molestation orders*, for protection from all forms of violence and abuse.

These orders are free-standing injunctions; that is, they can be applied for directly and do not have to be made ancillary to any other proceedings, such as divorce. Provisions for enforcement, through the attachment of powers of arrest, were strengthened. There are also a number of related new provisions under the Act, one of which is related directly to the risk of harm to a child:

- The court, when making an emergency protection order or interim care order for a child under the Children Act 1989, can exclude a person who poses a risk to the child.

- The Act makes provision for the transfer of tenancies between spouses and cohabitants.

- The Act allows a number of other connected provisions.

The related provisions for excluding suspected child abusers and for transfer of tenancies are discussed in Chapters Four and Seven, respectively.

6.3 Domestic Violence Crime and Victims Act 2004

Part IV of the Family Law Act 1996 has been amended further by the DVCVA 2004 to include the following provisions:

- Breach of non-molestation order will be a criminal offence.

- The definition 'cohabitants' is to include same-sex couples.

- With regard to cohabitants, the level of their commitment, rather than their unmarried status, should be the prime factor when determining rights of occupation of the home.

- The provision will be extended to include non-cohabiting couples.

- 'Associated persons' is to include cousins.

These measures are not yet implemented, but it is anticipated that they should be introduced during 2006 (see www.womensaid.org.uk).

6.4 Who can use the Family Law Act?

Eligibility for orders under the Family Law Act 1996 Part IV depends on the type of order and the relationship between the applicant and the other party (the respondent). The Act considerably extends the categories of people who may seek protection. It introduces the new concept of 'associated persons': to apply for a non-molestation order or an occupation order, the applicant must be 'associated' with the person against whom they wish to take out an order.

Section 62(3) defines 'associated persons' as people who:

- are or have been married to each other

- are or have been cohabitants (defined as a man and a woman not married to each other but living together as husband and wife)

- have lived in the same household (other than one of them being the other's tenant, lodger, boarder or employee); this, therefore, includes people in homosexual relationships and people sharing a house

- are relatives (this is defined to include most immediate relatives)

- have agreed to marry (evidenced by a written agreement, the exchange of a ring or a witnessed ceremony)

- are in relation to a child (they both are parents or have or have had parental responsibility for a child) (see Chapter Four for the definition of parental responsibility)

- are parties to the same family proceedings (other than under Part IV, but excluding the local authority).

When the DVCVA 2004 is implemented, 'associated persons' will be extended to include:

- two people who, although not married to each other, are living together as husband and wife (or, if of the same sex, are in an equivalent relationship[1])

- non-cohabiting couples who 'have or have had an intimate personal relationship with each other that was of significant duration'.

The definition of relatives is extended to include cousins.

Where a child has been adopted, two people are associated if they are the:

- natural parent/grandparent and adopted child

- natural parent/grandparent and adoptive parent.

Protection from violence or harassment for those not eligible to apply under the Family Law Act 1996 still has to be sought through common law actions in tort – that is, as ancillary to other legal actions, for example actions suing for assault or trespass or under the injunction provisions of the Protection from Harassment Act 1997 (see Chapter Five).

Within the Act, an order may be sought to protect from molestation or regulate occupation rights for the applicant and any 'relevant child'. A relevant child is defined under Section 62(2) as:

- any child who might be expected to live with either of the parties involved

- any child who is the subject of adoption or Children Act proceedings

- any other child whose interests the court considers relevant.

This extends the scope of previous remedies that were available that were limited to any 'children of the family'.

6.5 Non-molestation orders

Under Section 42 of the Family Law Act 1996, non-molestation orders reproduce and extend the previous powers of the courts to make orders prohibiting a person (the respondent) from molesting another person associated with the respondent or any relevant child. The term 'molestation' is unfortunate, as it tends to denote sexual molestation and can be confusing to potential applicants or respondents. However, as under previous legislation, an order prohibiting molestation can include both general and particular acts of molestation, none of which needs to be overtly violent, and can be used to order someone to stop using or threatening violence against (usually) a woman or relevant child or to stop intimidating, harassing or pestering the woman or child. The order can also have very specific instructions to suit a particular case; for example, it could order an ex-partner to stop telephoning or pestering the applicant at work.

The court can make an order either if the applicant is an 'associated person' or, by its own motion, within any family proceedings that the respondent is party to, if the court considers it of benefit to any other party or relevant child. Children under 16 years of age may apply for non-molestation orders with leave of the court [Section 43(1)] if the court decides the child has sufficient understanding.

In deciding the outcome of any application, courts must have regard to the health, safety and wellbeing of the applicant or any relevant child. 'Health' is defined broadly in Section 63(1) to include both physical and mental health.

An order may be made for a specified period (usually six months), for an open-ended period or until a different order is made if further provisions are needed. However, if the court decides of its own volition that an order should be made in the course of other family proceedings (e.g. under the Children Act 1989), then the order will cease to have effect if those proceedings are withdrawn or terminated.

6.6 Occupation orders

An occupation order regulates the parties' occupation of their present, former or intended home and replaces all previous legislation (see above) and terminology. Previously similar orders were known as ouster orders and exclusion orders.

An occupation order may take a number of forms, including:

- enforcing the applicant's right to remain in the house

- requiring the other party (respondent) to allow the applicant to enter and occupy the home

- prohibiting, suspending or restricting the respondent's right to occupy the house

- excluding the respondent from the house itself and/or from a defined area in which the house is situated.

These orders do not alter either party's financial interests in the home.

Occupation orders may be granted under five different sections of the Act, depending on the nature of the relationship between the parties and whether the applicant has an existing right to occupy the home. The parties must first be associated (see Section 6.4).

The Act introduces a new concept of 'entitlement'. An *entitled person* is someone who has some legal right to occupy the property, for example the person is the freehold owner, tenant, contractual licensee or someone with a beneficial interest, or has matrimonial home rights. The term 'matrimonial home rights' in the new legislation replaces the term 'rights of occupation' contained in the Matrimonial Homes Act 1983. Spouses of entitled persons automatically have matrimonial home rights under the Act. These rights are also sometimes obtained through the divorce process.

A *non-entitled person* has neither the legal right to occupy the property nor matrimonial home rights.

The main differences between the five different categories of order are:

- the range of people who can apply

- the criteria the court must use in assessing whether to grant an order

- the length of time the orders may last.

An application may be made as follows:

- Under Section 33 by a person who is entitled to occupy the home because that person is a legal owner or tenant or has matrimonial home rights in relation to the home against another person with whom he or she is associated, whether or not that person is also entitled to occupy the home. This provision will apply to most married couples and cohabitants and others who are sole or joint owners or tenants of their home. An order can be made for a specified period or until further order.

- Under Section 35 by a former spouse who is not entitled to occupy the home or who has matrimonial home rights in relation to it against his or her former spouse who is so entitled. An order under this section can be made only for an initial period of six months but can be extended for periods of up to six months on one or more occasions.

- Under Section 36 by a cohabitant or former cohabitant who is not entitled to occupy the home against the other cohabitant or former cohabitant who is so entitled. An order under this section can be made for six months and can be extended for one further period of up to six

months. In the case of non-entitled former cohabitants, this is an
extension of the previous law, as previously exclusion of a former partner
was not possible. However, restriction to a maximum of one year
discriminates against those who have cohabited for several years with a
partner and may well have made a substantial personal and economic
contribution to the family home.

- Under Section 37 by one spouse or former spouse against the other
  spouse of a former spouse where neither is entitled to occupy the home.
  This situation could include a couple lodging in a relative's or friend's
  house or squatting. An order can be made for up to six months and
  extended on one or more occasions for further periods of up to six
  months.

- Under Section 38 by one cohabitant or former cohabitant against the
  other cohabitant or former cohabitant, where neither is entitled to
  occupy the home. An order can be made for up to six months but can be
  extended for a further period of six months.

6.7 Grounds for making an occupation order

Sections 33, 35, 36, 37 and 38 each contain details of the matters that the court
should consider when deciding whether to make an occupation order. The criteria
differ somewhat between the sections, but in general courts must have regard to all
the circumstances of the case, including:

- the respective housing needs and resources

- the respective financial resources

- the likely effect of the order on the health, safety and wellbeing of the
  parties or any relevant child

- the conduct of the parties in relation to each other and otherwise.

If the application is under Section 35 (non-entitled former spouse), the court must
also take into account the length of time since the parties ceased to live together and
since the marriage ended, and whether other proceedings are taking place.

In an application under Section 36 (non-entitled cohabitant), the court should
also consider:

- the length of the cohabitation

- the length of time since separation

- whether there are any children

- the existence of any pending proceedings.

In addition, under Part IV, Section 41 of the 1996 Act, the court was required to have regard to the nature of the relationship, including the fact that the couple has not 'given each other the commitment involved in marriage'. This is now repealed by Section 2(1) of the DVCVA 2004. Additionally, where the court considers whether to give a right to occupy to a cohabitant or former cohabitant with no existing right (a non-entitled cohabitant), it should not only have regard to the nature of the parties' relationship but also consider the level of commitment in the relationship. It will be important to monitor the effectiveness of these new provisions when the DVCVA is implemented.

BALANCE OF HARM TEST

In addition to these provisions, Part IV of the Family Law Act introduces the balance of harm test, which in some cases will oblige the court to make an order. In applications by spouses, former spouses and applicants entitled under Section 33, it is mandatory for the court to apply the test, the results of which override other criteria.

> If it appears to the court that the applicant or any relevant child is likely to suffer significant harm attributable to conduct of the respondent if an order...is not made, the court shall make the order unless it appears to it that (a) the respondent or any relevant child is likely to suffer significant harm...if the order is made; and (b) the harm likely to be suffered by the respondent or child in that event is as great as, or greater than, the harm attributable to conduct of the respondent which is likely to be suffered by the applicant or child if the order is not made.

> *(Section 33(7), Part IV, Family Law Act)*

'Harm' is defined under Section 63 as 'impairment of health' (which includes both physical and mental health) or 'ill treatment' and in relation to a child means ill-treatment or the impairment of health or development.

In applications by cohabitants or former cohabitants under Sections 36 and 38, the court is required to have regard for the balance of harm test, but this does not override other criteria. The implications for implementation of the balance of harm test are discussed further below.

6.8 Further provisions

ANCILLARY ORDERS

The court can also make ancillary orders to occupation orders, imposing obligations on either party with regard to repairs and maintenance, discharge of rent or mortgage or other payments, and use or care of possessions or furniture. These must be made, however, with regard to the financial needs and resources, or the financial obligations, of the parties.

WITHOUT NOTICE (EMERGENCY) ORDERS (ALSO KNOWN AS 'EX-PARTE')

A court may make ex-parte non-molestation or occupation orders (without the normal period of notice to the respondent of the proceedings) if it considers it just and convenient to do so. The court must have regard to all the circumstances, including whether:

- there is a risk of significant harm to the applicant or child
- the applicant is likely to be deterred or prevented from making any application, if the order is not made immediately
- the respondent is evading service of notice of an 'inter-partes' hearing.

In all cases, a full hearing should follow as swiftly as possible in order to enable the respondent to have the opportunity to make representation.

UNDERTAKINGS

An undertaking is a promise made to the court to refrain from certain behaviour. In the past, the courts have tended to use undertakings as an alternative to granting orders. Although an undertaking made in court is intended to be taken as seriously as an order, and the respondent can still be committed for breach of such an undertaking, in practice undertakings are likely to be less easy to enforce, as no power of arrest can be attached, although the respondent can be committed for breach; research has shown how unsatisfactory such promises may be in affording protection from violence (Barron 1990). However, under Section 17 of the Family Law Act, the court cannot accept an undertaking if a power of arrest would (normally) be attached – that is, where (physical) violence has been used or threatened. Hence, this may be less problematic in the future than it has been in the past.

POWERS OF ARREST

The Family Law Act (Part IV, Section 47) states that a power of arrest shall be attached to one or more provisions of a non-molestation or occupation order where the respondent has used or threatened (physical) violence against an applicant or any relevant child unless the applicant or child is protected adequately without a power of arrest. This duty does not apply to ex-parte orders, but the court may still attach a power of arrest if:

- violence is used or threatened, and
- there is a risk of significant harm if a power of arrest is not attached immediately.

These provisions will be strengthened once the DVCVA 2004 has been implemented. Under this legislation, a breach of a non-molestation order will be a criminal offence: 'A person who without reasonable excuse does anything that he is prohibited from doing by a non-molestation order is guilty of an offence' and is liable to a fine or imprisonment of up to five years.

This should strengthen the power of court orders and means that in future the police will treat any breach of any order just like other criminal offences in cases of domestic violence (see Women's Aid Criminal Law briefing, www.womensaid.org.uk). However, the Act retains the option of returning to the county court or family proceedings court for contempt of court in the same way as now. It is not clear how this will work in practice, as this may now mean that powers of arrest will not need to be attached as a breach will automatically enable the police to arrest.

Occupation orders will be treated differently, and a separate power of arrest will still be needed.

OTHER PROVISIONS AND AMENDMENTS TO OTHER LEGISLATION

The Family Law Act 1996 made a number of other provisions, including changes to police powers, in relation to breaches and enforcement of orders, and others with direct reference to the protection of children:

- An important amendment to the Children Act 1989 under Section 52 and Schedule 6 enables the court when making an emergency protection or interim care order to make an order to exclude the suspected abuser from the house, removing the abuser instead of the child (this is discussed in Chapter Four).

- Within the general provisions of the Family Law Act 1996, children under 16 years of age may apply for orders if given leave of court to do so, for which the court must judge that the child has sufficient understanding.

- The Act brings in new powers under Section 53 and Schedule 7 to transfer joint tenancies into one party's name (see also Chapter Seven), a remedy not previously available for (heterosexual) cohabitants. This may enable an abused woman who is afraid to stay in her former home area to exchange her existing tenancy for a tenancy in another area, meaning women and children will have to spend less time in refuges and other temporary accommodation. However, these powers do not apply in the magistrates' court.

6.9 How much does Part IV of the Family Law Act help abused women and children?

The strengths of Part IV (especially once the DVCVA 2004 is implemented) are that the Act now enables a much larger group of applicants who have been abused, threatened or assaulted by someone with whom they are living or have (or have had) a family-type relationship to gain access to a uniform package of protective remedies in both magistrates' and county courts. The legislation is also now more accessible for users, advisers and legal professionals. The loopholes in eligibility for those who have never lived with their abuser, except where there has been a formal promise of future marriage or there is a child of whom both are parents or have parental responsibility, will change, although the effectiveness of the DVCVA 2004 has yet to be tested.

Similarly, although to date a homosexual partner can apply for occupation orders only if he or she has existing rights to occupy the home (i.e. is a tenant or owner), this will also change with the implementation of the DVCVA 2004.

Although other injunctive remedies are available under common law (the civil remedy against harassment introduced within the Protection for Harassment Act 1997 alongside the new criminal offences – see Sections 6.3 and 6.8), these orders are not likely to be as effective, as powers of arrest cannot be attached.

Nevertheless, Part IV was a significant improvement in many respects. For instance, powers of arrest could be attached as a matter of course whenever physical violence has been used or threatened to all orders made 'on notice', except where clear argument can be made as to why this is unnecessary. This should make more of these orders readily enforceable, as those with powers of arrest are lodged at police stations. Many advocates, however, still feel that the new law does not go far enough and that powers of arrest should also be mandatory in 'without notice' applications where violence has been used or threatened. Monitoring is needed to see whether powers of arrest will be attached with more regularity than heretofore. Anecdotal evidence suggests that practice is still very patchy and that there is a problem getting emergency occupation orders (to get the violent party out) because the courts will not attach powers of arrest until the violent party has been served notice and has a chance to come to court. This means that at the time of most vulnerability and risk (when female homicide statistics are highest), women are not protected fully, as their injunctions are not logged at police stations to enable fast action. This may change once breach measures under the DVCVA are implemented.

Some potentially retrogressive amendments were also introduced during the passage of the 1996 Act. In particular, in relation to occupation orders, the conduct of the parties (i.e. past behaviour) was reintroduced as a criterion. This means that even in cases of domestic violence, conduct not related to matters of safety and protection from violence may be a factor when considering whether to make an order. Research since 1978 has consistently confirmed how violent men frequently cite the conduct of the non-violent partner (in relation to domestic services, mothering or sexual fidelity) as 'provoking' or 'causing' the abuse (Barron 1990). Such justifications have also been accepted by courts as reasons not to grant occupation orders or, in more extreme cases within criminal law, as defences for killing a current or former female partner on grounds of 'provocation'.

On the other hand, consideration of conduct (i.e. violent or abusive behaviour) could be helpful in certain contexts. There has always been concern that in cases where women who are at risk of violence from their partners or ex-partners apply for orders after many years of abuse, the effects of that abuse on their mental or physical wellbeing may be used against them. For instance, the respondent might argue that his partner is mentally unstable and unfit to have care of her children, which is itself often a determining factor in who is permitted to occupy the property. In such cases, the removal of all considerations of past behaviour could lead to a snapshot picture at the time of application, without sufficient consideration of its causes, of harm in the past and of the potential for harm in the future. In practice, whether consideration of conduct proves to be positive or negative for abused women is likely to be related to the applicant's access to effective legal representation.

A second reference to conduct has been introduced into the balance of harm test (to be used when assessing the need for occupation orders). The balance of harm test is intended to be more effective in addressing not only physical violence and abuse but also mental and emotional cruelty. It also gives greater attention to the needs of children. However, any significant harm suffered by the applicant and any relevant child has to be attributable to the conduct of the respondent, whereas this is weighed against (any) harm likely to be suffered by the respondent or any relevant child. The effect of this appears to change the balance of harm test to favour the respondent (i.e. the violent partner), as all forms of potential harm (defined as impairment of health or ill-treatment) may be considered on his part, whereas only harm attributable to his behaviour may be considered in relation to the applicant. It has been pointed out that the fairness of the balance of harm test is now open to question, as this amendment could give unfair weight to an abuser's rights to occupation of the home over a survivor's rights to protection from violence through a temporary order. However, interpretation of this test remains to be challenged in court practice or by case law, which could consider the widest definition of harm suffered by the applicant attributable to the respondent's conduct. For example, if a woman is forced to leave her home, then the harm she suffers as a result of becoming homeless could be considered to be due to the respondent's conduct.

HELP WITH LEGAL COSTS

Even women who wish to obtain remedies under this Act may find that they are unable to do so because of the increasing difficulty in getting public funding (community legal services funding) to pay for the legal costs. There has been increasing concern about the difficulties of accessing public funding to pursue applications for injunctions.

FURTHER CONSIDERATIONS

Part IV of the Family Law Act 1996 in theory allowed new opportunities for a more holistic response to domestic violence, through the more effective linking of action under criminal law and protection for the future under civil law. Section 60 (which has never been implemented) offered the opportunity to pilot new powers by third parties to take out injunctions on behalf of abused women, for example for police to take out orders on behalf of women at the same time as going before magistrates for criminal proceedings. Such measures have been used very successfully in Australia and the USA (with the woman's consent) and carry a number of advantages, for example their speed and the removal of problems associated with legal aid.

The DVCVA 2004 should provide further opportunities for protection for survivors of domestic violence and improve on the existing provision within the Family Law Act 1996, but we have to wait for implementation of the Act to see how effective these will be in practice.

6.10 Summary

- In the early 1990s, the need for better protection from domestic violence under civil law was highlighted through a number of reports and enquiries. Research has shown that injunctions and protection orders were more often breached than not, and that enforcement was virtually impossible.

- Abused women face a number of problems within the legal process, including access to legal representation, lack of specialist services or interpreters for black and minority ethnic women, the trauma of the court process, and a lack of training of court staff on the impact of domestic violence on women and children and the reasons why many women stay with or return to a violent partner.

- A review of the law by the Law Commission led to recommendations for change, supported by many statutory and voluntary bodies, and eventually the introduction of the Family Law Act 1996, Part IV in October 1997.

- Part IV of the Family Law Act 1996 provides a single set of remedies available in all family courts, including the high court, county court and family proceedings (magistrates') court. There are two main types of order under the Act: occupation orders, which regulate the occupation of the family home, and non-molestation orders, for protection from all forms of violence and abuse.

- Eligibility for orders under the Family Law Act 1996 Part IV depends on the type of order and the relationship between the applicant and the other party (the respondent). The Act considerably extends the categories of people who may seek protection. It introduces the new concept of 'associated persons'. This is being extended under the DVCVA 2004 to include non-cohabiting couples and homosexual couples.

- Non-molestation orders reproduce and extend the previous powers of the courts to make orders prohibiting a person (the respondent) from molesting another person associated with the respondent or any relevant child. When DVCVA 2004 is implemented, breach will be a criminal offence.

- An occupation order regulates the parties' occupation of their present, former or intended home and replaces all previous legislation. An occupation order may take a number of forms, including enforcing the applicant's right to remain in the house or restricting the respondent's right to occupy the house. Occupation orders may be granted under five different sections of the Act, depending on the nature of the relationship between the parties and whether the applicant has an existing right to occupy the home.

- The court must consider a number of different criteria in deciding whether to make an occupation order, including the respective housing needs and resources, the respective financial resources, the likely effect of the order on the health, safety and wellbeing of the parties or any relevant child, and the conduct of the parties in relation to each other and otherwise.

- The Act also introduced the balance of harm test, which in some cases obliges the court to make an order. In applications by those entitled by legal right to occupy the home, it is mandatory for the court to apply the test, the results of which override other criteria.

- The court can also make ancillary orders to occupation orders, imposing obligations on either party with regard to repairs and maintenance, discharge of rent, mortgage or other payments, and use or care of possessions or furniture.

- A court may make without notice non-molestation or occupation orders (without the normal period of notice to the respondent of the proceedings) if it considers it just and convenient to do so.

- A court may accept an undertaking unless a power of arrest would (normally) be attached – that is, where (physical) violence has been used or threatened.

- Powers of arrest must be attached to one or more provisions of a non-molestation or occupation order where the respondent has used or threatened (physical) violence against an applicant or any relevant child unless the applicant or child is protected adequately without a power of arrest. (From DVCVA 2004 implementation, effectively there will be an automatic power of arrest as breach will be a criminal offence.)

- The Act makes a number of other provisions, including a specific amendment to the Children Act 1989 that enables the court, when making an emergency protection or interim care order, to make an order to exclude the suspected abuser from the house; a provision for children under 16 years to apply for orders if given leave of court to do so; and new powers to transfer joint tenancies into one party's name, a remedy not previously available for cohabitants.

- The strengths of Part IV are that it enables a much larger group of applicants who have been abused, threatened or assaulted by someone with whom they are living or have (or have had) a family-type relationship to gain access to a uniform package of protective remedies in both magistrates' and county courts; measures for enforcement have also been strengthened. The legislation is also now more accessible for users, advisers and legal professionals.

- Its weaknesses are, first, the loopholes in eligibility: the legislation does not extend to those who have never lived with their abusers, except where there has been a formal promise of future marriage, or if there is a child of whom both are parents or have parental responsibility; nor (except in the above circumstances) does it apply to non-cohabiting couples. Cohabiting homosexual partners currently can apply for an occupation order only if they have existing rights to occupy the home (that is as a tenant or an owner). All of the above should change with the implementation of the DVCVA 2004.

- Improved protection from violence still depends crucially on both access to public funding, which is now less accessible to people in paid employment, particularly those on low incomes, and its effective enforcement by the police and the courts.

- For a summary of the advantages and disadvantages of using the criminal versus the civil legislation, see Tables 6.1 and 6.2 (overleaf).

Table 6.1 Advantages and disadvantages for abused women of using the criminal law

Advantages	Disadvantages
State takes action: not left to women	Woman is passive witness: she may feel the situation is out of her control
Woman can feel that the violence is taken more seriously	Proceedings are held in open court (unless special measures are enacted)
Abuser can be arrested immediately and easily and held in custody for short periods	Law is intended to punish the perpetrator, not protect the victim
Abuser can be punished/removed from circulation for a certain period	Prosecution process can take a very long time
Clear indication of who is at fault	Woman might not want the man prosecuted for a number of reasons
Bail conditions can be more powerful than an injunction (but have limited duration)	Court personnel attitudes: can be a lack of understanding of nature and dynamics of domestic violence
Proceedings have a symbolic value: domestic violence is not acceptable	Risk of increasing the threat and danger to the woman and any children if effective interagency responses are not developed
No problems with costs or access to legal aid	Cannot deal with many non-physical aspects of domestic violence
Special measures available in court to make process easier and protect the victim from the perpetrator	
Changes in prosecution policy and coordinated intervention are improving safety and reducing time for cases to get to court in some areas	

Table 6.2 Advantages and disadvantages for abused women of using the civil law

Advantages	Disadvantages
Woman makes choice of what protection is sought	Limited access to legal aid
Can deal with a wide range of harmful behaviours	Some women are not eligible or do not have the same rights to protection
Court hearing is in closed court	Court personnel attitudes: can be a lack of understanding of nature and dynamics of domestic violence
Legal aid may be available	Pressure on court time and other factors means women may be pressed to accept undertakings instead
Woman can get immediate protection (in theory)	Reluctance to grant ex-parte occupation orders and ex-parte powers of arrest
Intended to protect the woman and her children and not punish the man	Penalties are non-custodial unless there is a severe and recurrent breach
Can offer protection for the future and a route to safe housing	Risk of increasing the threat and danger to the woman and any children if effective interagency responses are not developed

Note

1   This has probably been implemented by default due to the implementation of the Civil Partnership Act 2004.

CHAPTER SEVEN

PROTECTION AGAINST DOMESTIC VIOLENCE UNDER HOUSING LAW

The options for protection available under civil and criminal law have some limitations to their effectiveness, as discussed earlier; therefore, it is likely that many women will continue to rely on provision under homeless legislation for safe housing and longer-term protection from violence for themselves and their children.

Housing provision and resources, however, have been greatly reduced in many areas of the country in the past decades. The Housing Act 1996, although widening the definition of those eligible for emergency and temporary accommodation, set new limitations on local authorities' duties to help secure longer-term safe accommodation for women and children who are homeless through domestic violence. This has subsequently been amended by the Homelessness Act 2002, which requires local authorities to adopt a strategic approach in combating homelessness. The Act makes significant amendments to the main legislative provisions contained in the Housing Act 1996, but does not set out a new statutory framework for either homelessness or housing allocation. The Homelessness Act 2002 cannot, therefore, be read as a free-standing statute but has to be considered in conjunction with the Housing Act 1996. Among the major amendments brought in by this Act are changes to the statutory scheme of help for women who are homeless as a result of domestic violence, and changes to the arrangements for allocating local authority housing.

Accompanying this legislation, a new statutory instrument – the Homelessness (Priority Need for Accommodation) (England) Order 2002 – extends the categories of homeless person having 'priority need'.[1] A revised statutory Code of Guidance[2] supplements the Homelessness Act 2002 and the accompanying order.

7.1 Provisions of the Housing Act 1996, with amendments made under the Homelessness Act 2002

The Housing Act 1996 became law in January 1997 and made a number of major changes to public and private rented accommodation. The legislation is split into eight parts, each dealing with different areas of housing policy. Parts VI and VII of the Act affect decisions about who is housed in the social rented sector and are of particular relevance for women and children experiencing abuse.

The legislation removed the automatic link that used to exist between being homeless under the law and being given permanent housing. Under previous legislation, people who were unintentionally homeless and in priority need were eventually offered permanent accommodation. Part VII of the Housing Act 1996 gave local authorities a temporary, but renewable, two-year duty to house certain applicants. The Homelessness Act 2002 abolished this two-year period and replaced it with a duty to secure suitable accommodation until a settled housing solution is found. However, the duty to provide permanent accommodation has still been removed, and to obtain permanent accommodation the applicant must also apply through the council's normal waiting-list procedures under Part VI of the Act. (This may entail the applicant adding his or her name to the housing register.)

LOCAL AUTHORITY'S DUTY TO PROVIDE TEMPORARY HOUSING

Temporary housing is provided in two stages: interim accommodation and temporary accommodation.

Interim accommodation
If the local authority believes an applicant

- may be homeless or is threatened with homelessness, and
- is eligible for assistance, and
- is in priority need

then the local authority must secure interim accommodation, for example in a refuge or hostel, while it investigates whether it has a duty.

- The interim duty to accommodate arises regardless of whether there is a possibility of referring the application to another local authority.
- The interim duty ceases when the local authority conveys its decision to the applicant.
- If the applicant seeks a review of the decision, the local authority has a power but not a duty to continue the interim accommodation pending the review.

- If the local authority's decision is in the applicant's favour, the interim duty is likely to be superseded by a temporary duty to ensure provision of temporary accommodation.

Temporary accommodation

The local authority has a duty to ensure the provision of temporary accommodation to people who have a local connection with the area and are:

- homeless or threatened with homelessness, and

- eligible for assistance, and

- in priority need, and

- not intentionally homeless, and

- unable to access other 'suitable accommodation'.

Under the Housing Act 1996, this duty was for two years only. However, the Homelessness Act 2002 abolished this two-year period and replaced it with a duty to secure additional accommodation until a settled solution is found.

The duty ends earlier if the person housed under this Section:

- having been informed of the consequences unreasonably refuses an offer of housing under Part VI, or of other suitable accommodation

- ceases to be eligible for assistance

- ceases to use as his or her only or principal home the accommodation provided under this section

- accepts an offer of housing under Part VI.

7.2 Homelessness and threatened homelessness (1996 Part VII)

- A person is homeless if he or she has no accommodation available for occupation in the UK or elsewhere.

- A person is threatened with homelessness if this situation is likely to arise within 28 days.

- Accommodation is available for a person's occupation if he or she has a legal right to it, such as freehold or leasehold ownership, a tenancy including a statutory tenancy, or an express or implied licence, and only if it is suitable for that person together with anyone who normally resides, or might reasonably be expected to reside, with the person as a family member. It is not available if the person cannot secure entry to it, or if it is a movable home (and there is nowhere to place it and live in it legally), or if it would not be reasonable for him or her to continue to occupy it.

- Accommodation would not be reasonable to continue to occupy if the applicant's continued occupation of it would be likely to lead to violence directed against the applicant or someone who lives, or might reasonably be expected to live, with the applicant.

The Housing Act 1996 has broadened the definition of homelessness for women experiencing domestic violence. Part III of the 1985 Housing Act accepted only violence or threats of violence from people living in the home. In the Housing Act 1996, domestic violence is defined as violence or threats of violence from a person who is associated with the person under threat. An 'associated person' is defined in the Code of Guidance to the Act (and the definition is the same as under Part IV of the Family Law Act 1996 – see Chapter Six) and, therefore, also includes people who are or have been married, engaged or living together in the same household; relatives; people who are parents of a child under the age of 18 years or who have shared parental responsibility for such a child; and civil partners and those who are or have been living with partners of the same sex as themselves.

A further extension of the provisions of the homelessness legislation is included in Section 10 of the Homelessness Act 2002, which identifies people who cease to live in their accommodation because of violence or threats of violence from anyone as being both homeless and in priority need – that is, the violence is no longer confined to that within a 'domestic' context. This means that a local authority now has a duty to accommodate anyone at risk of violence using both the Homelessness Act 2002 and the Housing Act 1996 (see 'People who are at risk of violence' below).

PRIORITY NEED FOR ACCOMMODATION

The following homeless people are in 'priority need' under Section 59 of the Housing Act 1985:

- a pregnant woman or a person with whom she resides or might reasonably be expected to reside
- a person with whom dependent children reside or might reasonably be expected to reside
- a person who is vulnerable as a result of old age, mental illness, handicap or physical disability or other special reason, or with whom such a person resides or might reasonably be expected to reside
- a person who is homeless or threatened with homelessness as a result of an emergency such as flood, fire or other disaster.

Under the provisions of the Homelessness Act 2002, additional categories of priority need have been added. In particular, as mentioned above, Section 10 of this Act specifies that people who are at risk of violence are in priority need:

- a person who is vulnerable as a result of ceasing to occupy accommodation by reason of violence from another person or threats of violence from another person that are likely to be carried out (see 'People who are at risk of violence' below).

Further additional categories of priority need dovetail with social services' duties to care leavers under the Children (Leaving Care) Act 2000 and use the same definitions; that is, relevant child/former relevant child:

- a person who is aged 16 or 17 years old and is not a relevant child or a child in need to whom a local authority owes a duty under Section 20 of the Children Act 1989

- a person aged 18, 19, 20 or 21 years and who is a former relevant child (i.e. a young person aged 18–21 years who has been a 'relevant child' because he or she was in care for a total of at least 13 weeks from age 14 years, some of which time was when he or she was 16 or 17 years)

- a person who is vulnerable as a result of having been looked after, accommodated or fostered, within the meaning of Section 24 of the Children Act 1989 (as amended by the Children (Leaving Care) Act 2000); that is, a person under the age of 21 years who may not qualify as a former relevant child but at some time since the age of 16 years has been in some form of care, for example private care

- a person who is vulnerable as a result of having been a member of Her Majesty's regular naval, military or air force

- a person who is vulnerable as a result of:

  o having served a custodial sentence (within the meaning of Section 76 or the Powers of Criminal Courts (Sentences) Act 2000)

  o having been committed for contempt of court or any other kindred offence

  o having been remanded in custody (within the meaning of paragraph (b), (c) or (d) of Section 88(1) of that Act).

PEOPLE WHO ARE AT RISK OF VIOLENCE: HOMELESSNESS ACT 2002 (SECTION 10)

The effect of this Section is to produce an (almost) level playing field for all victims of actual or threatened violence. This category includes people fleeing any violence and is not confined to violence in a family or 'domestic' context.

The Department for Communities and Local Government has produced revised guidance[3] on good practice in assessing vulnerability. In the guidance, local authorities are reminded that the test of vulnerability is whether the applicant is less able to fend for him- or herself when homeless or in finding and keeping accommodation so that he or she would suffer injury or detriment in circumstances where a less vulnerable person would be able to cope without harmful effects.

The guidance also stresses that the priorities should be the safety of the applicant and ensuring that confidentiality is maintained. It suggests considerations that should be taken into account when deciding whether a person is vulnerable as a result of ceasing to occupy accommodation because of violence or threats of violence that are likely to be carried out. These considerations are:

- the nature of the violence or threats of violence (there may have been a single but significant incident or a number of incidents over an extended period of time which have had a cumulative effect)

- the impact and likely effects of the violence on the applicant's current and future wellbeing

- whether the applicant has any existing support networks, particularly by way of family or friends.

In cases of domestic violence, the revised guidance makes it clear that authorities should not provoke further violence, and that 'the safety of the applicant and ensuring confidentiality must be of paramount concern'. At different points, the Code of Guidance states that 'it is not advisable for the housing authority to approach the alleged perpetrator' (6.17) and later adds, 'inquiries of the perpetrators of violence should not be made' (10.28). The Code of Guidance also states that local authorities may seek information from police, social services, friends and relatives – but that corroboration may not be available.

Under the Homelessness Act 2002, local authorities may also secure accommodation for homeless applicants who are not in priority need, although they do not have a duty to do more than provide advice and such assistance as they think reasonable.

INTENTIONAL HOMELESSNESS

Once the local authority has established that the applicant is homeless and in priority need, the authority must then decide whether the applicant is homeless intentionally:

> A person becomes homeless intentionally if she/he deliberately does or fails
> to do anything in consequence of which she/he ceases to occupy accommo-
> dation which is available for his/her accommodation and which it would
> have been reasonable for him/her to continue to occupy.

(Housing Act 1996)

In making its decision, the local authority is likely to consider:

- whether the loss of 'suitable' accommodation happened because of the applicant's deliberate act or failure to act

- whether it was reasonable for the person to have continued to occupy the accommodation

- whether the person was aware of all the facts

- whether the person colluded to bring the accommodation to an end (this could apply to an applicant who has been asked to leave by a friend or relative or by a landlord)

- whether the person has been given advice and assistance in order to get accommodation but failed to secure it.

Where an authority is satisfied that other suitable accommodation is available in its district for occupation by the applicant, but the applicant unreasonably fails to secure such accommodation, the applicant shall be treated as having become intentionally homeless. However, the Code of Guidance (see below) states that such a finding on this ground would not be justified unless the authority was satisfied that alternative accommodation was both suitable for and available to the applicant (particularly with regard to affordability), and there was no good reason why the applicant did not obtain it.

A local authority must give advice and assistance to those who are found to be intentionally homeless and must ensure that they have accommodation for 28 days while they find somewhere else to live.

LOCAL CONNECTION

Local connection is established by current or previous voluntary residence, current employment, family association or other special circumstance. If no one in the applicant's household has any connection with the local authority to which the application was made, then the authority may refer the household to another local authority with which at least one member of the household has a connection, provided that no one in the household runs a risk of domestic violence in the other area. An applicant can ask for a review if he or she objects to the referral. The applicant must be given accommodation by the first authority pending the outcome of the review.

7.3 Provision of temporary accommodation

A local authority can satisfy a duty under Part VII to secure accommodation by:

- providing the accommodation itself

- obtaining an offer of accommodation from some other body, such as a registered social landlord[4]

- providing the applicant with sufficient advice and assistance to enable him or her to obtain accommodation.

The Homelessness Act 2002 repeals the main duty in the 1996 Act requiring local authorities to provide temporary accommodation for priority homeless people for only two years. It removes this time limit and replaces it with a requirement to provide temporary accommodation until the applicant has been provided with settled accommodation.

It is, therefore, a concern that women and children experiencing domestic violence who are rehoused by a local authority under the homeless legislation may be placed in the worst housing on run-down estates. It is advisable for homeless families seeking rehousing because of domestic violence to apply for permanent accommodation either through nomination to a housing association or from a local authority's housing stock. (This may mean putting their names on the housing register, where this applies.)

OTHER 'SUITABLE' TEMPORARY ACCOMMODATION

A local authority *may* fulfil its duties to homeless applicants by temporarily housing them in its own accommodation or by giving advice and assistance to help applicants secure access to private rented accommodation if the authority is satisfied that suitable accommodation is available in its area. However, under the Homelessness Act 2002, the authority no longer has an obligation to do this. Many housing authorities now hold a 'housing options interview' before making an appointment with a homelessness officer. This interview outlines the options available and provides (often minimal) information about the local authority's duty to provide temporary accommodation for anyone at risk of violence. The interview is often aimed at reducing the number of homelessness allocations. The options offered may also include provision of a Sanctuary Scheme but this is a choice and does not have to be accepted.

Anecdotal evidence shows that childless women survivors of domestic violence have more difficulty in being accepted as homeless. Housing officers may often be more willing to accommodate domestic violence survivors who have children, since that is an additional category of 'priority need'.

The local authority may assist an applicant to secure the accommodation with rent guarantees or help with deposits while providing interim housing. 'Suitable' accommodation must be available for at least a two-year period, and preferably longer, in order to avoid recurring homelessness. The accommodation must be adequate to accommodate the needs of the family and should take into account medical and social needs. People on low incomes are not expected to take on a rent above the housing benefit level. The local authority must take into account the characteristics and circumstances of the applicant and the state of the local housing market; for example, a woman and children who are escaping domestic violence may not be in a position to take on private accommodation.

REVIEW OF LOCAL AUTHORITY DECISIONS

Within 21 days of being notified of the decision (or longer, if the local authority agrees), the applicant can request a review of any decision made by a local authority concerning:

- whether the applicant is eligible for assistance under Part VII
- whether a duty is owed and, if so, which duty
- whether the case should be referred to another authority.

If requested under Section 202, the authority must review its decision and notify the applicant of the result, giving reasons if the decision is not in the applicant's favour. Notification must be in writing, must inform the applicant of the right to appeal under Section 204 and must be sent to the applicant or left for a reasonable time for collection at the authority's office.

If the applicant is dissatisfied with the outcome of a review or has not been notified of the result within the time limits, the applicant has 21 days to appeal to the county court on a point of law. The court may uphold, vary or quash the local authority's decision.

PROTECTION OF PROPERTY

Where a local authority is under a duty to an applicant under the legislation, it must (if the applicant is unable to do so) take such reasonable steps as it considers necessary to prevent any loss of or damage to property belonging to the applicant's household. The local authority may make a reasonable charge, and failure to pay such a charge may lead to its disposal.

This means that the local authority must store the property of women and children who leave their homes because of violence, either within their own storage facility or elsewhere. There is a small charge made for this, which can be claimed by the woman from the Benefits Agency. Family pets can be defined as property and can, therefore, be kennelled. (This has been achieved successfully by some domestic violence organizations on behalf of women and children in their refuges.)

7.4 Help with permanent housing

Part VI of the Act determines who gets access to permanent accommodation in the social rented sector. It requires local authorities to decide who does and who does not qualify for rehousing. People who must qualify are unintentionally homeless people in priority need. Asylum seekers and people from abroad who are subject to immigration control will not qualify.

Under the Homelessness Act 2002, local authorities are no longer required to maintain a housing register, although many of them may still choose to do so.

The local authority must have an allocations scheme for deciding who gets priority when it allocates its own tenancies and its nominations to registered social landlords. Preference must now be given to all people who are homeless within the meaning of Housing Act 1996 Part VII, including those:

- accommodated under Section 190(2) as intentionally homeless people

- occupying unsatisfactory accommodation

- who need to move on medical or welfare grounds

- who need to move to a locality in the district where failure to meet that need would cause hardship.

The 2002 Act also identifies factors that an authority's scheme may take into account when determining priorities within the reasonable preference categories. These include:

- the financial resources available to meet the housing costs

- any local connection that exists between a person and the authority's district.

Allocation schemes differ between authorities, but each allocation scheme must be accompanied by a policy explaining how it works. There is a new power under the Homelessness Act 2002 to exclude altogether from the allocation schemes those applicants considered to be unsuitable (by virtue of their behaviour or the behaviour of a member of their household) to be a tenant of the authority. It also allows local authorities to give a lower priority to applicants whose behaviour may not have been sufficiently serious to exclude them from the scheme but who may still be considered to be entitled to less preference than a 'model tenant'.

Local authorities are being encouraged to give priority to married couples with children and vulnerable individuals living in unsuitable housing. A copy of the scheme must be available for public scrutiny.

Where local authorities maintain a register, people on the register are entitled to information about their place on the register, so that they can work out how long it will take for them to be rehoused. Where there is no register, people eligible for housing through the allocation scheme are entitled to information about the scheme in order to be able to assess:

- how their application is likely to be treated under the scheme

- whether appropriate housing accommodation is likely to be made available

- the length of time that it is likely to take for the allocation to be made and accommodation to become available.

The Housing Act also encourages local authorities to:

- provide translations of forms for applicants whose first language is not English

- provide audiotapes or Braille copies for people with visual impairment

- provide help with filling in the application form where required

- adopt an equal opportunities policy relating to all aspects of the allocation process.

7.5 Implementing the Housing Act 1996 and Homelessness Act 2002: the Code of Guidance

The Code of Guidance (Department for Communities and Local Government 2006) gives guidance to local authorities on how they should implement the Housing Act 1996 and Homelessness Act 2002. The Code does not have force of law, but local authorities should have regard to it in exercising their functions relating to homelessness and the prevention of homelessness. The Code makes a number of specific references to the needs of women and children experiencing domestic violence. For example, the Code states:

VIOLENCE

6.17 Under Section 177, it is not reasonable for the applicant to continue to occupy accommodation if it is probable that this will lead to domestic violence or other violence against him or her, or against a person who normally resides with him or her as a member of his or her family, or any other person who might reasonably be expected to reside with him or her. Violence means violence from another person or threats of violence from another person which are likely to be carried out.

8.19 ... Domestic violence is violence from a person who is associated with the victim and also includes threats of violence that are likely to be carried out. Domestic violence is not confined to instances within the home but extends to violence outside the home.

8.20 Section 178[5] provides that, for the purposes of defining domestic violence, a person is associated with another if:

 a) they are or have been married to each other

 b) they are or have been civil partners of each other

 c) they are or have been cohabitants (including same-sex partners)

 d) they live or have lived in the same household

e) they are relatives, i.e. father, mother, stepfather, stepmother, son, daughter, stepdaughter, stepson, grandmother, grandfather, grandson, granddaughter, brother, sister, uncle, aunt, niece or nephew (whether of full blood, half blood or affinity), of that person or of that person's spouse or former spouse. A person is also included if he or she would fall into any of these categories in relation to cohabitees if they were married to each other

f) they have agreed to marry each other, regardless of whether that agreement has been terminated

g) they have entered into a civil partnership agreement between them, whether or not that agreement has been terminated

h) in relation to a child, each of them is a parent of the child or has, or had, parental responsibility for the child (within the meaning of the Children Act 1989). A child is a person under the age of 18 years

i) if a child has been adopted or freed for adoption (s.16(1) Adoption Act 1976), two persons are also associated if one is the natural parent or grandparent of the child and the other is the child of a person who has become the parent by virtue of the adoption order (s.72(1) Adoption Act 1976) or has applied for an adoption order or someone with whom the child has been placed for adoption.

8.22 An assessment of the likelihood of a threat of violence being carried out should not be based on whether there has been actual violence in the past. An assessment must be based on the facts of the case and devoid of any value judgements about what an applicant should or should not do, or should or should not have done, to mitigate the risk of any violence. Inquiries into cases where violence is alleged will need careful handling. (See 'Making enquiries' below and paragraph 6.17 of the revised Code of Guidance.)

8.23 In cases involving violence, housing authorities may wish to inform applicants of the option of seeking an injunction, but should make it clear that there is no obligation on the applicant to do so. Where applicants wish to pursue this option, it is advisable that they obtain independent advice, as an injunction may be ill-advised in some circumstances. However, housing authorities should recognize that injunctions ordering people not to molest or enter the home of the applicant may not be effective in deterring perpetrators from carrying out further violence or incursions, but should make it clear that there is no obligation on the applicant to do so. Where applicants wish to pursue this option, it is advisable that they obtain independent advice, as an injunction may be ill-advised in some circumstances. Consequently, applicants should not automatically be expected to return home on the strength of an injunction. To ensure applicants who have experienced actual or threatened violence get the support they need, authorities should inform them of appropriate organizations in the area, such as agencies offering counselling and support as well as specialist advice.

8.24 When dealing with cases involving violence or threat of violence from outside the home, housing authorities should consider the option of improving security of the applicant's home in order to enable him or her to continue to live there safely, where that is an option that the applicant wishes to pursue.[6] In some cases, immediate action to improve security within the victim's home may prevent homelessness. A fast response combined with support from the housing authority, police and voluntary sector may provide the applicant with the confidence to remain in the home. When dealing with domestic violence within the home, where the local authority is the landlord, housing authorities should consider the scope for evicting the perpetrator and allowing the victim to remain in the home. However, where there would be a probability of violence if the applicant continued to occupy the present accommodation, the housing authority must treat the applicant as homeless and should not expect the applicant to return to the accommodation. *In all cases involving violence, the safety of the applicant and his or her household should be the primary consideration at all stages of decision-making as to whether or not the applicant remains in their own home.* (Emphasis in original.)

MAKING ENQUIRIES

During the period when the local authority is providing interim accommodation, for example within its own Homeless Persons' Unit or by referral to a Women's Aid refuge, the local authority carries out enquiries to establish whether a woman fleeing violence is eligible for assistance. The Code of Guidance states that the authority may make enquiries to discover:

- whether the applicant is eligible for assistance
- whether any duty is owed to the applicant and, if so, what duty [Section 184(1)]
- whether a local connection exists with the area of another authority in England, Wales or Scotland (Section 184) (see 'Local connection' above).

The Code of Guidance also states (6.15–6.18):

- 'The obligation to make enquiries rests with the authority. It is not for the applicant to prove his or her case' (6.15).
- Authorities will wish to ensure that their enquiries are always undertaken quickly, sympathetically and, as far as possible, in confidence.
- The authority may request another relevant body to assist in discharging the enquiry duty under Section 213 (cooperation between relevant housing authorities and bodies). If so, the other body is under a duty to cooperate in rendering such assistance in the discharge of the function to which the request relates, as is reasonable in the circumstances.
- Enquiries should not be over elaborate or overlong.

- Women fleeing violence can be accompanied during interviews (in recognition that they are often under stress).

- Authorities should ensure access to competent interpreters for community languages of the area and have access to intermediaries for people with hearing and/or speech disabilities.

- In cases of domestic violence, applicants should be given the option of being interviewed by an officer of the same sex if they so wish.

- If the applicant reports violence or threats of violence, it is not advisable for the authority to approach the alleged perpetrator, since this could generate further violence and may delay the assessment.

INJUNCTIONS

The Code informs local authorities that:

> 8.23 In cases involving violence, housing authorities may wish to inform applicants of the option of seeking an injunction, but should make it clear that there is no obligation on the applicant to do so. Where applicants wish to pursue this option, it is advisable that they obtain independent advice, as an injunction may be ill advised in some circumstances. However, housing authorities should recognise that injunctions ordering persons not to molest, or enter the home of, the applicant may not be effective in deterring perpetrators from carrying out further violence or incursions and applicants may not have confidence in their effectiveness. Consequently, applicants should not be expected to return home on the strength of an injunction. To ensure applicants who have experienced actual or threatened violence get the support they need, authorities should inform them of appropriate organizations in the area, such as agencies offering counselling and support as well as specialist advice.

REFERRALS TO ANOTHER AREA (LOCAL CONNECTION)

> An applicant cannot be referred to another housing authority if he or she or any person who might reasonably be expected to reside with him or her would be at risk of violence in the district of the other housing authority.

WOMEN'S REFUGES

Authorities are recommended to develop close links with local women's refuge services. They should not delay in securing suitable accommodation elsewhere in the hope that she might return to her partner. The Code stresses that places in refuges must be available to others in need (i.e. they should not 'silt up' because of lack of move-on) (16.27). If a refuge organization terminates a licence to occupy because the household no longer needs to be in the refuge, then the authority has a duty to secure alternative accommodation straight away.

VICTIMS OF VIOLENCE OR ABUSE OR SEXUAL AND/OR RACIAL HARASSMENT

The Code states that local authorities should consider whether women without children are vulnerable as a result of having suffered violence from people with whom they are associated, or whether they are at risk of further violence or abuse if they return to those people. They should also consider whether those who have suffered or are under threat of harassment or violence on account of their gender, race, colour, ethnic or national origin or religion are vulnerable and, therefore, in priority need as a result. (See 10.28 and 17.6 of the Code of Guidance.)

7.6 Transfers and exchanges

The Housing Act 1985 gave local authority tenants the right to apply to live in another empty property belonging to the local authority within the same area. Applications are considered on the basis of need and priority. To get on the priority list, either medical or other evidence is usually required. Individual authorities have different ways of interpreting need, and each has a policy outlining how it prioritizes people for transfer.

For women with joint tenancies, however, until the introduction of Part IV of the Family Law Act 1996, transfers could be completed only on divorce, as the tenancy had to be in the woman's name only. However, county courts now have the power to transfer certain tenancies from one party to another under the Family Law Act 1996 Part IV Section 53 (which provides that Schedule 7 to the Act shall have effect). (Previously, this power had existed only in respect of spouses and former spouses, but the new Act has extended the provision to cohabitants and former cohabitants.)

Tenancies that can be transferred are:

- protected or statutory tenancies

- secure tenancies.

Assured shorthold tenancies (duration of six months only) are not included.

Spouses or former spouses can apply for a transfer of tenancy order under Schedule 7 if they are entitled or jointly entitled to occupy the home and are applying for a divorce or are divorced. (They cannot apply if they have remarried, and a transfer of tenancy order cannot take effect before decree absolute.)

Similarly, cohabitants or former cohabitants can apply for a transfer of tenancy order if they are entitled or jointly entitled to occupy the home. However, there are no restrictions on the time within which an application may be made, and they do not lose their right to apply if they marry someone else.

Once the tenancy has been transferred to the woman's sole name, this can then enable her, if she wishes, to use her existing tenancy to access alternative safe accommodation, either through a transfer or through an exchange (see below).

CRITERIA FOR MAKING AN ORDER TRANSFERRING A TENANCY

When deciding whether to make an order, in all cases the court must have regard to a number of factors, including:

- how the tenancy came into being and to whom it was granted
- the respective housing needs of the parties and any relevant child
- the respective financial resources of the parties
- the effect of an order (or not) on the health, safety or wellbeing of the parties and any relevant child
- the suitability of the parties as tenants (this allows the court to take account of the landlord's interests).

For cohabitants and former cohabitants, where only one of the parties is a tenant, the court must also have regard to:

- the nature of the relationship
- the duration of the cohabitation
- whether there are children for whom they are responsible
- the length of time since they ceased to live together.

PAYMENT

The court can also order that one party makes a payment to the other party in the event of a transfer of tenancy. In deciding whether to exercise this power, the court must take into account all the financial affairs of each party and consider the case carefully.

EXCHANGES

There are also a number of exchange mechanisms by which women experiencing domestic violence may be able to access new, safe accommodation:

- The Housing Act 1985 gave local authority and housing association tenants the right to mutually exchange houses anywhere in England and Wales, provided that each tenant obtained the written consent of their respective landlord.

- It is also possible to arrange reciprocal transfers between local authorities – that is, where two authorities each agree to house a woman from the other area in one of their empty properties.

- Housing Mobility and Exchange Services (HOMES), a government-funded organization set up to work with local authorities and housing associations to help people move home, operates two schemes: Homeswap, which is a national mutual exchange scheme, and the Homes Mobility scheme, through which people are 'nominated' by one landlord to another.

- Exchanges may also be arranged informally by advertising in local newspapers and shops of both areas or at local offices of councils and housing associations in the home area and new areas. After an exchange partner has been identified, it is important to go through the proper channels with both housing bodies in order to ensure that security of tenure is safeguarded.

The tenancy status of individuals wishing to transfer or exchange was affected by the Housing Act 1988. It is important to check before making a transfer or exchange whether security of tenure or other housing rights will be affected. Exchanges, transfers and mobility schemes all take time. They are not overnight solutions to immediate housing difficulties.

7.7 Homelessness reviews and strategies (Sections 1–4)

Sections 1–4 of the Homelessness Act 2002 introduce two new concepts: the 'homelessness review' and the 'homelessness strategy'. Local authorities were given the necessary statutory power to formulate a homelessness strategy for their area and formulate and publish a homelessness strategy based on the results of that review. Homelessness reviews on which strategies will be based are defined in Section 2 of the 2002 Act. A local authority must review:

- the levels and likely future levels of homelessness

- the resources available to a range of bodies (including other organizations and other people)

- activities carried out in their district for preventing homelessness, securing that accommodation is or will be available for people who may become homeless, and for providing support for those who become homeless and those who need support in order to prevent them becoming homeless again.

The 'homelessness strategy' (Section 3) is to be formulated by the local housing authority and must cover:

- the prevention of homelessness

- the securing of suitable accommodation for people who are or may become homeless

- the provision of satisfactory services to people who are actually or potentially homeless.

A local authority's homelessness review and strategy must be made available at the authority's principal office for inspection by members of the public.

Social services departments and housing departments are recognized by the 2002 Act as key players in the homelessness review process and the development of homelessness strategies. The local authority should also consider action by any other public authority, voluntary organization or other person whose activities are capable of contributing to the achievement of the three key objectives.

BEST VALUE PERFORMANCE INDICATOR 225

The requirement for local authorities to address domestic violence has been increased through the development of this performance indicator introduced in April 2005. In the past, local authorities have been required to show how many refuge spaces they had in their area per 10,000 population. This indicator has now been extended to include 12 measures that relate to different aspects of addressing domestic violence. The following are those aspects that relate to housing and homelessness provisions:

- 225.2 Is there within the local authority area a minimum of one refuge place per 10,000 population?

- 225.7 Has the local authority developed, launched and promoted a 'sanctuary' type scheme to enable victims and their children to remain in their own homes, where they choose to do so, and where safety can be guaranteed?

- 225.8 Has there been a reduction in the percentage of cases accepted as homeless due to domestic violence that previously had been rehoused in the past two years by that local authority as a result of domestic violence?

- 225.9 Does the council's tenancy agreement have a specific clause stating that perpetration of domestic violence by a tenant can be considered grounds for eviction?

Although raising the issue of domestic violence in relation to performance is welcome, there are a number of concerns about the effectiveness of these indicators to address domestic violence:

- There is still chronic underfunding and lack of provision of refuges, and although 225.2 refers to refuge places per population, this does not always result in implementation.

- There is debate within the domestic violence sector about the effectiveness of 'sanctuary schemes'. Although the Best Value Performance Indicator (BVPI) is worded carefully to state choice, support from a specialist domestic violence service and the guarantee of safety, it is possible that women and children may still be at risk in their sanctuary, for example if the perpetrator sets fire to the house.

- The requirement to reduce the percentage of cases of homelessness due to domestic violence is of particular concern, since many specialist domestic violence services and forums have identified homeless and housing provision as a key element of provision to increase the safety of women and children survivors of domestic violence.

- Domestic violence services supporting women have often found that local authorities do not evict perpetrators, and in many cases this would be welcome.

The impact of these indicators therefore needs to be monitored closely and modified accordingly.

Further information is available from the Local Government Association Domestic Violence Unit at www.lga.gov.uk/ProjectHome.asp?ccat=976.

7.8 Implementation of housing law: limitations and problems for women and children experiencing domestic violence

Research has documented the continuing need of women and children experiencing domestic violence for safe permanent housing and safe emergency accommodation and, in particular, the continuing importance of access to local authority and social rented housing (Malos and Hague 1993a, 1993b). This research showed that some authorities interpret their duties very narrowly, for example by adopting a stance of 'minimum legal compliance' with the law and attempting to deter women from pursuing their applications; by pointing women in the direction of legal remedies that have been ineffective; or by demanding a high degree of 'proof' and conducting stringent and detailed investigations into the violence women have experienced (often very distressing for women in these situations, because of the private and intimate nature of the abuse experienced). Some authorities would not consider rehousing women escaping violence who did not have dependent children with them, or interpreted the 'local connection' clause of the homelessness law more narrowly than the law prescribes in situations involving domestic violence. This might involve the authority attempting to refer women on to another authority, even if they might be in danger there, or keeping women in uncertainty about whether they would be accepted for rehousing for very long periods of time.

Similarly, a study commissioned by the Department of the Environment demonstrated the significant part played by local authority housing entitlement for women experiencing violent relationship breakdown (Bull 1993).

More recent research was commissioned by the former Department of the Environment, Transport and the Regions (DETR), later the ODPM (Office of the Deputy Prime Minister), and now renamed Department for Communities and Local Government (DCLG), in 1998 in cooperation with the Women's Equality Unit and the Department of Health, and published in 2002 in advance of introducing the Supporting People programme. This research concluded the following:

- Domestic violence and fear of violence add an extra dimension to a household's housing needs. There is a need not only for safe and secure accommodation but also focused and appropriate support to enable people to rebuild their lives.

- Many local authorities in the study were making efforts to avoid using inappropriate accommodation, such as bed and breakfast hotels, for households experiencing domestic violence. Housing professionals in some areas had no choice because of a shortage of housing, a lack of suitable alternative temporary accommodation and an inability to meet the specific needs of some households, such as large families and women with mental health problems.

- Although there was widespread recognition of the range of support provided for women in refuges, it was generally felt that households in other forms of temporary accommodation fared less well in terms of accessing support. There was some evidence of outreach services providing support in some areas.

- Refuge services were perceived by users and professionals as providing a unique and highly regarded service for households experiencing domestic violence. Refuge users particularly valued the holistic support and support from other residents. It would be difficult to replicate this model to other forms of temporary housing, especially where households with a variety of circumstances are being accommodated together.

This research also confirms the existing evidence that local authority responses vary widely from one area to another, in terms of the use of their discretion under the homelessness legislation to accept or attempt to limit their acceptance of homeless people (Evans 1991; Evans and Duncan 1988; Thomas and Niner 1989). Women who become homeless because of domestic violence are no exception to this pattern. Further information is available at www.communities.gov.uk.

As noted earlier, local authorities that operate a housing register may now offer permanent housing only to those on this register. Homeless families, including women and children made homeless by domestic violence, will initially be placed in temporary accommodation. Local authorities are required when offering permanent accommodation to give preference to those who are 'homeless' and 'in priority need', the definitions of which have been extended under the 2002 Act. Women escaping violence and women staying in refuges should, therefore, ensure that – where a housing register exists – they are included on the register; failure to do so could mean their being moved on repeatedly from one temporary home to another. There is some evidence from refuge services that, where local authorities are operating what Hague and Malos called 'minimal legal compliance' (2005, p.113), women are returning home rather than living in short-term, inadequate private sector accommodation.

The legislation also allows local authorities to refuse accommodation to those whom they believe to have suitable accommodation available elsewhere. This provision particularly affects some women from minority ethnic groups, who might be deemed to have access to accommodation in another country; as before, women who have no permanent right of residence in Britain, perhaps because they have stayed with their abusing partners for less than 12 months, have 'no recourse to public funds' and, hence, no right to assistance under the law. Current attention by the government to this issue may, however, result in improvements in the near future.

There is also a concern that, in some areas, existing residents in refuges are unable to move on to safe permanent accommodation within a reasonable period of time because of shortages of housing stock.

Concern has been expressed by practitioners from a number of agencies about the impact of the Family Law Act 1996 on local authority housing policy and practice. There is some anecdotal evidence that since the introduction of Part IV, pressure by local housing departments on abused women to return home with injunctions has increased, which may put their lives, and their children's lives, at risk. Concerns have also been expressed that where Part IV is used to exclude an abusive partner or to transfer the tenancy to the woman's sole name, this must be followed up quickly with transfers to other accommodation by local authorities, if those experiencing domestic violence are to be effectively protected from abuse.

Abused women may also feel under pressure to apply for occupation orders as a means of avoiding the risk of losing their children at court in contested residence applications. If they cannot access refuge or safe temporary accommodation while this is happening, or obtain housing benefit to cover both rents, then they may have to return home with the injunction, even if they do not feel safe to do so, while waiting for an exchange or transfer, because this might seem the only option to keep both a secure home and their children.

The new homelessness legislation and accompanying Code of Guidance has put further emphasis on the need for local authorities to provide for survivors of domestic violence, but many housing authorities do not have the resources to make appropriate provision. The Supporting People programme is becoming more problematic in terms of funding for refuge provision and floating support for survivors of domestic violence, since this funding is being reduced and local authorities are having to source funding from existing budgets. Anecdotal evidence from refuge providers suggests that, in many areas, there is no money for new projects or to maintain existing provision. Supporting People funds support only for adults, and so domestic violence organizations have to seek alternative funding to provide support for children in refuges, mainly through trusts and other charities, since there is no dedicated statutory provision available. This means that although recognition of domestic violence is further strengthened legislatively, there are still not the resources to provide for it adequately.

Overall, the homelessness safety net has been strengthened. For example, the definition of 'domestic violence' has been widened and the categories of 'priority need' have been increased.

The new approach to homelessness puts a lot of emphasis on joint working in undertaking reviews, preparing a strategy and delivering the strategy once it is finalized. For example, social services are now required to give 'reasonable assistance' to help housing authorities prepare the strategy, and the local authority is required to consult widely before adopting or changing its strategy. Housing associations will also have a key role to play in this.

There are benefits associated with homelessness strategies; for example, local authorities should now have more accurate information on the scale and nature of homelessness in their areas and should know what additional resources can be used to tackle homelessness. There is, however, no indication of where such additional resources will come from.

If an authority makes a decision not to house someone, then securing accommodation pending a review of an adverse decision will still require an application to the High Court. Although blanket exclusions by local authorities in their allocations and lettings are no longer permitted, the 'unacceptable behaviour' test will be difficult to apply in practice and may lead to conflict between applicants and authorities.

7.9 Summary

- The options for protection available under civil and criminal law have some limitations to their effectiveness, and therefore it is likely that many women will continue to rely on provision under homeless legislation for safe housing and longer-term protection from violence for themselves and their children.

- The Housing Act 1996 made a number of major changes to the provision of public and private rented accommodation. Parts VI and VII of the Act affect decisions about who is housed in the social rented sector and are of particular relevance for women and children experiencing abuse.

- This was further amended by the provisions of the Homelessness Act 2002.

- The legislation removed any automatic link that existed between being homeless under the law and being given permanent housing. Whereas under previous legislation people who were unintentionally homeless and in priority need were offered permanent accommodation, now Part VII of the Housing Act 1996 gives local authorities only a number of temporary duties.

- The local authority has a duty to secure interim accommodation, for example in a refuge or hostel, while it investigates whether it has a further duty if it believes an applicant may be homeless or is threatened with homelessness and is eligible for assistance and is in priority need.

- The local authority has a duty to house certain applicants who fit all the following criteria: homeless or threatened with homelessness; eligible for assistance; in priority need; not intentionally homeless; unable to access other 'suitable accommodation'; and with a local connection with the area.

- The duty to provide permanent accommodation has been removed. To obtain permanent accommodation, the applicant must apply through the council's allocation scheme (which may be managed through a housing register under Part VI of the 1996 Act).

- The Housing Act 1996 has broadened the definition of homelessness for women experiencing domestic violence. 'Domestic violence' is defined as violence or threats of violence from a person who is associated with the person under threat, and should be understood to include threatening behaviour, violence or abuse (psychological, physical, sexual, financial or emotional) between persons who are, or have been, intimate partners, family members or members of the same household, regardless of gender or sexuality.

- An 'associated person' is defined in the Code of Guidance to the Act (and the definition is the same as under Part IV of the Family Law Act 1996) and now includes civil partnerships and same-sex partners.

- Under Section 10 of the Homelessness Act 2002, a person who ceases to occupy accommodation by reason of violence or threats of violence from any other person (whether or not this is defined as 'domestic' violence under the above definition) may also be regarded as homeless and in priority need.

- Homeless people are in 'priority need' for accommodation if they fulfil any of the criteria listed in the Housing Act 1996 or Homelessness Act 2002.

- Once the local authority has established that the applicant is homeless and in priority need, the authority must then decide whether the applicant is homeless intentionally. A local connection is not needed if the applicant is homeless because of violence and would be at risk of violence if the applicant was sent to an area where he or she has a local connection.

- A local authority can fulfil its duties to homeless applicants by temporarily housing them in its own accommodation or by giving advice and assistance to help applicants secure access to private rented accommodation, if it is satisfied that suitable accommodation is available in its area.

- Local authorities should have regard to the Code of Guidance in implementing the Housing Act 1996 and Homelessness Act 2002. The Code of Guidance makes a number of specific references to the needs of women and children experiencing domestic violence, including good practice recommendations on making enquiries, injunctions, local connection and referrals to another area, women's refuges, and the vulnerability of women without children who are at risk of violence.

- For women with joint tenancies, it is now possible to apply under Part IV of the Family Law Act 1996 for the tenancy to be transferred to the woman's sole name. This then enables her, if she wishes, to use her existing tenancy to access alternative safe accommodation through a transfer or an exchange. It is also possible to arrange reciprocal transfers between local authorities.

- There are also a number of exchange mechanisms by which women experiencing domestic violence may be able to access new, safe accommodation. Research has documented the continuing need of women and children experiencing domestic violence for safe permanent housing and safe emergency accommodation and, in particular, the continuing importance of access to local authority and social rented housing. However, inconsistent interpretation throughout the country has meant that while some local authorities have recognized the serious nature of domestic violence and consequent homelessness, and have developed good practice guidelines and domestic violence policies to govern their practice, others have taken a much harsher view of the law, leaving many women in insecure and dangerous situations.

Notes

1   This follows a similar order that took effect in Wales in 2001.

2   Further revised in July 2006, and implemented 4 September 2006: Department for Communities and Local Government: Homelessness and Housing Support Directorate (2006) *Homelessness Code of Guidance for Local Authorities.*

3   Department for Communities and Local Government: Homelessness and Housing Support Directorate (2006) *Homelessness Code of Guidance for Local Authorities.*

4   That is, any organization that is allowed to receive transfers of local authority housing and to administer it, such as housing associations, building societies and non-profit-making private companies.

5   As amended by the *Homelessness Code of Guidance for Local Authorities.* (Revised July 2006, following the implementation of the civil partnership legislation.)

6   In some areas a Sanctuary Scheme may be available to provide increased security with support from a specialist domestic violence service if chosen by the applicant.

Notes

PART THREE

Practice Interventions

CHAPTER EIGHT

SOCIAL CARE RESPONSES TO DOMESTIC VIOLENCE AND ABUSE OF CHILDREN

This chapter provides an insight into the development of positive social care and related practice with regard to children living with domestic violence. As detailed in Chapter Three, there is compelling evidence for thinking that domestic violence is a context where child abuse is likely to take place. Also, where there are child protection or safeguarding issues, adult carers may also be at risk of abuse. Consequently, social care and other services dealing with the protection and safeguarding of children need to be aware of the possibility that abuse is taking place between adults (in particular, against the mother) in the same family.[1] Establishing safety and providing support to non-abusive carers (usually mothers) can be a particularly effective child protection strategy in the context of domestic violence, and this is detailed below.

Mullender (1997), in her overview of the social work response to domestic violence, identifies two main directions that social work practice has taken since the 1980s:

- In the 1980s, the expectation that an abused woman should stay with the violent man 'for the sake of the children' was particularly prevalent.

- During the 1990s, the onus on women to protect their children was increasingly translated into demands that an abused woman leave the violent man or have the children accommodated due to a perceived 'failure to protect'.

In the 1990s, there was an increasing focus in social work on child protection and prevention of abuse, and practice moved away from keeping children with both parents to an emphasis on removing children from situations where there was risk of significant harm. This general approach is still the most prominent as we write in the first decade of the twenty-first century.

8.1 Different histories: child protection and domestic violence work

It has to be recognized that the work of child protection services has a very different history from those organizations and agencies that focus more specifically on domestic violence. This has, at times, made it difficult for social workers and other child protection staff to take into account domestic violence. Child protection agencies have the child as the central focus of their work and have developed a welfare approach that emphasizes 'partnership with parents' while apparently decriminalizing abuse of children (Ball 1995). The prevalent social work view has been to see the family, and in particular 'dysfunctional' families, as central to the problem. Within this approach, the focus is on the child and the main carer, usually the mother. Consequently, there has been a tendency to see the mother 'as colluding with the man's behaviour and failing to protect her children' (Parton 1990, p.15). In contrast, organizations and agencies working with domestic violence, such as refuges and providers of advocacy, have the adult victim/survivor as their central focus and are working in a context where there has been increasing criminalization of and intervention with perpetrators of domestic violence.

These differences between child protection and domestic violence services create tensions and contradictions and have made it more difficult for coherent and consistent practice to be developed that takes into account needs for safety of both children and adults. Hester (2004) (see also Radford and Hester 2006) has argued that child protection and domestic violence work may actually be perceived as operating on separate 'planets', with different histories, culture, laws and sets of professionals on the two planets. It is these structural factors that have made it especially difficult to integrate practice across the two areas and has resulted in child protection work where there is a tendency to see mothers as failing to protect their children rather than as the victims of domestic violence, and where violent male perpetrators are often ignored.

It is hoped that the greater emphasis on multi-agency working in relation to the safeguarding of children, which (at the time of writing) is in the process of implementation, will help to embed closer links between agencies working on child protection and domestic violence and thus overcome some of the 'planetary problems' alluded to above. (The establishment of local safeguarding children boards is discussed further in Chapter Eleven; see also Chapter Four for legal framework.)

8.2 'Failure to protect'

The 1980s approach of keeping families together 'for the sake of the children' made it especially difficult for women to leave violent men and thus created difficulties with regard to safety for both women and children. Both Maynard (1985), in her study of social work case files, and Dobash, Dobash and Cavanagh (1985), in their interviews with women experiencing domestic violence, found numerous examples of social workers discouraging women from leaving their violent male partners. For instance:

> I went to the welfare to get somewhere to stay but they couldn't help me. Mrs Jones [the social worker] told me I would have to stay and I said, 'I just can't', and they said, 'You'll just have to stay for the sake of the wee ones.'
>
> *(Woman quoted in Dobash et al. 1985, p.161)*

Moving from an expectation that women and children should stay with violent men to a recognition that women and their children may be better off by leaving such men has clearly been a positive step forwards in social care practice and has developed alongside a greater public awareness of domestic violence. However, many women experience this current 'failure to protect' approach as especially punitive.

The problem is that all the responsibility for protecting children has been placed on mothers rather than tackling those responsible for the violence – male abusers. Moreover, the dynamics involved in domestic violence, and the impacts on and needs of the women living in violent relationships (as detailed in Chapter One), often have not been understood by professionals. This has led to frustration about why women don't 'just leave'. Professionals, whose prime focus is on protecting children, have tended to respond by threatening accommodation of the children, perhaps seeing this as a means of pushing women to leave violent relationships. Or professionals may decide that a woman is no longer able to parent effectively for her children in the context of the violent relationship and, therefore, remove the children into care. These may appear sensible courses of action, but in reality they have been counterproductive because they have largely ignored the (primarily male) abusers and have created fear for women that their children will be taken away if they disclose domestic violence. Farmer (2006) argues:

> Relying on women to protect their children is clearly a flawed policy... When women who live with violent men are clearly unable to protect themselves, the chances of their being in a position to protect their children may be remote.
>
> *(Farmer 2006, p.125)*

A number of studies provide evidence of child protection professionals using a 'failure to protect' approach (see Farmer and Owen 1995; Forman 1995; Hester and Radford 1996, 1997a, 2000):

- Forman (1995) found, in her study of 20 mothers of sexually abused children, that all the women and children had been through the child protection system. Despite all the women having separated the child from the abuser, social work departments placed the children on the child protection register or took them into care (in five cases), or referred to children's panels, or did all of these things. Forman suggests that these interventions were linked to the notion that the woman would not be able to keep the abuser away from the house and from the child.

- In Hester and Radford's (1996) study, two mothers were told by social services that they must ensure no contact between the children and their father after separation and that, in the event of a reconciliation, the children would be placed into care. However, no support was provided to ensure that contact between the children and the abusive fathers was stopped formally via a Children Act Section 8 order.

- In Humphreys' (1997a) study, the local authority appeared to expect women, in over half the cases involving domestic violence, to protect their children by not associating with the abusive male partner. Moreover, a quarter of the women were threatened with removal of their children if the abusive man returned.

- McGee (2000) found that fear of losing their children was possibly the main reason for women not contacting outside agencies for help or for denying that they were experiencing violence from their partners.

- In Humphreys and Thiara's (2002) study of women using domestic violence outreach services, 44 per cent had contact with social services' children and families' teams. Concerns of social workers about child protection issues led to a significant number of these women being coerced into leaving their abusive partners before they were ready or without the support needed to carry through such a difficult and dangerous process.

8.3 Focusing on mothers and avoiding violent men

Research in the UK looking at social work practice indicates that social workers tend to be uncomfortable working with domestic violence and may have no policies or guidelines on domestic violence to which they can refer (Farmer 2006; Humphreys *et al.* 2000; Mullender 1997; O'Hagan and Dillenburger 1995). Social workers are likely to ignore perpetrators of domestic violence, focusing instead on the women and children, who are more accessible, with whom they are more familiar and more confident, and who possibly are more open to the influence of social work. Some professionals also assume that women are able to influence or prevent the men's violence against them (Armstrong 1994; Farmer 2006; James 1994).

In Farmer and Owen's study on child protection practice, they note that not only was there a striking shift in focus 'away from an abusing father figure on to the mother' in relation to physical and emotional child abuse but also that this 'shift of focus from men to women often also allowed men's violence to their wives or partners to disappear from sight' (Farmer and Owen 1995, p.223). This appeared to be based on an assumption about parenting by social workers that mothers, but not fathers, were responsible for the children's wellbeing (Farmer and Owen 1995, p.223). Similar findings have been highlighted in other studies; for example:

- In an Australian study, Goddard and Carew (1988) noted what was termed the 'hostage effect' in some social workers, who failed to openly acknowledge and address the high level of violence within a family. According to Stanley and Goddard (1993), this meant that the social workers unconsciously adopted the viewpoint of the abuser in order to protect themselves and, therefore, did not protect the children (or, one presumes, the woman).

- James's (1994) study of Children Act Section 8 reviews highlighted that the work being carried out in child protection focused on women and asked 'where were the invisible men?' (see also Armstrong 1994).

- In relation to child protection conferences, Humphreys (1997a) found that where fathers who had been violent to the mothers attended conferences, in 9 of 11 cases the domestic violence was either not mentioned in the case plan or conference or was minimized. Moreover, in the two cases where the domestic violence was discussed, the 'recommendations made in the case plan would have put the woman at risk of further abuse' (Humphreys 1997a, p.iv).

Milner (1996) points out that even where violence from men to their partners is acknowledged, this tends to be excused as unintentional, as a one-off act or resulting in the woman being used as a scapegoat. Moreover, unlike women on the receiving end of the violence, the violent men themselves are not challenged by being told that their behaviour might lead to them risking losing their children. Because of their own intimidation and fear of violence, social workers also avoid challenging interactions with these men and often time their initial visits to ensure that the man is not present (Mullender 1997).

Clearly, childcare professionals avoid violent men or minimize their behaviour for a number of reasons, including their assumptions about parenting and concerns regarding their own safety. It could be argued that without adequate resourcing and safety precautions, social workers are partly justified in their reticence in dealing with violent men. As Milner (1996, p.123) points out: 'Confrontation is an entirely acceptable strategy when used by high-status men in a safe environment... In the home or at case conference, confrontation is a dangerous and ineffective strategy.'

Farmer (2006) discusses the ways in which violent men assist in deflecting the focus of social work away from themselves and on to mothers. For instance, they might be absent when the social work visit takes place, refuse to discuss with the social worker issues concerning the child, or be intimidating to (often female) professionals. In Farmer and Owen's (1995) study of child protection cases, there were three main ways in which the attention of social workers was deflected away from the violent male abusers and on to their female partners:

One occurred when the social worker considered the father figure to be a serious risk to the child and tried to arrange for him to move out. If no charge had been brought by the police, workers could only try to put pressure on mothers to exclude their partner. If…unsuccessful, workers might concentrate their attention…on the mothers and on general child-care issues.

(Farmer 2006, p.127)

A second process…was when a male social worker became strongly identified with the father's view of the family situation…that the children were disobedient. The father's abuse was reconstructed as discipline, albeit occasionally excessive.

(Farmer 2006, p.127)

The third process occurred where, either because the man denied causing the child's injury or because, in the absence of any direct evidence, it was unclear which parent had abused the child, the worker focused on some other area of family difficulty.

(Farmer 2006, p.127)

8.4 'Implacable hostility'

The research concerning 'failure to protect' provides examples of the problems women and children face after they have left violent men. However, the difficulties are made even more complex where both (public law) child protection and (private law) arrangements for children post-separation of the parents intersect (see also Chapter Six). As Humphreys (1997b) points out, mothers have to be seen by social services to be actively – indeed, 'aggressively' – protecting their children. Yet in relation to divorce and separation, the message is very different. Mothers may not be perceived to attempt to 'aggressively protect' their children from the direct or indirect abuse of a violent father (Hester and Pearson 1997b). Within divorce proceedings, mothers who bring up problems related to domestic violence or child abuse within that context have often been construed as 'implacably hostile' or 'unreasonably hostile' and seen to be acting against the children's best interests of contact with the father (e.g. Re O [1995] 2FLR 124; see Radford and Hester 2006).[2]

As a result, contradictory outcomes may be established where there may be, on the one hand, an expectation that mothers should protect their children but, on the other hand, formally constituted arrangements for contact that do not adequately take into account that in some instances mothers and children may experience further abuse (Hester and Pearson 1997b; Hester and Radford 1996; HM Inspectorate of Court Administration 2005; Radford and Hester 2006; Wade and Smart 2002) (see also Chapters Two and Four).

This is an area where interagency working around domestic violence needs to be developed in order to encourage positive and safety-oriented practice, especially links between domestic violence, child protection and family proceedings professionals. A number of legislative and policy frameworks may provide the basis for this. The Family Law Act 1996 provides a legal framework whereby civil remedies will require partnership between women, children and statutory agencies to ensure that women and children are protected and remain at home in safety (see Chapter Four for legal details). The new safeguarding boards are also supposed to have representatives from social care, the Children and Family Court Advisory and Support Service (CAFCASS) and domestic violence services.

8.5 Working with and supporting mothers as a positive response

Since the early 1990s, supporting non-abusive mothers to be safe has increasingly been considered as the most positive approach in child protection where domestic violence is an issue (see London Borough of Hackney 1993; Mullender and Debbonaire 2000; Mullender and Morley 1994). The Department of Health circular on Part IV of the Family Law Act suggests, for instance, that '[w]here domestic violence may be an important element in the family, the safety of (usually) the mother is also in the child's welfare' (Department of Health 1997, p.12). With appropriate protection and support to be safe, many mothers who are being abused by their male partners can be enabled to protect their children. As the Social Service Inspectorate report on domestic violence and social care pointed out: 'Protection and empowerment of non-abusing women is effective child protection' (Ball 1995, p.5) (see also Box 8.1 below).

Such an approach also fits with the new emphasis on safeguarding children, where childcare staff have been encouraged to place child protection work within a wider context that includes prevention, protection and support for children in need as well as an holistic approach to domestic violence. For instance, recent guidance for local commissioners of children's services highlights the focus on non-abusing parents, stating:

> The most effective intervention for ensuring safe and positive outcomes for children living with domestic violence is usually to plan a package of support that incorporates risk assessment, trained domestic violence support, advocacy and safety planning for the non abusing parent who is experiencing domestic violence in conjunction with protection and support for the child. The focus of this guidance is children and young people, but commissioners will need to ensure corresponding services and safeguards are in place for the abused parent and to assess and manage the risk an abusive parental partner presents.

(Local Government Association 2005)

There is some evidence from evaluation research, largely in the USA, that interventions focusing on advocacy and support for women decrease the detrimental impact of domestic violence by reducing depression and increasing self-esteem (Sullivan 2001). When combined with parenting training, such approaches may also have positive effects on the impacts children have suffered as a result of domestic violence, including behaviour problems (Ducharme, Atkinson and Poulton 2000; Jouriles *et al.* 2001).

A number of social care services and other childcare agencies have begun to adopt approaches that involve the protection and support of mothers in child protection. Humphreys (1997a) found instances of change towards such practice in her study of child protection practice in Coventry. Where this practice had been introduced, it was having a positive effect. For instance, in one case, the work originally carried out ignored the man's behaviour towards his partner and 'the father was seen as the cornerstone of the family' while his ongoing domestic violence, constituting 'mental abuse, isolation, multiple pregnancies and undermining of the woman', was ignored (Humphreys 1997a, p.7). Another worker (a student on placement) changed the orientation of the work to include an emphasis on domestic violence: 'Through careful and sensitive support work with the woman, the domestic violence was named, and the woman supported in finding alternative housing. She then separated from her husband and she and the children are progressing well' (Humphreys 1997a, p.6).

The NSPCC team in Hester and Pearson's (1998) study, which was doing recovery work with abused children, had also decided to incorporate work to support both mothers and their children in cases of domestic violence. This was considered especially positive for all concerned, as it placed the support and protection – and, therefore, recovery – of the child within a context where the key carer (the mother) was also supported. As one team member explained:

> ...if a child has been abused, it's what happens next in terms of the help, of an acceptance from particular key carers...that will determine the outcome in terms of the child's recovery... So, therefore, if we can work with women as well as children, carers as well as children, taking account of domestic violence...of the power dynamics around, and the frequency with which men abuse women we know about just in a factual way, then I think that we can start to create with those carers safer environments for them and their children.
>
> *(Childcare worker, quoted in Hester and Pearson 1998, p.38)*

Working with mothers to protect children often requires the involvement of a number of agencies working in unison. It can be difficult, however, to ensure that the outcome is safety rather than further risk. Mullender and Debbonaire (2000) point out some of the problems that may arise:

Where one parent is being abused by the other, any process of child protection can in many cases undermine rather than support the safety of the non-abusing parent and consequently risk affecting the safety and welfare of the child. This can be due to agencies or individuals failing to identify the risks to the non-abusing parent, interviewing parents together so that the woman does not feel safe to speak, holding case conferences with both parents present so that again, the woman's participation is limited or contradicts what she may have said before.

(Mullender and Debbonaire 2000, p.19)

There are also examples in Hester and Pearson's (1998) NSPCC study of practice issues that need to be dealt with. One instance, in particular, showed up the dilemmas and difficulties that may arise for childcare professionals when attempting to work supportively with mothers across agencies. In this case, the mother, who had previously stayed in a refuge, had returned to the violent partner. (It has to be recognized that women who are under extreme threat of further violence from their ex-partners may return as a part of their 'safety strategy' – see Chapter One.) The team wanted to support both mother and child, so the mother would be enabled to protect and support the child and so the mother and child could stay together. This needed to be carried out in a way that recognized the increased danger of abuse for the woman if she was seen to be in direct contact with any agency. The team felt, however, that social workers were more likely to focus on protection of the child without supporting the mother, as the former was not as difficult:

She's not going to go back into the refuge. So, short of people telling her that she must go into a refuge, which people obviously have, it's about how you're going to match the two together. And all of a sudden it becomes too difficult which is probably why she hasn't had any help... You've either got to do one – protect the children at the cost of herself, which she knows and feels very guilty about, or try and work with both, and you need an awful lot of time and resources don't you, plus the fact that you've got to find a way of getting to her because she can't come here.

(Childcare worker, quoted in Hester and Pearson 1998,
unpublished interview)

Many local authorities have produced, or are producing, guides related to the safeguarding of children. As stressed by the guidance on commissioning referred to earlier (Local Government Association 2005), it is important that an emphasis on supporting non-abusive carers is built into any assessments and assessment mechanisms. Clearly, in child protection cases, working with and supporting mothers who have experienced domestic violence can be hard work but is likely to have more positive outcomes in the longer term than more traditional 'mother blaming' approaches.

Box 8.1 How should social care services respond when women suffer violence from known abusers?

- Develop and implement policy: violence against women is a crime. Women from all backgrounds experience violence. Men from all backgrounds are perpetrators of violence. Protection and empowerment of non-abusing women is effective child protection.

- Develop and implement good practice guidelines.

- Monitor use of services by women experiencing domestic violence.

- Include the issue in basic practice: referral forms, community care assessments, community care plans, child protection investigations, child protection conferences and in supervision.

- Ensure awareness of domestic violence is integrated into existing provision of services.

- Develop in-house practical services and options for women and children – women's and children's drop-in centres and groups, women's groups in day centres and residential establishments, crisis centres, counselling/play with children, use of mental health hostels as safe houses, and provision of counselling services to women in hospital.

- Ensure awareness of domestic violence is integrated into provision of non-statutory services – for example, enabling discussion about domestic violence in mother and toddler groups and craft and cookery groups.

- Finance non-statutory services and options for women and children – Women's Aid's work with children and counselling services.

- Use current legislation by displacing the man as the nearest relative (Section 29, Mental Health Act), by recommending that courts attach injunctions or prohibited steps orders to Section 8 orders, by using the Children Act (Schedule 1, Para. 5) with regard to removal of perpetrator, by using the Children Act (Section 17) for finance to enhance safety (e.g. for new locks, travel to a refuge and installation of a telephone).

- Multi-agency liaison to provide up-to-date information on delivering services and referral and to clarify the role of each agency.

- Publish and provide information for the public and staff – posters, leaflets, help cards, directories of services.

- Training – professional training, both induction and specialized.

- Personnel policy to cover both the safety of workers and staff experiencing violence from abusers.

(Adapted from Ball 1995)

8.6 Working with and supporting mothers as a positive response: the case of abusive mothers

Women may also be abusive to children. Mothers may abuse children physically, emotionally or sexually. Such abusive behaviour may require statutory intervention (Farmer 2006; Farmer and Owen 1995; Mullender 1996a; Saradjian 1997; Violence Against Children Study Group 1990).

Domestic violence may be an important part of the equation where women are being abusive to children and should, therefore, always be seen as a possibility. For instance, a mother's parenting capacity may be affected so severely by her experience of domestic violence that she may for a time be unable to meet her child's essential needs, including the need for protection. It has been found that mothers experiencing domestic violence may be particularly punitive in their behaviour towards children in the presence of a man who is carrying out domestic violence towards them or may be withdrawn from their children (Rivett, Howarth and Harold 2006) (see Chapter One for discussion of the impact of domestic violence on parenting). Where domestic violence is an issue, the woman's abuse of the children may stop once the man is no longer there or may stop in the longer term. As Mullender points out:

> Where women have actually abused or neglected their children, it is always important to ask how much of this has been coerced by the male abuser, or has in other ways directly resulted from his behaviour, since, where this is the case, it may immediately, or with help, stop in his absence.
>
> *(Mullender 1996a, p.105)*

Supporting a woman so that she and the children become safe from the male abuser, and helping her to create a new life, can in such circumstances prove to be positive. Clearly, the feasibility and type of support needed will require careful assessment. The support, such as counselling, advocacy and parenting support, may need to take into account that 'one or more of the children is identified in her mind with the abuse' (Mullender 1996a, p.105). For instance, the child may have been forced to take part in the mother's abuse, may have been conceived through marital rape or may look or behave like the abuser.

8.7 Assessing levels of risk and need

Chapter Four outlined safeguarding, child protection and children in need issues, as related to the Children Act 1989 and 2004. Domestic violence is an important indicator that a child is 'in need' and may be likely to suffer significant harm. Also, it is important for childcare professionals to know whether a child who is being abused is living in a context where the carer is also experiencing violence and abuse, as this has direct implications for practice. The problem is that there are no specific indicators of the impact of domestic violence on children, although the impacts and behaviours listed in Chapter Three provide some important indicators:

- The effects of domestic violence on children's development, behaviour and wellbeing can be similar to the effects resulting from child abuse without a context of domestic violence.

- Children living with domestic violence, but not being physically or sexually abused, may exhibit similar difficulties to children who are being so abused.

- Some children may not exhibit difficulties and may have developed coping strategies that involve being high achievers. Such children may still be in need of support and protection with regard to domestic violence.

It is crucial, therefore, to ascertain from the adults and/or children concerned whether domestic violence is an issue. As Debbonaire explains:

> The clearest indicator of domestic violence is still a woman or child saying that it is happening. The professional role in this is to create the conditions and trust that make it possible for a woman or child to say this, and help to make this process positive and useful, rather than using a checklist of behaviours.
>
> *(Debbonaire 1997, p.57)*

Chapter Nine provides details concerning disclosure of domestic violence and safety planning with regard to children. Here, the focus is on enabling disclosure of domestic violence from adults, and women in particular.

8.8 Disclosing domestic violence and abuse of children

ROUTINELY ASKING WOMEN ABOUT DOMESTIC VIOLENCE

Asking women directly about domestic violence has been found to be positive practice in a number of areas, including health and social care (Hester 2006b; Hester and Westmarland 2005). Asking routinely is also known as 'routine enquiry' or 'screening' and is defined by the Department of Health as 'asking about the experience of domestic violence of all people within certain parameters' (Department of Health 2000, para. 3.11). The very act of asking about domestic violence conveys an important message to women and children that practitioners are aware of its existence and relevance. This may facilitate disclosure by women trying to seek help. It may also enable women who do not see themselves as being in a domestically abusive relationship, or who are minimizing the abuse, to disclose their experiences for the first time and, thus, allow intervention or even early intervention.

In communicating with the woman, it is important to relay to her:

- that she is not at fault
- that you are concerned about what is happening to both her and to her child(ren)
- your willingness to help by providing information and other support
- that living with domestic abuse is also detrimental to her child(ren)
- that although she thinks the children do not know what is going on and this has protected them, they are very likely to be aware of the violence
- that help is available and there are agencies and organizations where she can go.

(Adapted from Mullender 1994, p.235)

The process of disclosure might be facilitated partly by ensuring that offices and agency waiting rooms display posters about domestic violence, including information about where women and children can obtain practical help and refuge accommodation if required. This in itself conveys a message to women that domestic violence is not condoned or viewed as 'normal' behaviour that they are simply expected to tolerate.

The fact that domestic violence can be overlooked unless specifically asked about was demonstrated in Hester and Pearson's (1998) project with the NSPCC. A major feature of this project was the establishment of screening for domestic violence as one means of incorporating questions about the possibility of domestic violence into all aspects of the team's work with children. In the scheme, staff members were expected to ask about possible violent and abusive behaviour in the relationship of the parents (or equivalent carers). A form was devised to remind and help staff to routinely ask about domestic violence every time they met with clients and referrers. In practice, the process was used most frequently with adults. It was found that the incidence of domestic violence in those cases accepted for service rose from one-third to nearly two-thirds as a result of asking routinely about domestic violence in every case. This is not to say that the research resulted in more referrals involving domestic violence but that domestic violence became more acknowledged and recognized where previously it had been hidden.

In another study, involving evaluation over a two-year period of the use of routine enquiry by health visitors and social care services (Hester 2006b), the practitioners involved found that their practice was both more effective and more rewarding as a result. As with the NSPCC, routine enquiry by health visitors and social workers resulted in a trebling of the number of cases where domestic violence was identified. The staff involved felt that using routine enquiry had helped to empower some of the women, in particular because it allowed a naming of the violence and abuse they were experiencing. They were also using the Duluth power and control wheel (see www.duluth-model.org) with the women as part of the enquiry process and to help them identify the abuses they were subject to in their relationships.

Despite the importance of enquiry about domestic violence, a UK-wide survey of social services departments indicated that only 40 per cent of social services departments ask these questions at some point in the child protection process, and in only 14 per cent of cases are the results recorded systematically (Humphreys *et al.* 2000).

It is essential that professionals who use routine enquiry about domestic violence have adequate training to do so. The evaluation of health visitors and social care services implementing routine enquiry (Hester 2006b; Hester and Westmarland 2005) and research with general practitioners (Westmarland *et al.* 2004) found that a minimum of two days' training was needed. This training should comprise of:

- domestic violence awareness

- how to ask about domestic violence

- linking with and appropriate referrals to other local agencies.

HOW TO ASK

It has to be remembered that many women minimize their experiences and/or may not define them as domestic violence. For instance, if there is no physical violence – which is perceived as the stereotypical experience of domestic violence – women may be reluctant to see their experience of abuse in this way. Therefore, it is not helpful to simply ask the woman whether there is or has been any domestic violence, as this might provide a negative, possibly false, response. Instead, a range of areas of questioning might need to be pursued in order to gain a more complete picture. Some agencies have developed such domestic violence 'screening' approaches (e.g. Department of Health 1997; Hester and Westmarland 2005; Hester *et al.* 1997). Suggestions for questions to open up the issue of domestic violence include the following (adapted from Department of Health 1997, p.20):

- How are things at home?

- How are arguments settled?

- How are decisions reached?

- What happens when you argue/disagree?

- Do you feel/have you ever felt frightened of your partner?

- Do you feel/have you ever felt threatened or intimidated by your partner?

- What happens when your partner gets angry?

- Does your partner shout at you, call you names, put you down?

- Has your partner ever physically hurt you? How? What happened?

- Has your partner ever thrown things?

- Has your partner ever destroyed things you care about?

- Has your partner ever forced you to have sex or engage in any sexual activities against your will?

- What do the children do when (any of the above) is happening?

- How do the children feel when (any of the above) is happening?

Despite being given the opportunity to reveal domestic violence in this way, some women will be very wary of the response and may test out the practitioner's reaction in order to ensure that they will be believed and that they will be safe (Mullender 1996a). Some women feel able to disclose their experiences only over a period of time. Thus, it is important to continue asking sensitively about domestic violence, even if it does not emerge immediately. In Hester and Pearson's (1998) study regarding NSPCC practice, they found that in one instance the experience of domestic violence was disclosed only at the fourth session with the woman concerned. The form from the first session indicated that domestic violence was 'suspected'. The third form indicated 'don't know yet', and the fourth form itemized seven forms of domestic violence experienced by the same woman – which included physical, sexual, psychological, emotional and verbal abuse, threats to kill and isolation. This raises concerns about situations, such as duty social work, where women will usually be seen only once and where any domestic violence issues, especially extremely controlling behaviour by the abuser, may remain hidden. In the Suffolk project (Hester 2006b), it was found that incorporating routine enquiry about domestic violence into initial social care assessments was especially effective.

WHERE TO ASK: SEPARATE INTERVIEWS

It is essential that asking about domestic violence is carried out with care and sensitivity and in a way that does not further endanger the woman and children. Disclosure is not very likely to occur when the woman is in the presence of her abusive partner, as her fear of the possible repercussions may prevent her from revealing any violence. Therefore, joint interviews and meetings should be avoided, especially for initial sessions. This has been recognized, for instance, in the National Standards for family court advisory work (Home Office 1994), in relation to mediators affiliated to national family mediation (Hester et al. 1997) and highlighted in research on in-court conciliation (Trinder et al. 2006).

In recovery work with children who have experienced abuse, the professionals involved may use sessions where all of the family, or a variety of family members, are expected to be present. Hester and Pearson (1998) found in their study of NSPCC practice that there were occasions when workers felt it was especially inappropriate or unsafe to ask about domestic violence. This included instances where the family was seen together and the male partner, in particular, was present:

> Sometimes when I have a family in and there's been no reference to domestic violence at all within the referral, I find it difficult to talk about… Where I've been working though with just mothers, or mothers and children, or just children, or families where domestic violence has been part of the referral, it's been a lot easier… I suppose it's because the man is there – that's what makes it difficult.

> *(Hester and Pearson 1998, p.10)*

On the other hand, asking and talking about domestic violence when both the mother (who has experienced violence from her male partner) and the children (who have also lived with the experience) are present is more likely to be positive and can help facilitate recovery.

Mary McKay (1994) has pointed out that this is also a practice issue for child protection workers, who need to know about the existence of domestic violence if they are to make accurate risk assessments in relation to children. McKay recommends use of separate interviews:

> …interviewing both parents together to assess the risk to the child appears to be a detriment to determining if domestic violence is present… Given the seemingly strong link between spouse abuse and child abuse, interviewing each parent separately seems always indicated.

> *(McKay 1994, p.34)*

Where there is a history of domestic violence, the survivor should be centrally involved in deciding whether any further interviews or sessions should be joint and how safety might be ensured if joint sessions do go ahead. Some professionals may be wary of seeing women separately in order to raise the issue of domestic violence, partly fearing that this may be time-consuming or may invite malicious allegations (e.g. Hester 2006b; Hester *et al.* 1997). It is vital, however, that the possibility of separate meetings is explored in order to ensure effective and safe interventions for women and children.

8.9 Fear of what professionals will do

It is essential that:

- questions about the existence of domestic violence are asked and framed in a non-blaming and sympathetic manner
- professionals are clear about wanting to know about domestic violence in order to provide support rather than punishment.

Many women and children living with domestic violence have learned to keep the violence a secret and go to great lengths to conceal it, especially in relation to authority figures who are perceived as being powerful (Farmer and Owen 1995; Mullender 1996a; Mullender *et al.* 2002) (see also Chapters Three and Nine). Mullender *et al.* (2002) found that keeping domestic violence a secret is especially strong in communities where criticism of the family's honour would be shameful, such as some South Asian communities. Mullender (1997) has suggested that domestic violence is rarely given by women as a reason for requesting a social work service and that information about the violence is usually hidden behind other presenting concerns, such as childcare or mental health issues (Stanley and Penhale 1999). Farmer and Owen (1995) found in their interviews with families involved in the child protection process that women kept incidents of violence concealed from social workers. In half the cases involving domestic violence, the domestic violence had not been known to the initial child protection case conference: 'In some cases they revealed [the extent of violence from partners] in interview with us, but withheld the information from their social worker' (Farmer and Owen 1995, p.240).

In the NCH study (Abrahams 1994), mothers talked of the difficulty of telling professionals 'about the problems their children were having because of violence at home'. Three-quarters of the mothers were afraid that their children would be taken away, and four-fifths said it 'was because they felt guilty' (Abrahams 1994, p.4).

There is an overrepresentation of black and minority ethnic, in particular African Caribbean, children in public care, and black and minority ethnic women have a justifiable fear of a heavy-handed response from social services (Batsleer *et al.* 2002; McGee 1996). Lesbian mothers may also have well-founded fears of prejudicial interventions (Harne and Rights of Women 1997).

8.10 Fear of what the abuser will do

As discussed in Chapter One, domestic violence can have an impact on a mother's ability to discover, recognize and report child abuse (Forman 1995; Hester and Radford 1996; Hooper 1992; Radford and Hester 2006). Forman (1995), for instance, found that although the women in her study acted in various ways to protect their children, they did not necessarily report the abuse to the authorities for fear of what the abuser would do.

The domestic violence experienced by mothers can also reduce their awareness of what else is happening around them. In her small in-depth study of mothers of daughters who had been abused by their fathers, Tyler Johnson (1992) concludes that the mothers were rendered unaware or incapable of discovering the abuse to their children, partly as a result of the violence they were experiencing from their partners:

> The mothers…were all physically or psychologically absent or incapacitated around the time the incest began… However, this absence or incapacity

cannot be viewed simply as an active abandonment or a turning away from the family or the needs of their daughters. It was related much more to a number of reality factors...[including] all of the mothers' responses to physical and psychological abuse [from their partners].

(Tyler Johnson 1992, p.107)

Hooper (1995) similarly described women as being so preoccupied with their own daily survival that this restricted their awareness of what was happening to the children. That the children were living with domestic violence also provided an alternative explanation for any difficulties the children appeared to be experiencing. However, once suspicions of sexual abuse had arisen, the woman's own experiences of abuse from the same man helped to facilitate the children's process of disclosure and belief.

Some men will exploit women's fears that the children will be removed in order to stop the women reporting child abuse. For example, in McWilliams and McKiernan's (1993) study, one of the women who was interviewed explained:

I came home with Bob when he was a few days old, I'd been indoors half an hour when there was a row...he threatened to call social services to say that I was an unfit mother. In fact he picked up the phone and pretended to dial the number, pretending he was speaking to somebody and was saying I was an unfit mother.

(Quoted in McGee 1996, p.6)

Similarly, Humphreys and Thiara, from their study of outreach services, report:

...there was a high rate of concern by women (58%) who had contact with statutory child welfare services that their children would be taken into care. This is often the result of a tactic of control used by perpetrators who frequently tell women that they will report them to child protection authorities and that they will lose care to their children.

(Humphreys and Thiara 2002, p.81)

8.11 Monitoring and recording of domestic violence

Domestic violence should be included as a specific category in all social work referral and assessment forms and in duty records. Routinely monitoring and recording domestic violence as a specific intake category can:

- help to establish a more accurate picture regarding the scale of the problem
- ensure that existing resources are targeted effectively.

Agencies are increasingly expected to record and monitor domestic violence, although a survey in 2000 found that very few social care services did so and that domestic violence was monitored systematically in only a fifth of children's organizations. Agencies and organizations linked to mediation services were the most likely to record and monitor domestic violence (Hester *et al.* 1997; Humphreys *et al.* 2000).

8.12 Summary

- Practice in relation to domestic violence varies between childcare professionals, and there are examples of both positive and negative practices.

- Research in the UK indicates that social workers tend to be uncomfortable about working with domestic violence and often have no policies or guidelines on domestic violence to which they can refer.

- There is often an expectation in child protection work that women should leave violent partners in order to protect children. This not only places undue responsibility on mothers for men's violence and abuse but also ignores the reality that the violence may not cease despite the separation of the partners.

- Contradictory outcomes for children may result where there is an expectation that mothers should protect their children but where formal arrangements for contact do not adequately take into account that mothers and/or children may experience further abuse in such circumstances. This is an area where interagency working around domestic violence needs to be developed in order to encourage positive and safety-oriented practice.

- Childcare professionals often avoid violent men or minimize their behaviour for a number of reasons, including assumptions about parenting and concerns regarding their own safety.

- Increasingly, supporting non-abusive mothers to be safe is being considered as the most positive approach in child protection where domestic violence is an issue. Such an approach also fits with the safeguarding agenda where childcare staff members have been encouraged to place child protection work within the context of wider services for children in need.

- Women may also be abusive to children. Domestic violence may be an important part of the equation in such circumstances and should always be seen as a possibility. Where domestic violence is an issue, the woman's abuse of the children may stop once the man is no longer there or may stop in the longer term.

- There are no specific indicators of the impact of domestic violence on children. The effects of domestic violence on children's development, behaviour and wellbeing can be similar to the effects resulting from child abuse without a context of domestic violence.

- Good practice consists of asking all women routinely about domestic violence in every case. A range of areas of questioning might need to be pursued in order to gain a more complete picture.

- Disclosure is not very likely to occur when the woman is in the presence of her abusive partner, as her fear of the possible repercussions may prevent her from revealing any violence. Therefore, joint interviews and meetings should be avoided, especially for initial sessions. The survivor should be centrally involved in deciding whether any further interviews or sessions should be joint and how safety might be ensured where joint sessions do go ahead.

- Many women and children living with domestic violence have learned to keep the violence a secret and go to great lengths to conceal it, especially in relation to authority figures who are perceived as being powerful. Black and minority ethnic women have an especially justifiable fear of a heavy-handed response from social services.

- Domestic violence should be included as a specific category in all social work referral and assessment forms and in duty records.

Notes

1   As Cawson (2002) found in a retrospective study of child maltreatment, domestic violence was reported by most of the victims (80%) of serious physical abuse, by almost two-thirds of the young people sexually abused by parents (62%) and by 88 per cent of the young adults neglected in childhood (see Chapter Three).

2   Hester (2004) argues that practice regarding child contact is an area that may be considered to be on a third 'planet' – with yet another history, culture, laws and set of professionals compared with the other two 'planets' of domestic violence and child protection.

CHAPTER NINE

PRACTICE AND INTERVENTION WITH CHILDREN IN CIRCUMSTANCES OF DOMESTIC VIOLENCE

Chapters Two and Three outlined how children are likely to be at risk of direct physical, sexual and emotional abuse in the context of domestic violence and that the effect of witnessing domestic abuse to their mother or other carer may in itself lead to emotional harm to the children concerned. Chapter Four highlighted that emotional abuse resulting from witnessing domestic violence is now identified in law for consideration as significant harm. This chapter provides an overview of practice issues regarding children who live or have lived with domestic violence. The chapter covers the following areas of work:

- disclosure
- risk assessment and safety planning
- using reframing to incorporate domestic violence
- behavioural difficulties
- individual work
- group work
- work in refuges
- preventive work in schools.

Adults in a variety of settings may encounter children who are living with or have lived with domestic violence, including doctors, health visitors, solicitors, social workers, family centre workers, foster/adoptive carers, teachers, youth workers and mental health practitioners. The practice issues described below are of relevance to all of these professionals and individuals. Anyone with an understanding of the dynamics of domestic violence may feel able to apply the practice ideas regarding disclosure and safety planning. The discussion about reframing similarly provides ideas for incorporating domestic violence as an issue in childcare work. The sections on behavioural difficulties, individual work and group work with children will be of specific interest to those who already have some knowledge and skills in these areas, but they are also of relevance to anyone who works with children. The final sections in this chapter, concerning work with children in refuges and preventive work in schools, will be of direct relevance to refuge workers and teachers, respectively, but also to others working with children.

We have separated individual work and group work with children into two sections for the sake of clarity. This is not intended to suggest that children should be offered either individual or group work; in reality, children may benefit from both. Moreover, work with children may also incorporate adults and, in particular, mothers (see also Chapter Eight). For individual children, a combination of individual work, group work with other children and/or sessions involving them and their mothers may be the most appropriate. In reality, what (if anything) children are offered will depend on the resources and what is available in their locality. The aim here is to provide childcare and other professionals who work with children ideas for extending and enhancing their practice by incorporating the issue of domestic violence.

In recognition of the evidence linking the existence of domestic violence with various forms of harm to children, some countries, including the USA and Canada, have developed a variety of coordinated services for children in order to address the needs of children who have experienced domestic violence and to break the silence surrounding the issue. These services have included treatment programmes with individual children, support groups for children and educational group work in schools. The initiatives have been accompanied by the expansion and development of services for children in shelters or refuges, often with financial support from government.

By contrast, there have been comparatively few developments in the UK concerning specific intervention strategies for these children. Over the past 20 years, the main providers of services in the UK for children living with domestic violence have been Women's Aid and other refuges. These have managed to provide much innovative work for children and have built up a body of knowledge and expertise without sufficient funding or recognition from the statutory authorities. In a national survey of support for families experiencing domestic violence, Humphreys et al. (2000) found that 69 per cent of refuges in England and 89 per cent in Wales, Scotland and Northern Ireland employed specialist children's workers (mostly part-time). Work with the children included one-to-one work, group work, advocacy, after-school clubs and holiday activities. Specific services for black and minority ethnic children were offered by 12 per cent of refuges in England and by 4 per cent of refuges elsewhere in the UK. A small number of refuges – about 5 per cent – also attempted to provide services for children with special needs, such as children with disabilities.

The major UK children's organizations were also surveyed by Humphreys *et al.* (2000).[1] It was found that although about three-quarters (73.9%) provided services for children and their families living with domestic violence as part of their overall work, only a tiny number (1.3%) provided specific domestic violence services, and nearly a fifth (19.4%) did not consider domestic violence relevant to their client group. Services related to domestic violence were, not surprisingly, most often aimed specifically at children (60.1%), and more than half of the projects also worked with mothers and children together (53.5%). The projects involved in child protection were most likely to consider as relevant the provision of support to families experiencing domestic violence. Projects working with disabled children and projects engaged in fostering and adoption appeared least likely to see domestic violence as relevant to their work. According to Humphreys *et al.* (2000, p.9): 'One adoption project commented that adoptive parents would risk losing the child if they revealed domestic violence, yet the project did not seek such information despite possible risk to the child.'

As in the case of refuges, the children's organizations provided a range of one-to-one work, group work and advocacy provision and also counselling or other therapeutic interventions.

The interventions with children and their appropriateness for different situations and age groups are discussed below.

9.1 Children's disclosure of domestic violence: general issues

If children's behaviour raises anxiety of any kind or there is social work involvement because of child protection concerns, then the issue of domestic violence may be an important, key aspect of the picture. It is, therefore, important to:

- always bear in mind the possibility that children may be living with domestic violence

- ask children about domestic violence whenever this is possible and appropriate (i.e. both safe and confidential)

- not assume that disclosure will be immediate – it may be necessary to find out or to ask over a period of time.

Mullender (2004) stresses that children who are disclosing domestic violence should always be listened to and believed (see also Department for Education and Skills 2003). Moreover, professionals should have knowledge about what is available for children and their mothers and be familiar with the guidance on dealing with children who have been abused, for example, *What to Do if You Are Worried about a Child Being Abused* (Department of Health 2003a).

It is important to remember that the impact on children of living with domestic violence can manifest itself in a variety of ways (as outlined in Chapter Three), and there is no specific set of indicators. Many children do not give overt cause for concern and may have learned their own ways of dealing with the violence. At school, children may be truanting and displaying disruptive behaviour, or they may be overly compliant, eager to please and anxious to achieve.

9.2 Children's disclosure of domestic violence: hiding

Some children may have difficulty in disclosing domestic violence to others and may go to great lengths to hide it, for various reasons:

- the child is protective of the mother

- the child is protective of the abusing parent/parent figure

- the child is extremely fearful of the consequences of sharing the family 'secret' with anyone; this may include fears that it will cause further violence to the mother and/or the child.

One 11-year-old girl, who was receiving therapeutic work from the NSPCC in connection with physical abuse from her father, when asked about the context of domestic violence (gross physical, sexual and emotional abuse of her mother) within which she had lived, wrote that she found it both upsetting and frightening to talk about because of the potential dangers of disclosure: 'I thought if I tell someone then they go and tell someone and they will come and hurt me' (Hester 2000, p.104). However, being enabled to talk about the domestic violence in a safe context, which included a safe location for her mother and herself away from the violent man, proved positive.

9.3 Children's disclosure of domestic violence: asking

There may be some resistance from adults to the notion of asking children directly about domestic violence issues. This might be linked to concerns that addressing issues with children may evoke painful memories and 'make matters worse' (Catchpole 1997, p.151). It may be thought that, given time, children will simply forget their painful and difficult experiences and, therefore, recover from them. Adults may find disclosure from children too painful to hear (Silvern and Kaersvang 1989, p.427). Evidence suggests, however, that children's recovery and wellbeing can be aided by greater openness about their experiences (Harris Hendriks et al. 1993; Mullender 2004).

Children also stress the need to talk about their experiences and to be believed (Jaffe, Wolfe and Wilson 1990; McGee 2000). In interviews with children about living with domestic violence, Mullender et al. (2002) found that the key messages are that children need to be safe and want someone to talk to. They conclude that children:

> ...generally want far more opportunities to talk to other people about what is going on at home. They also want others to discuss things with them, giving them information and seeking their opinions. This applies to their mothers and also to helping agencies.

(Mullender et al. 2002, p.210)

It is important that domestic violence issues are discussed and acknowledged if children are to make sense of their experiences and gain appropriate support. The practitioners need to ask the 'right' questions, to show a sympathetic attitude and to be patient if the child is to feel able to disclose any information. This might include reassuring the child that he or she is not alone in witnessing or experiencing violence and allowing the child to reveal information at his or her own pace, which may necessitate the development of trust over several interviews.

Silvern, Karyl and Landis (1995), in their individual psychotherapy work with traumatized children of abused women, found that a direct approach to asking about domestic violence can be beneficial. They found that children often display feelings of avoidance and numbness and need to be given the opportunity to disclose the violence to their mothers that they have witnessed. Silvern and colleagues suggest that this is best achieved by a process of straight talk:

> It is necessary to ask specific questions and to draw explicit conclusions about the traumatic event. Directness is necessary to provide cognitive structure, to interrupt avoidance about the details of the trauma...and to explore and reframe beliefs about guilt, helplessness...

(Silvern et al. 1995, p.55)

According to Silvern *et al.*, children usually respond well to the need for 'a little straight talk' rather than to indirect or polite questions about the violence. They acknowledge that this might appear overly directive but argue that without such explicit invitations to disclose the violence, children will continue to see the issue as taboo and assume that adults do not want to hear about it. This will result in isolation for the child and an inability to resolve the trauma.

Similar conclusions have been drawn by Hurley and Jaffe (1990) in relation to their work at children's mental health centres. They found that issues of domestic violence for children could remain hidden unless they were asked about specifically. Hurley and Jaffe conclude that, for mental health professionals (although this is also applicable to other professionals), 'questions about violence need to be asked as routinely as questions about developmental milestones and temperament' (Hurley and Jaffe 1990, p.475).

Depending on the age and development of the child, disclosure may be facilitated by sensitive questioning or through play and artwork. Mullender and Morley (1994) cite a list of question areas drawn up by practitioners in Canada, which may be useful to consider when children in any setting are suspected of witnessing violence against their mothers. An adaptation of this list is given in Box 9.1. The very fact of raising such issues is crucial in showing children that practitioners are aware of the existence of domestic violence and gives children permission to disclose the violence in the knowledge that they will be believed.

Box 9.1 Suggested questions to ask when you suspect a child is experiencing domestic violence

- What happens when your mum and dad (mum and stepdad, dad and stepmum) disagree?
- What does your dad do when he gets angry?
- Did you ever hear or see your dad hurting your mum? What did you do?
- Who do you talk to about things that make you unhappy?
- What kind of things make you scared or angry?
- Do you worry about Mum and Dad?

(Adapted from the Children's Subcommittee
of the London Coordinating Committee
to End Woman Abuse 1994, p.233)

9.4 Children's disclosure of domestic violence: child abuse in circumstances of domestic violence

The dynamics of disclosure are particularly complex when the child is also being physically or sexually abused by the perpetrator of domestic violence. The child may have been threatened (either directly or implicitly) that any disclosure of the abuse will lead to more violence to the mother and/or siblings and/or the child him- or herself (Mullender *et al.* 2002; Peake and Fletcher 1997) (see also Chapters Two and Three). For this reason, children do not necessarily tell their mother or anyone else that they are being abused, especially as they may be fully aware of the violence of which their father is capable. In Forman's (1995) study, there were several examples of children believing that their mother would be killed by their father if they revealed that they were being sexually abused by the father. Both Forman (1995) and Kelly (1988) have also pointed out that children will deliberately not disclose their own sexual abuse in order to not add to their mother's distress. This means that disclosure about the child's abuse may occur after the partners have separated, when the child perceives that there may be more safety and when the mother is no longer having to deal so directly with her own abuse (Hester and Radford 1996; Mullender *et al.* 2002). This was also acknowledged by one of the mothers in Forman's study: '…the disclosures came after we separated… They protect the mother, they protect the mother's feelings, because she's going to be upset' (Forman 1995, p.24).

Hooper (1987) has suggested that because of the complexity of such situations, disclosure will not necessarily follow a straightforward linear pattern but might ebb and flow over a timespan of up to several years.

9.5 Children's disclosure of domestic violence: taking domestic violence seriously

Linked to the idea of safety for children living with domestic violence is the importance of consulting with children about what they have seen or experienced – and then taking this seriously. This is particularly vital in relation to child protection work, where previous child death inquiries have shown the repercussions of a failure to do this (see Chapters Two and Eight for more details of such inquiries). O'Hara (1994) has pointed out how the inquiries in relation to the deaths of Sukina Hammond and Toni Dales found that neither child was asked specifically about her experiences of witnessing attacks on her mother. Each child had also expressed fears about her father to social workers and to hospital and nursery staff, and yet these fears were ignored rather than explored. In the case of Sukina Hammond, who had also experienced physical violence from her father, Harris Hendriks et al. (1993, p.32) suggest that particular care and skills would have been needed to pick up the indicators of what was happening and how this was affecting the child: '...children like Sukina may be particularly at risk because they become so compliant, silent and eager to please that they give no clues, or only negative ones, about what they are experiencing and so become even more vulnerable.'

9.6 Children's disclosure of domestic violence: emphasis on safety

In whatever setting a child discloses that he or she is witnessing or experiencing domestic violence, the primary focus must be on the child's safety and protection from abuse. Any aims to provide therapeutic support or to achieve changes in behaviour at this stage will not succeed if the child does not feel safe at home (Jaffe, Wolfe and Wilson 1990; Mullender 2004). Because domestic violence can take many forms, and children's experiences of it and reactions to it can be very varied, it is important that any disclosure is handled in such a way as to elicit as much information as possible from the child. At the same time, the information that the child provides should not be used inappropriately. Mullender (2004, p.9), discussing findings from evaluations of Home Office projects on crime reduction programmes for domestic violence, provides a 'worst case example' where 'social workers [referred the child] to the group, largely to try and extract information about the perpetrator's continuing involvement in the family rather than because they thought the child could benefit from the group.'

9.7 Assessing safety and risk

An important aspect of handling any disclosure is the need to make a thorough assessment of the child's immediate safety needs. If the disclosure is made in the context of social work involvement of any kind, then the social care services department has a statutory responsibility to carry out such a safety assessment. Disclosure may give rise to some difficult issues regarding confidentiality, especially if the child discloses information indicating that the child could be exposed to a potentially dangerous situation. In such circumstances, professionals have a duty (moral rather than mandatory in the case of those professionals not linked to social care service departments) under the Children Act 1989 to report any concerns about risks of significant harm to a child.[2] If possible, it is preferable for this to be made clear to the child from the beginning.

Again, assessing safety (and, thus, dealing with risk) of the child will probably require some careful questioning in order to acquire the necessary information; some suggestions are given in Box 9.2.

Box 9.2 Assessing the child's safety

- When was the most recent incidence of violence or abuse?

- Can you give some details about this incident?

- Were any weapons used or threatened to be used? Have any weapons been used or threatened to be used in the past?

- Was your mother locked in a room or prevented from leaving the house? Has either of these things happened before?

- Was any substance abuse involved?

- How often do violent incidents or abuse occur?

- Have the police ever come to your house? What happened?

- What do you do when there is violence? Do you try to intervene? What happens?

- Where were your brothers and sisters during the violence?

(Adapted from the Children's Subcommittee
of the London Coordinating Committee
to End Woman Abuse 1994, p.234)

Once such information has been obtained, it is possible to develop a personal safety plan with the child, reflecting the child's age and understanding. This should be a straightforward and practical strategy that aims to help the child stay safe, especially if the mother is being physically attacked in some way. The strategy might include:

- asking the child to identify a safe place to go if there is further violence

- asking the child to identify a person he or she can go to if necessary

- ensuring that the child knows how to contact the emergency services

- ensuring that the child understands that it is neither safe nor his or her responsibility to intervene in an attempt to protect the mother.

In Mullender *et al.*'s (2000) study on children's perspectives, children came up with advice and things children should consider in relation to staying safe. These include who to talk to, what to do and how to talk to their mothers.

It cannot be stressed enough that the approach to safety with a child will also affect the safety of the mother/non-abusing parent and in turn have implications for the safety and welfare of the child. As Mullender and Debbonaire point out with regard to child protection procedures:

> [Where] one parent is being abused by the other, any process of child protection can in many cases undermine rather than support the safety of the non-abusing parent and consequently risk affecting the safety and welfare of the child. This can be due to agencies or individuals failing to identify the risks to the non-abusing parent, interviewing parents together so that the woman does not feel safe to speak, holding case conferences with both parents present so that again, the woman's participation is limited or contradicts what she may have said before.
>
> *(Mullender and Debbonaire 2000, p.19)*

9.8 Practice interventions with children: general issues

It has been found that children can recover from the detrimental exposure of domestic violence, or the effects can be minimized, provided that the violence is eliminated from their lives and opportunities for recovery are provided (Mullender 1996b; Rossman 1998).

> A…possibility for improved practice is for positive and healing work with children who are survivors of living with abuse. Once they are safe, children can be helped to come to terms with the past and with the continuing confusions of the present.
>
> *(Mullender 1996b, p.13)*

Effective intervention involves:

- elimination of violence

- recovery work, treatment or just 'talking to someone'

- supporting the mother to be safe as a positive approach in child protection

- supporting the mother to be a well-functioning residential parent
- building on coping and resilience strategies.

Such an approach recognizes:

- the existence of violence
- the impact of the violence
- the need for a significant other
- other protective factors.

The needs of children who have lived with domestic violence are as many and as varied as the children themselves and may be affected by factors such as age, race and disability. Some children may have lived with violence or the threat of violence for most or all of their years of childhood. All will have been affected in some way by living with violence. Some children may need interventions that are both challenging and supportive, especially when they have learned to excuse their father and blame their mother for the violence (Kelly 1994; Rivett *et al.* 2006). As Rivett *et al.* point out from a review of the research literature:

> …children exposed to domestic violence require help to accurately understand and respond to events that occur around them. This will help minimize their distress and the subsequent problems they manifest as a result of this distress. In particular, they need to be helped to understand who is to blame for the violence.
>
> *(Rivett* et al. *2006, pp.118–119)*

Peled (1997, p.288) indicates that all children require support to deal with the aftermath of their experiences: 'The cessation of violence is not sufficient for healing from its effects. Child witnesses of violence need emotional support both during and after witnessing the violence.'

It is essential that, regardless of its form, the support is provided by professionals who have an understanding of the dynamics of domestic violence and the effects of these on children (see Chapter Three). This applies even in those situations where domestic violence is compounded by other difficulties that the child (and the mother) may be experiencing. The continuum of support needed ranges from low-key interventions consisting of validation and affirmation of children's experiences through to long-term therapy, and may include:

- empowering (rather than punitive) work with the mother
- interventions that serve to validate and acknowledge children's difficult experiences and that reassure them that they are not alone and not to blame

- more long-term 'therapeutic' interventions in order to help children make sense of their experiences and understand the impact they have on them

- support that takes account of children's cultural/ethnic needs.

Rivett *et al.* (2006, p.119) suggest in addition that programmes should:

- help children differentiate between non-violent and violent conflict so that they can moderate their levels of threat accordingly

- teach children strategies to reduce the level of threat they experience

- build on coping and resilience behaviour by teaching children relaxation techniques.

Given the prevalence of domestic violence and the large numbers of children affected by it, it is clear that many children currently do not receive any support in recovery. The new safeguarding approach as laid out in *Every Child Matters* (Department for Education and Skills 2003) is intending to provide more strategic, targeted services that include support for children living with domestic violence. The commissioning document for children's directors and those working through children's strategic partnerships or children's trusts specifies with regard to domestic violence:

> Children and young people vulnerable as a result of domestic violence...should be identified and supported wherever possible within the universal setting, e.g. in Children's Centres, or by peer mentors etc. Vulnerable children and young people whose needs cannot be met within that setting should be able to be referred to specialist services including community-based domestic violence support, group work and advocacy services. Children and young people with complex needs whose lives are (or have been) seriously disrupted by domestic violence...and children with acute needs who are at risk of death or serious harm from an abusive parental partner...should, dependent on need, have access to:
>
> - individual support, advocacy and counselling with skilled practitioners knowledgeable about domestic violence; and
>
> - a group work programme suited to their needs.
>
> *(Local Government Association 2005)*

9.9 Practice interventions with children: work with children in refuges

A study by Hague, Kelly *et al.* (1996) was the first to detail the history of children's work in refuges in the UK and to examine at a national level the age-specific needs of the children living there. The study also highlighted the innovative and creative work being carried out by children's workers in refuges and indicated that this work is often restricted by a chronic lack of resources and insecure or inadequate funding.

Since the inception of the refuge movement in the early 1970s, refuges have provided protection for both women and children, although initially there were few facilities specifically for children (Binney *et al.* [1981] 1988). This changed gradually over the years, with the development of policies relating to work with children and the employment of specific children's workers during the early 1980s. By 1986, Women's Aid Federation of England (WAFE), the national coordinating body for refuges in England, had introduced an additional aim that refuges should provide specific support for children. This was followed in 1990 by the funding of the post of National Children's Officer. In the same year, an evaluation of children's workers in nine WAFE refuges was carried out, highlighting the value of their role as children's advocates and in offering support to children who had been physically or sexually abused (Ball 1990). The children themselves were positive about the children's workers and enjoyed the activities and play sessions provided. The main area of difficulty identified by the children's workers was the lack of time to explore children's feelings and anxieties more fully on a one-to-one basis – a lack confirmed in Saunders *et al.*'s (1995) retrospective study of adults who spent time in refuges as children.

By the 1990s, most refuges saw the provision of services to children as an important priority, and this was accompanied by the production of an information pack on work with children in refuges (Women's Aid Federation of England 1992). In 1993, WAFE adopted a policy for children's rights in refuges (Debbonaire 1994, pp.164–169).

Against a backdrop of ongoing financial constraints and uncertainties, refuges have been determined to provide improved services and facilities for children. Women's Aid has developed important training packs and other materials aimed at children and those who work with them (Ellis, Stanley and Bell 2006; Hague *et al.* 2000). Higgins (1994) and Debbonaire (1995) have outlined some of the reasons for this commitment to separate work and advocacy for children, as follows:

- Children constitute two-thirds of refuge populations.

- Coming into a refuge can be a traumatic experience for children.

- Living in a crowded refuge can be stressful.

- Children will often have experienced physical and/or sexual abuse themselves.

- Children's needs are different from their mother's.

- The children's and mother's wishes may be in conflict.

A variety of age-appropriate work and activities has been developed over the years to meet the needs of children in refuges. These have been underpinned by the two key principles of a commitment to promoting the rights of children living with domestic violence and a belief in the healing value of play (Debbonaire 1994; Hague *et al.* 2000). Some of the work provided by children's workers is summarized by Debbonaire:

> There is no single job description that reflects the range of work going on with children in refuges but most children's workers will provide all or some of the following:
>
> - Play sessions for different age groups, including painting and other messy play, cooking
> - Outdoor activities, e.g. trips to park and further afield
> - Holidays for children, e.g. outward bound, outgoings to seaside, camping in France
> - Provision of advice and information specifically for children
> - Encouraging and helping children to help each other, through developing peer support, holding separate children's meetings, discussions on refuge rules, e.g. why women only
> - One to one support sessions with children
> - Organising parties for birthdays and religious festivals
> - Holiday play and activity schemes
> - Work with mothers and children on a range of matters: problems in parent–child relationships, non-violent punishment
> - Information on local advice and counselling services, youth and sporting activities etc.
> - Advocacy – supporting women in getting school and nursery places, access to health care for children, statements for children with special needs
> - Involvement in case conferences or giving evidence in court in support of child/mother
> - Liaison with local schools about general domestic violence issues, confidentiality, security.
>
> *(Debbonaire 1995, p.63)*

Much of the work with children carried out in refuges has been innovative, with one of the earliest innovations being the development of structured work with individual children. The aim of such individual work has been to help children recognize and understand their experiences of domestic violence by supporting them in talking about it and in dealing with the complexity of their emotions. Such work is undertaken carefully with an agreement between mother, child and worker and with clear policies on limits to confidentiality if there is any disclosure of abuse (Higgins 1994).

Attempts are made to ensure that the work is age-appropriate and flexible in approach and that it reflects WAFE's commitment to anti-racist and anti-discriminatory practice (Women's Aid Federation of England 2006). This may be achieved by means of a multicultural playroom, by sharing other languages and cultures and by discussing race awareness in children's meetings. This is supplemented by working with children in a way that is supportive of difference and diversity and encouraging equality of treatment for boys and girls and for children with impairments and learning disabilities (Hague *et al.* 2000; Higgins 1994). At Hammersmith Women's Aid, the children produced their own anti-discriminatory policies (Box 9.3).

Box 9.3 Children's anti-discriminatory policies at Hammersmith Women's Aid

This is our anti-racism statement!

- Do not make fun of other people's accents.
- Do not make fun of their religion.
- Do not make fun of other people's food, and make noises about it.
- Do not make fun of people's hair and what they look like, calling names, etc.

Anti-sexism statement!

- We want boys and girls to play together.
- Don't make fun of boys when they play with dolls and stuff.
- Boys are not to take over the playroom.
- Girls for football and rugby.
- Club for both girls and boys.

(Higgins 1994, p.173)

9.10 Practice interventions with children: reframing to take into account domestic violence in child abuse interventions and practice

Hester and Pearson (1998) examined the practice of an NSPCC team that was making a concerted effort to incorporate domestic violence into its recovery work with abused children (see also Hester 2000). The team felt that asking about and incorporating domestic violence as part of the picture had enhanced its overall practice. For instance, thinking about both child abuse and domestic violence enabled the team to reflect more thoroughly on its use of particular approaches, largely due to many of the underlying issues being the same or overlapping because both domestic violence and child abuse involve one person exerting power and control over another.

Having a practice framework that included an understanding of domestic violence was also seen to enhance practice and partnership work with parents because it allowed a better understanding of what was going on in many of the cases: 'This framework of domestic violence explains a lot to us – it explains a lot of people's actions, or could help to explain them… I think it can only help us work in partnership much better' (Hester and Pearson 1998, p.38).

As part of its attempt to introduce a 'domestic violence focus' in its work with children, the NSPCC team re-examined and reframed some previously finished cases where domestic violence had not been disclosed or apparent but where it might have been a possibility. This involved the exploration of the effect that taking domestic violence into account might have.

For instance, in one case the team had investigated an allegation that the key worker of a 16-year-old girl in residential care was involved with her in a sexual relationship. This allegation was made by the girl and was subsequently retracted. The man involved was consequently suspended for abusing his position of authority. The team had identified the case as involving child sexual abuse, even though the girl concerned considered herself in some ways to be in a relationship with this man. As the investigation by the team progressed, it learned more details about the girl's relationship with this man, including instances where he had put his hands around her throat in a very threatening way. On at least two occasions, she reported that when he was displeased with her 'he was rough and angry…he pushed her, but did not hit her' (Hester and Pearson 1998, p.14). In another instance, 'he frightened her by shaking her violently' (Hester and Pearson 1998, p.14). There were also suggestions that he was being sexually coercive; she described how 'he wouldn't leave her alone' (Hester and Pearson 1998, p.14).

Reframing did not alter the impropriety or nature of the man's behaviour. Reframing did, however, provide an additional way in which the team could have carried out recovery work with the girl and would have allowed the team to work in a person-centred way that incorporated the girl's own apparent perspective. Incorporating domestic violence into the picture would also have allowed information regarding refuges and other support for women experiencing domestic violence to be imparted with regard to safety planning with the girl.

This use of reframing to incorporate domestic violence proved a very useful mechanism for the integration of work around both child abuse and domestic violence. As one team member explained, it was these re-examinations of cases that had in particular clarified for her how the 'domestic violence lens' could enhance her own practice in relation to children:

> …the thing that brought it home to me was that session we had when we looked at some cases, we traced the domestic violence, we traced the problems back…and it sort of really brought it home to me that there we all were,

all the different agencies, running round in circles basically trying to help families, not actually considering the issue of the domestic violence and how problems that had either arisen from that or been exacerbated by that, and that in fact we probably had to go back and deal with that domestic violence issue to make any headway at all and to get people in a stable sort of settled environment, to be able to benefit from some therapy and get their lives back on course.

(Hester and Pearson 1998, p.13)

Thus, incorporating domestic violence as a possible feature in the lives of the children concerned provided a much wider view and context for understanding their presenting behaviour. It also resulted in more effective work.

9.11 Practice interventions with children: behavioural difficulties

Children may be referred to social care services or other practitioners as a result of behavioural difficulties. Alongside other abusive experiences, this may be an indication that the child is or has been living in a context of domestic violence (see Chapter Three). Jaffe, Hurley and Wolfe (1990, p.468) noted that domestic violence may be in the backgrounds of many children with emotional or behavioural difficulties referred to children's mental health professionals, and yet this is seldom the presenting problem: '…the presence of violence in the family is often overlooked. At times, "the family secret" is kept from mental health professionals or, more commonly, the issue is never raised or actively pursued.'

Several case examples are given where the domestic violence that children witnessed was not raised or addressed in the clinical assessment of the children (Hurley and Jaffe 1990). As a result, the focus of interventions remained on the behavioural or emotional difficulties of the children without addressing the possibility that domestic violence might be an underlying feature. As Hurley and Jaffe (1990) point out, such interventions fail to meet the needs of children and serve to 'silently condone' violence against women and children. Mullender *et al.* (2002) also found that the physical and behavioural changes children exhibit as a consequence of domestic violence may be misinterpreted by the range of professionals they come into contact with, whether in education, healthcare, child protection, family support or youth offending.

The London Borough of Hackney's (1993) good practice guidelines for responding to domestic violence included the recommendation that whenever a child with behavioural and emotional difficulties is referred to social services, social workers should be aware that such difficulties may be a result of the child's experiences of domestic violence.

Hester and Pearson (1998), in their study of NSPCC practice, found that in cases involving children with behavioural difficulties, workers' awareness of domestic violence could help to provide a more complete understanding and, thereby, achieve effective change. In one example, a child whose behavioural difficulties were initially assumed to be symptomatic of sexual abuse began to be understood more fully in the therapeutic sessions when the child enacted scenes of domestic violence. In another example, a child's angry behaviour was resolved positively in therapy by incorporating the domestic violence that both the child and the mother had experienced. By bringing the issue of domestic violence into the sessions, the child was able to understand the effect on the mother of the domestic violence, and that the effect continued despite them having left the violent man:

> [Mother] was having difficulties with her little girl's behaviour…she's very angry because her father wouldn't let her have any of her belongings ever. He's still got all her toys – everything. And Mum kept saying things like, but I'm sure you're too big for them. And she started kicking and biting and scratching her mum again. And I said, well maybe she sees you as the strong person now and forgets what it was like – so she doesn't see why you can't go and get them, so just talk to her about what [the experience of the domestic violence] was like… So just explore that anger with her and tell her, you know, mummy is angry too, mummy can't have any of her things. So that's what she did the next time she got angry and, yes, it worked, and the little girl kind of had a long conversation with her mother about [it].

> *(Hester and Pearson 1998, pp.13–14)*

Thus, having a framework that included an understanding of domestic violence enhanced practice by providing insights into children's behaviour.

Even where domestic violence is known to be a factor in the backgrounds of children referred for therapeutic work, the therapist or practitioner may need to be very patient before the impact of this emerges. Silvern and Kaersvang (1989) give one example of an eight-year-old boy, Jon, who was referred for psychotherapy because of his occasional uncontrollable outbursts of aggression against other children, including attempts to choke them. After seven months in therapy, Jon finally described how he had once awoken to see his father choking his mother and how he had felt powerless to intervene. His mother was unaware of this, and Jon did not want to upset or embarrass her by telling her about it. This sense of powerlessness had led to a strong sense of self-loathing, and Jon's rages could be understood as his way of reliving the traumatic event – but with him in charge. Without an understanding of the impact of domestic violence, the focus of the work being carried out with Jon would have remained on his behaviour, which in turn would have remained incomprehensible and difficult to modify. Instead, one year after completion of therapy, there had been no repetition of Jon's violent outbursts. Silvern and Kaersvang (1989, p.433) conclude: '…current understanding of the inexorable impact of unresolved trauma suggests that it is dangerous to leave children unsupported in their efforts to master the experience of witnessing spousal abuse.'

9.12 Practice interventions with children: individual work

As in the case of Jon, described above, many children would benefit from the opportunity to express (either verbally or through play or art) what living with domestic
violence has meant for them.

Individual work with children can be carried out in a variety of both formal and
informal ways and can be undertaken by a number of different practitioners, such as
social workers, teachers and youth workers. In many cases, this work consists of
giving children the time and space to reflect on their experiences and to express any
feelings of anger, hurt, fear and confusion that they might have. This helps to relieve
the children of the burden of the secret they have been holding and enable them to
understand that they are not alone or at fault. The basic requirements are to validate
children's experiences, to believe what they say and to take their situation seriously
without needing to provide solutions. This is identical to the needs of children who
are referred for clinical assessments: 'The children we have interviewed are almost
universal in their need to be listened to, believed and supported. They usually are not
looking for solutions but an opportunity to share their fears' (Jaffe, Wolfe and
Wilson 1990, p.83).

There are occasions where the impact on the child of the domestic violence
necessitates therapeutic work. This might include situations where the child's behaviour is such that there is concern for the safety of the child or of others or where
concern for the child has persisted over time. This distinction between the thresholds
of children whose needs can be met by 'talking with' someone and those who require
therapy is an issue that will need careful assessment by the professionals and adults
concerned and are similar to the thresholds used in other child abuse contexts.

Any individual or therapeutic work must have a focus on some of the specific
effects on the child of witnessing domestic violence. This might include some of the
same elements as outlined in Sections 9.1–9.7; that is, consideration of basic safety
needs, an exploration of some of the confusion and ambivalent feelings that the
violence has evoked, and ensuring that children learn to understand that they are not
responsible for the violence. This must be accompanied by messages that violence is
never an appropriate way to resolve conflict and that children are not inevitably
going to model such behaviour. Children need help in understanding that it is
acceptable to be angry but unacceptable to express this by means of violence. Jaffe,
Hurley and Wolfe (1990, p.468) point out that 'children are often frightened by their
own anger and feel that the cycle of violence is inevitable', and it is important to
explain that there is no inevitability about them becoming violent adults.

In individual work with children, it is also important that the diversity of such
children is acknowledged and addressed. Silvern *et al.* (1995) argue that race, ethnicity, economic status, family structure and the sexual orientation of the child's carer
should all be given consideration if the child is to perceive the service provided as
safe and accessible.

Mullender (2004, p.4) suggests that individual ('one-to-one') work can be used with children of 'any age from about four or five upwards', and needs to be carried out 'by a professional who has been specifically trained to work with children who have witnessed domestic abuse'. Mullender (2004, p.4) identifies two main types of individual work:

- in-depth work 'focused around a particular issue'

- an unstructured approach, 'going where the child wants to take it, at the child's pace and only as far as they want to go, using free expression through art, play or other forms of therapy designed to help "unravel complex feelings"'.

Individual work may also be used as a precursor to attending group work.

In the Home Office Crime Reduction Programme of domestic violence evaluations (Hester and Westmarland 2005), some of the projects also used individual work with children; mothers usually commented positively on this work. Box 9.4 gives an example of the type of work provided.

Box 9.4 Individual work with children

In [one] project, an initial four-week block of individual sessions is booked for each child, with a review with the child's mother at the end of this period to determine whether to stop, continue or refer elsewhere. The child is also asked to indicate how he or she is now feeling, how well supported s/he is, whether there are people to talk to elsewhere and how well they are coping. The majority of children continue to be helped, sometimes over many months, for example if there are protracted court proceedings or contact issues through which the child needs support. There can be simultaneous referrals to Sure Start or other agencies. Planning and evaluation are undertaken before and after each session. Work may be done on self-esteem, self-protection, the family unit, schools, feelings and/or past experiences. It is to some extent led by what the children themselves want and is also dependent on age. Techniques include various forms of art work: painting, drawing, collage materials, clay and plasticine, feelings sheets. Other techniques involve the use of books on self-esteem and being safe, worksheets, puppets and dolls, therapeutic and also 'fun' games.

(Mullender 2004, p.5)

INDIVIDUAL WORK WITH CHILDREN WHO HAVE BEEN PHYSICALLY, SEXUALLY OR EMOTIONALLY ABUSED IN THE CONTEXT OF DOMESTIC VIOLENCE

Children living with domestic violence who have been physically, sexually or emotionally abused may benefit from a range of levels of therapeutic interventions. Catchpole (1997), talking about therapeutic work with abused children generally, has pointed out that some parents and professionals have reservations about the effectiveness of such interventions. Clearly, forcing children against their will to talk about difficult experiences will be counterproductive. However, as highlighted above, for some children retelling their story can in itself be of therapeutic value. For younger children, therapy may be indicated even though the children may not recognize the need for it. Farmer and Owen (1995) found in their child protection study that the offer of some direct work was helpful to children who had been sexually abused. Social workers who could offer even a few sessions were reported to have made a difference. In refuges, such individual work with children has also been developed, as discussed later in this chapter.

As in the examples above, intervention with these children can range from low-level support to more intensive work and can include any of the following (Catchpole 1997):

- therapeutic play
- the use of toys and books to help children express their feelings
- the use of puppets so that children can distance themselves from the conversations enacted through them
- the use of videotaped sessions.

Whatever the approach adopted, it is vital that the work is undertaken at the child's pace, otherwise there is a danger of reinforcing the child's lack of control or of the child being overly compliant, as is often the case with children who have been (sexually) abused.

9.13 Practice interventions with children: group work

In some countries, including the USA and Canada, there has been a much longer history than in the UK of the existence of groups specifically for children who have witnessed the abuse of their mothers (Mullender 1994). There are several reasons why group work is perceived as a valuable method of working with children who have experienced domestic violence; among these is the fact that children welcome the use of such groups. Research in the UK has suggested that the majority of children who have lived with domestic violence would prefer to talk to other children with similar experiences (Humphreys *et al.* 2000; McGee 2000; Mullender *et al.* 2002). This is partly because adults are seen to talk and think differently from children, as one 12-year-old girl explained to McGee:

I think because adults think differently to children so it's easier for children to talk to people like friends or maybe cousins or brothers and sisters, but hard to talk to adults because their minds are different in a way.

(McGee 1996, p.8)

Peake and Fletcher (1997) outline some of the advantages of group work for children who have been sexually abused, many of which are equally applicable to child witnesses of domestic violence. These advantages include the following:

- Children are given the opportunity to talk about their experiences.

- Children learn that they are not alone in their experiences.

- Sharing experiences with others helps children to understand that they are not responsible.

- Children may have been isolated and, therefore, lacking in interpersonal skills; group work can offer a safe space to practise these skills.

- Individual work can appear to replicate the abusive situation for the child, in that the child is having to deal with a powerful adult.

- Therapy and treatment that involves videos and one-way screens can appear to the child to replicate the secrecy and lies of the abusive situation.

- In group work, children outnumber adults and can gain a sense of empowerment and control from this

- Children can learn from each other ways of keeping safe in the future.

In the UK, recognition of the effects and consequent needs of children living with domestic violence was (as discussed above), for a long time, largely confined to the refuge movement. As a result, group work for children who have lived with domestic violence developed initially within refuges. Such group work for children has, more recently, begun to be developed outside refuges, in particular by the voluntary sector (Mullender 1996b). Several of the children's charities (e.g. NSPCC, Barnardo's, Children's Society) have contributed to these developments and services (Humphreys *et al.* 2000). Developments in group work for children have also grown out of interagency initiatives (Hague, Malos and Dear 1996; Hester and Westmarland 2005; Mullender 2004). Examples of these included an innovative support group for child witnesses, called AWAKENS, created by Keighley Domestic Violence Forum. In Cleveland, similar group programmes were developed by the local interagency forum and run jointly by the NSPCC and the social services department. The Home Office Crime Reduction Programme projects on domestic violence also included some of the examples of group work with children (Hester and Westmarland 2005).

Evaluations of group work have indicated that such an approach may benefit children in a variety of ways, especially with regard to self-esteem, confidence and understanding of domestic violence, although there have been few long-term outcome studies. A small pilot study in Canada by Jaffe, Wilson and Wolfe (1986), for instance, suggested that group programmes created some improvements in children's self-esteem, attitudes about violence and safety skills. In a later study, 64 children (aged between 7 and 13 years) were assessed by means of interviews pre- and post-attendance at the group sessions and by completion of standardized measures. This was supplemented by obtaining similar information from the children's mothers (Jaffe, Wolfe and Wilson 1990, p.89). This showed that children enjoyed the group and led to improvements for them in terms of safety skills and their perceptions of each parent, but there were no apparent changes in behavioural or emotional difficulties. According to 88 per cent of the mothers, the children enjoyed the group and they also perceived positive adjustment changes. The group programme also resulted in improved interagency liaison and a more integrated community response.

Jaffe, Wolfe and Wilson (1990, p.89) conclude that the group programme is best suited to children 'with mild-to-moderate behaviour problems' and that other children (especially those who have been exposed to long-term repeated acts of violence) may require more extensive individual counselling. This confirms the view of the authors of the original intervention model (Wilson *et al.* 1989), who suggested that attitudes and behaviour realistically could not be changed in the course of a ten-week programme. They suggested that some children would require further group sessions.

A more recent evaluation of the same group treatment model, using a control group, was carried out by Wagar and Rodway (1995). This found significant differences between the children pre- and post-group attendance, especially in relation to attitudes about and responses to anger and in an understanding of where the responsibility for the violence should lie.

In the USA, Peled and Edleson (1992) carried out a more formal qualitative evaluation of the children's group programmes run by the Domestic Abuse Project (DAP) (see Hester, Pearson and Harwin 2000, Chapter Nine). They found that all the children interviewed and observed in groups had, to some extent, succeeded in the aim of breaking the secret of the abuse with which they had lived. The group programme had also mostly achieved the other stated aims of developing children's protection and safety skills, increasing self-esteem, understanding violence and responsibility, encouraging the expression of feelings, and experiencing the group as a safe and fun environment. They also found some unintended outcomes: some children, for instance, respected the confidentiality of the group to the extent that they would not talk about the group with their mothers, thus frustrating the mothers' hopes that the issues would begin to be discussed more openly. For other children, the emotions stirred up by the reliving of painful events led to tensions and stress between the children and other family members. The role of the mothers, therefore, is crucial in understanding and supporting the children through their group work experience (see also Rivett *et al.* 2006).

There are differences between individual children as to how effective the group process can be, and this will be affected by factors such as personality, family background, and each child's personal experiences of direct and indirect abuse. In their evaluation, Peled and Edleson (1992) reported the difficulties experienced by one girl in the group because of her perception of being different because she had been physically abused by her father. Care needs to be taken in the planning of the group composition in order to reflect the diversity of backgrounds and experiences of the children involved. Particular attention needs to be paid in this respect to issues of race and disability in order to ensure that children are not isolated and marginalized within groups.

In the UK, a few of the domestic violence projects evaluated as part of the Home Office Crime Reduction Programme also included group work (Hester and Westmarland 2005; Mullender 2004). As a general principle, for referral to a group, children had to be living in a safe environment, with both mother and child being happy about the child attending the group. In one example, group work was offered for seven- to ten-year-olds, with children younger than seven years being offered play therapy instead. The first group ran for eight weeks, but the children felt that they would have benefited from longer, so this was then extended to 12 weeks. This allowed more time to be spent on protective behaviours and dealing with angry feelings. One boy suggested having continuing support meetings every few months, one of which was subsequently planned. The structure of the group was preplanned, but with flexibility to pursue the children's own issues. Worker debriefing and planning took place between each session. Membership of the groups was limited to ten people. Material for use in the group was gathered from earlier work, both locally and beyond, from general group work exercises from Women's Aid and health promotion, and from ideas gleaned from a social work-qualifying programme. Both the group workers and the children evaluated the group after each session and at the end, and the children were asked to reflect on their level of satisfaction in various regards. According to this feedback, all the children enjoyed the group. They liked the venue and found it easy to get to. They enjoyed most of the activities and felt they had been listened to, although one boy did not like talking about the violence. Mothers also reported positive gains from the group, with children talking more, appearing able to cope better with their feelings and showing improvements in behaviour.

9.14 Primary prevention: work with children in schools

The final frontier in dealing with violence in our society which most often leaves women and children as victims is the potential role of primary prevention programmes... Hope may lie in primary prevention programmes

within school systems which ensure that children...are made aware of this
issue.

(Jaffe, Hurley and Wolfe 1990, p.469)

Primary prevention relates to the prevention of violence before it occurs by examining and changing the attitudes, beliefs and behaviours that lead to violent behaviour. Research on primary prevention in education settings indicates that violence prevention programmes may change attitudes (Hague, Mullender and Kelly 2001). What is less well known is whether there is a link between raised awareness and any long-term impact on violence reduction. There is some evidence, however, that supportive anti-violence work in schools may play a role in setting out guidelines for healthy relationships (Mullender 1994, 2001). Primary prevention in schools has been particularly developed in Canada, Australia and New Zealand, and such innovative work in schools is now becoming more widespread in the UK (Ellis *et al.* 2006).

With regard to policy, the National Healthy Schools Scheme (Hampshire Inspection and Advisory Service undated) now mentions domestic violence specifically, and other government information and consultation documents regarding domestic violence have begun to recognize these issues. For instance, both *Living without Fear* (Home Office 1998) and *Safety and Justice* (Home Office 2003) recognize the role of education and consciousness-raising both among the statutory services and in the public in general in tackling violence against women. The new safeguarding approach, which has prevention as a key issue, also acknowledges domestic violence as a specific problem to be addressed (Department of Health 2004).

9.15 Primary prevention: violence prevention in Canada

Violence prevention work in schools in Canada continues to be particularly advanced, and development of the approach is thus worth outlining here. The work began around 1988, due partly to the presence and influence of a dedicated 'champion'.[3] Following a conference on the issue, a decision was taken that violence prevention should be addressed in schools. Training was given to school heads and designated teachers before five pilot schools each held a day-long event on the issue, including plays, films and speakers. Counsellors were made available for children who made disclosures or who found the material distressing.

This was followed in 1989 by a large day workshop on violence, which was attended by 680 secondary school pupils and staff from 21 school boards across the region. Subjects covered at the workshop included:

- rape and violence in teenage dating relationships
- where to turn for help
- breaking down the isolation

- the establishment of student-run hotlines
- supporting and helping others
- the need for more teacher awareness and concern.

The success of the workshop proved that school was an appropriate environment in which to tackle and prevent violence. This was coupled with an acceptance by the Ontario Ministry of Education that domestic violence had an impact on children's learning, thereby making it an issue of concern for education. The work was soon expanded, and by 1991 all secondary schools in London, Ontario, had held similar workshops. This was followed by local and regional developments and initiatives, with a set of procedures to use for teachers when children disclose living with violence, including:

- the distribution of resource kits and videos to every school
- the publication of a monthly violence prevention newsletter
- the distribution of leaflets on domestic violence for students and teachers
- information sessions for classes and staff groups
- presentations in school for pupils, staff and parents
- a violence awareness week.

Some of the initiatives were aimed at elementary schools and kindergartens as well as secondary schools. A violence awareness week, for example, might include age-specific activities, such as 11-year-olds helping six-year-olds to draw anti-violence posters and kindergarten children being given information by shelter workers on how to call for help if their mother was being attacked. Gamache and Snapp (1995) provide a more detailed account of violence prevention programmes for elementary schools, and Sudermann, Jaffe and Hastings (1995) describe programmes for secondary schools that have been used in the USA. In effect, such work has provided a combination of both prevention and intervention.

In addition to these developments, the Ontario Ministry of Education promoted a policy of no tolerance of violence in schools and required every school to develop a violence-free policy. This was accompanied by active cooperation with women's organizations such as the Women's Community House in London, described above. Loosley (1994) describes how, since 1989, part of the children's programme of this organization has been to provide schools with a violence awareness programme. This was initially aimed at 6- to 12-year-olds but has now been expanded to include the 4 to 18 years age range; it covers a number of issues related to attitudes and beliefs about violence, particularly in relation to violence against women. Through discussion groups, puppet shows and plays, children are encouraged to think about safety planning and to identify alternatives to the misuse of power and control in relationships: 'It is through mutual community efforts like this program, and the promotion of an open awareness and understanding of woman abuse and issues of

violence, that those involved with children can make a difference in their lives'
(Loosley 1994, p.186).

As the violence prevention work has developed, there have been increasing
attempts to integrate this work into the general school system. In London, Ontario,
this has resulted in the production of a video and training pack, entitled 'A
School-based Anti-violence Programme' (ASAP). This comprehensive pack covers a
wide range of issues, including:

- the need to involve the whole school and local community in violence
  prevention

- prevention and intervention strategies for elementary and secondary
  schools

- how to create a safer school climate

- how to promote gender equality

- positive responses to disclosure (from children and staff)

- further available resources.

Mullender (1994) suggests there are some omissions to the ASAP manual, especially
in relation to its lack of integration of racism awareness and its failure to mention
homophobia or the fact that schools and school staff may be abusive. Nonetheless,
evaluation of the work to date has shown that for the majority of pupils, it has had a
significant impact on their awareness of abuse issues and on the sources of help available, as well as positive changes with regard to respect in relationships (Hague
et al. 2001).

9.16 Primary prevention: work in the UK

An exciting amount has been achieved there [Canada] and, as a general approach, it would be highly transferable to the British context. This makes the
relative inactivity here look inexcusable and dangerous in comparison.

(Mullender 1994, p.257)

By the mid-1990s, work in the UK on violence prevention in schools and in youth
work was largely undeveloped and ad hoc rather than coordinated (Mullender
1994). This has been changing gradually at a local level, often as a result of the influence of interagency initiatives. A number of education authorities have now
produced, or are in the process of producing, education packs on violence prevention. In addition, some of the work on conflict resolution now being carried out in
some schools includes an acknowledgement of domestic violence. A study in
England, Wales and Northern Ireland found that by 2003, primary prevention
programmes were being, or had been, delivered in 102 local authorities and focused

in particular on urban areas (Ellis *et al.* 2006). Most of these programmes had been established after 2000, when funding from, for instance, the Children's Fund and the Home Office became available for this purpose. Thus, some of the domestic violence projects evaluated as part of the Home Office Crime Reduction Programme also included primary prevention activities in schools (Hester and Westmarland 2005). Examples of these programmes are discussed in more detail below.

Much of the earlier impetus for the preventive work in the UK has come from Women's Aid groups, which have given talks in schools and provided teachers with training to raise their awareness of the issues. In some cases, refuge workers have joined with teachers to plan anti-violence work, which has also focused on bully-ing and racism within schools. Higgins (1994), for instance, described how Hammersmith Women's Aid built strong links with local schools and provided workshops for teachers and helpers on the effects of domestic violence. The refuge was also involved with a joint project on bullying and ran a workshop with 14- and 15-year-old girls on positive images for young women, which raised issues concern-ing sexism, racism and violence against women. Some schools have also included as-pects of violence-free conflict resolution in their curriculum (Debbonaire 1994). Women's Aid was again an important instigator (along with Rape Crisis) in the more recent development of primary prevention programmes (Ellis *et al.* 2006).

Hague, Malos and Dear (1996) identified a growing trend for some of the inter-agency initiatives to develop preventive work in schools and youth projects. Inter-agency projects in Leeds, Islington and Keighley provided support work in schools, which was developed further by the production of comprehensive education packs and training modules – still some of the best materials available to date. In Leeds, a Home Office-funded programme for primary schools was developed and tested alongside teachers in the classroom. In Keighley, the Home Office funded the devel-opment of a resource pack on gender issues and violence for use in schools and youth clubs. In Islington, interagency initiatives led to the publication in 1995 of the manual *S.T.O.P Domestic Violence* (London Borough of Islington 1995) for use in schools. This is a thorough and comprehensive manual, including advice and infor-mation, training modules, curriculum material and ideas on raising awareness. In addition, forums have produced plays and workshops for schools and youth groups. These materials have continued to be used and developed in the recent expansion of primary prevention, with newer materials being *Violence Free Relationships* (Sandwell Against Domestic Violence Project 2000), the Westminster programme (Debbonaire and Westminster Domestic Violence Forum 2002) and the Protective Behaviours approach (Protective Behaviours undated) (see Ellis *et al.* 2006 for an overview).

Generally, however, schools and youth and community services in Britain remain an untapped source of potential for work on violence prevention and educa-tion. Recommendations for further development include the following (Ellis *et al.* 2006; Hague, Kelly *et al.* 1996; Holder, Kelly and Singh 1994):

- all schools to develop policies recognizing domestic violence

- schools and colleges to have policies on confidentiality and safety

- regular input from refuges to all teachers and youth workers about domestic violence and the work of the refuge

- partnerships between refuges, colleges and youth services to develop curricula/programmes/activities on sexism, power, gender and non-violent relationships

- schools and youth clubs to develop skills work on assertiveness, conflict resolution and problem-solving

- schools, colleges and youth services to develop peer networking, advocacy and education to provide support for young people

- educational systems to recognize the impact of domestic violence on children's and young people's learning, which may necessitate additional support.

The implementation of these recommendations would serve to act as both intervention and prevention. The breaking down of the secrecy surrounding domestic violence would enable those children and young people already living with it, or who have lived with it, to gain support and help with safety. All would learn the impact of violent behaviour and, we hope, understand that the power and control that such violence exemplifies is not acceptable in any relationship.

9.17 Primary prevention: examples of UK projects

Providing children and young people with awareness of domestic violence and the necessary skills required to build relationships based on mutual respect and understanding was a core or partial aim of five projects evaluated as part of the Home Office Crime Reduction Programme (Hester and Westmarland 2005). The projects built, to different extents, on previous research that has indicated that a multi-goal curriculum may be the best strategy to reduce violence, since a change in attitudes does not necessarily affect behaviour (Sudermann et al. 1995). Also, the most effective strategy for violence prevention is probably a school-wide effort, rather than a stand-alone class-based curriculum programme.

School-wide activities were used in three of the projects including drama interventions and a mass media programme. One project, in Thurrock, used the Edinburgh Zero Tolerance Respect pack (see Hester and Westermarland 2005, Chapter 2), while a project in Southampton devised its own curriculum materials so that they fitted personal, social and health education (PSHE) guidelines. Projects in Bridgend, Cheshire and Thurrock all made use of drama, with Cheshire being particularly ambitious in its coverage. A further project, in Camden, carried out more limited community awareness work on domestic violence for children and young people.

The projects were evaluated for one or two years. Comparison across the projects indicated that pupils enjoy these types of activity and welcome the opportunity to discuss relationship issues and these activities appear to have some impact on knowledge about violence against women and, possibly, with regard to attitudes. However, the impact may be only short term and is likely to depend on the extent to which the issues are embedded within the curriculum and wider school activities in the longer term. An example of the work is provided in Box 9.5. (For further details, see Hester and Westmarland 2005, Chapter 2).

Box 9.5 Primary school

The project in Cheshire developed a drama piece named Can You Keep a Secret based on story-telling, about a violent relationship within a family and to illustrate points about secret-keeping. The production made links between bullying at school and domestic 'bullying' and was accompanied by workshops, teacher packs, guidance for schools, lesson plans, support around child protection issues, guidance on handling disclosure and teacher training, teacher support and evaluation materials. Support for the productions was provided by a range of local services. They were followed up with children's workshops, class by class, in which the pupils discuss the issues raised in practical ways, alongside special activities and lesson plans. The work was positively received by pupils and their mothers, and there was some evidence of changes in attitudes, increased knowledge about violence in relationships and awareness of bullying.

(Hester and Westmarland 2005, pp.22–23)

Another evaluated UK project, the Healthy Relationships Schools Programme, was developed in northern England (Ellis *et al.* 2006). It was designed for use in schools with children aged 12–13 years on an inner-city housing estate characterized by social exclusion. The focus was on 'positive behaviour in relationships, although issues of gender, power and inequality were also identified' (Ellis *et al.* 2006, p.76). A local theatre company was commissioned to provide a drama production and to develop a series of related workshops, with general emphasis on reflecting PSHE curriculum requirements. Initial evaluation of the programme indicated that it had been effective in increasing awareness and understanding of domestic violence among the pupils involved and that messages about disclosure and help-seeking had also been absorbed. Further evaluation a year after implementation, however, indicated that although some changes had been sustained over time, 'there was also evidence that some of the messages and information from the programme had not been retained' (Ellis *et al.* 2006, p.78). As was the case in the Home Office evaluation (see above), the researchers in this instance also conclude that 'Programmes need to be embedded in the PSHE curriculum if they are to have a long-term impact' (Ellis *et al.* 2006, p.78).

Another finding related to the gender content of the programme. It was found that using an approach that encouraged 'girl power' and 'we can do it too' in the attempt to empower the young women led to a perception that women should use violence and aggression to get their own back. This was clearly problematic in a programme that was attempting to question and reduce the use of such behaviour. The researchers conclude in this respect: 'Future programmes need to address gender issues in an appropriate and sensitive way and be wary of encouraging girls to approve assertive models of behaviour which could encompass violence' (Ellis *et al.* 2006, p.78).

9.18 Summary

- Adults in a variety of settings will encounter children who are living with/have lived with domestic violence. This will include doctors, health visitors, solicitors, social workers, family centre workers, foster/adoptive carers, teachers, youth workers and mental health practitioners.

- Whenever children's behaviour raises anxiety of any kind, or where there are child protection concerns, it is important to bear in mind the possibility that the issue of domestic violence may be an important (and key) aspect of the context for the child. This may be particularly so for children who present with emotional or behavioural difficulties.

- Incorporating an awareness and understanding of domestic violence in this way can enhance practice and improve partnership work with parents because it allows a fuller understanding of the overall family picture.

- It is important to ask children about domestic violence whenever this is possible and appropriate, and it may be necessary to find out or ask over a period of time, as children might be fearful of the consequences of disclosure, and/or protective of their parent(s) and/or have learned to keep the 'family secret' from others.

- When a child discloses experiences of domestic violence, the primary focus must be on safety and protection from abuse.

- The needs of children who have lived with domestic violence are varied and may be affected by factors such as age, race and disability.

- Some children may have learned to excuse their father and blame their mother for the violence and may need interventions that are both supportive and challenging.

- Support for children must be provided by professionals who have an understanding of domestic violence dynamics and of the effects of these on children. The continuum of support needed will range from low-key interventions consisting of validation and affirmation of children's experiences through to long-term therapy.

- Some children, especially those who have also experienced sexual and/or physical abuse from the perpetrator of the domestic violence, will benefit from individual therapeutic work. This work must include a consideration of basic safety needs, an exploration of some of the confusion and ambivalent feelings the violence has evoked, and ensuring that children learn to understand that they are not responsible for the violence.

- Group work is a valuable method of working with children who have experienced domestic violence, especially as children themselves welcome the use of such groups. Such work addresses issues such as breaking the secret, strengthening self-esteem, defining violence and assigning responsibility, protection planning and learning to express feelings.

- In the UK, individual and group work for children who have lived with domestic violence developed initially within refuges and is still in its infancy outside refuges. Several of the children's charities (e.g. NSPCC, Barnardo's, Children's Society) have developed projects to provide these services.

- Primary prevention programmes that aim to examine and change the attitudes, beliefs and behaviours that lead to violent behaviour are becoming more widespread in schools in the UK.

- In some areas, such violence prevention work has been developed further by the production of comprehensive education packs and training modules.

Notes

1   The organizations included Barnardo's, the Children's Society, the NSPCC and NCH Action for Children.

2   Carers now also have a legal responsibility to report if a partner is causing harm to the child (see Chapter Four).

3   The 'champion' was academic Peter Jaffe, who was on the Board of Education for the City of London, Ontario.

CHAPTER TEN

INTERVENTION WITH MALE PERPETRATORS OF DOMESTIC VIOLENCE

Previous chapters have indicated the need for practitioners to take into account the safety of both women and children if children are to be protected from harm. This also necessitates that the activities, behaviour and whereabouts of perpetrators is taken into account.

In the UK, the provision of services to men who are violent to their female partners is a relatively recent development. The provision began to develop partly as a result of policies aiming to increase the criminalization of domestic violence and partly to a growing recognition that more interventions need to be aimed at men as the cause of domestic violence (Hague and Malos 1993; Hester *et al.* 2006; Mullender 1996a). The evidence suggests that tackling domestic violence effectively involves a coordinated approach that includes the victim/survivor, the child(ren) and the perpetrator. Although multi-agency responses to domestic violence have been established for a long time (see Chapter Eleven), the separate development of child protection work on the one hand and domestic violence work on the other (see Chapter Eight) has also meant that these three aspects (victim/survivor, perpetrator, children) are rarely considered together. For instance, in social work practice, little attention has been paid to challenging the behaviour of the violent man (Farmer 2006; Farmer and Owen 1995; Humphreys 1997a; Mullender 1996a; O'Hagan and Dillenburger 1995) (see also Chapter Eight). Moreover, many of the programmes aimed at challenging and changing the behaviour of men who are violent and abusive do not appear to address the impact of men's behaviour on children, even though most of the men concerned are probably fathers (Humphreys *et al.* 2000).

Perpetrator programmes have been the main interventions in the UK to challenge and change the behaviour of men who are violent and abusive, and these are the main focus of this chapter. Such programmes have tended to be run by the voluntary sector or probation services or in partnership with these sectors (Hague, Malos and Dear 1996; Scourfield and Dobash 1999). In 2000, there were around 30 per-petrator programmes, and a mapping survey by Humphreys *et al.* (2000) indicated that most of these were run by probation services. The most rapidly developing area continues to be probation-led, with a new nationwide probation programme having been implemented from 2005. It has to be recognized, however, that probation-based projects will exclude many perpetrators of domestic violence. Only 12 per cent of incidents of domestic violence are ever reported to the police (Walby and Allen 2004), and of those incidents reported only about a quarter result in arrest (Hester 2006a). Consequently, many men do not appear before the courts, and few are placed on probation. Similar problems arise for those voluntary projects taking only court mandated referrals.

Where the probation service already provides group work for male sex offend-ers, it is important to recognize that many of these men will also be perpetrators of domestic violence (see Chapter Two). This will help to avoid perpetuating the false dichotomy between abusers of children and abusers of women, and allow such groups the additional opportunity to tackle men's violence on a wider scale and to make the connections between various misuses of male power. This approach might be useful across all agencies. Hearn (1996b), for instance, asks:

> Would it be appropriate to create (anti-)violence workers who would be able to follow through the inter-agency interventions that are necessary in work-ing against violence? Focusing on men's violence also means taking up the problem of violence in a consistent way throughout agencies.

(Hearn 1996b, p.111)

Men who are violent and abusive to their partners are also likely to come into contact with health services, social care services and other agencies, and this is discussed briefly below.

10.1 Intervention approaches with perpetrators of domestic violence

Any interventions that endeavour to change the behaviour of violent men will, to some extent, be influenced by beliefs about the causes and reasons for this behaviour. There are various theories and explanations of why men are violent to women, some of which are summarized by Scourfield (1995) (see also Hague and Malos (2005) for an overview):

- seeing the violence as biological (men are 'naturally' violent)
- systems theory (emphasises the 'dysfunctional' family unit as the cause of the violence)
- psychodynamic (violence is caused by problems in the man's past)

- social learning (violence is learnt through observation/modelling)
- social structural (violent men are fulfilling their dominant gender role)
- feminist (violence is rooted in patriarchy and in men's need to have power and control over women).

(Scourfield 1995, pp.5–7)

These different perspectives lead to a number of different approaches to working with violent men, which can be broadly categorized as follows:

- anger management

- cognitive behavioural work

- individual therapeutic work

- family therapy work

- pro-feminist approach.

Some of these approaches are examined in more detail in the remainder of this chapter. It will be apparent that different approaches, such as cognitive-behavioural, learning theory and pro-feminist work, may be drawn on within one programme. It has to be recognized that work with violent men, whatever the approach, requires specific skills, which may be somewhat different from the usual social work skills. It is essential, therefore, that adequate training and safety measures are introduced before challenging violent men (RESPECT 2004). O'Hara (1994) points to the need for using only experienced workers for such work. It is also important to be aware of existing agencies that offer programmes for violent men and to make referrals where necessary.

Whoever attempts this work must ensure the centrality of the message that violence is not acceptable and must aim to challenge, stop and prevent further violence. This requires skilful intervention, given that many men deny or minimize their violence (Hearn 1996a) (see also Chapter One) and explain it in terms of anger problems. The UK association for domestic violence perpetrator programmes, RESPECT, states: 'The primary aim in working with perpetrators of domestic violence is to increase the safety of women and children. Every intervention and decision made in this work must be chosen with this in mind' (RESPECT 2004). The secondary aims are to:

- hold men accountable for their violence towards women
- promote respectful egalitarian relationships
- work with others to improve the community's response to domestic violence.

(RESPECT 2004)

There are concerns that perpetrator programmes might give women false, unsafe hopes about staying with or returning to violent partners and that attendance at such programmes may be used in some cases in order to enhance men's positions in contested residence or contact cases (Morley 1993; Mullender 1996a). Attending such groups may also be used as a manipulative ploy by men to gain reconciliation with their partners (e.g. Hester and Radford 1996; Radford and Hester 2006).

There is also concern that the development of services for men will be at the expense of the funding and provision of supportive and protective services for women (Mullender 1996a; Pringle 1995; RESPECT 2004). Other debates have centred around the use of such men's programmes as a diversion from criminal prosecution; some authors are concerned that this may be seen as a 'soft' alternative for men and serves to decrease the seriousness of domestic violence as a crime (Hague and Malos 2005; Mullender 1996a). RESPECT argues that not only is domestic violence a criminal act and a legitimate concern of the criminal justice system, but also projects must ensure that men do not use their attendance on a perpetrator programme to avoid the legal consequences of their behaviour. Projects should engage proactively with criminal justice agencies in order to ensure that this does not happen.

ANGER MANAGEMENT

The use of anger management techniques is deemed inappropriate as a main focus when working with violent men (RESPECT 2004). There is often a confusion among professionals, the judicial system and the general public on the difference between anger management and domestic violence intervention for perpetrators. The real issue in domestic violence is power and control on the part of the perpetrator and not anger, as perpetrators attack or are abusive when their control is threatened. The social learning theory underpinning the anger management approach does not adequately challenge men's assumptions about, and their attempts to use, violence to control and dominate women with whom they have relationships. As Mullender explains:

> An overall objection to the concept of anger management is that it feeds into men's habitual denial and minimisation of their behaviour. A 'problem with my anger'…does not sound criminal, unacceptable or commensurate with the physical and emotional damage inflicted on women.

> *(Mullender 1996a, p.230)*

Barnish (2004), in an overview of the relevant research, also comments that poor control of anger is not the main problem for many perpetrators:

> The finding that the heart rates of some domestic violence perpetrators decrease, indicating inner calm and possible feelings of disgust, whilst these men are simultaneously looking and sounding angry, aggressive and

contemptuous towards their partners...suggests that for this group at least, poor control of anger arousal is not part of their problem.

(Barnish 2004, p.107)

10.2 Interventions with violent men: individualist approaches

In the USA and Canada, there has been a longer history of agencies providing services to men who are violent to their female partners. The early programmes tended to adopt models of intervention that were mostly informed by the more individualist theories of male violence. Adams (1988) provides an overview of these earlier clinical treatment models, which he labels the 'insight model', the 'ventilation model', the 'interaction model', the 'cognitive-behavioural model' and the 'psychoeducational model'. All of these models are criticized for not taking into account gender and power, overly empathizing with men and not necessarily placing responsibility for the violence with the man: '...some of these approaches collude with batterers by not making their violence the primary issue or by implicitly legitimizing men's excuses for violence' (Adams 1988, p.177).

These approaches also reflect what Dobash and Dobash (1992) refer to as the 'therapeutic society', which they see as especially prominent in North America. This is characterized by the belief that all social, economic and political problems are seen to be rooted in individual difficulties that can be solved through therapy. These individualist approaches are seen to be problematic in work with violent men because they are not adequately challenging of men's behaviour:

> Despite their apparent diversity, therapeutic approaches to violent men have a number of common elements...the basic assumption is that the fundamental cause of violence is faulty personality or psychopathology... No individual man is accountable for his violence; the family, faulty backgrounds or situational factors are the causes.

(Dobash and Dobash 1992, p.239)

Mullender (1996a) echoes Dobash and Dobash's concerns about another individualist model of male violence, used especially in earlier American interventions. This can be broadly categorized as the intrapsychic model, which explains men's violence in terms of unresolved past problems and is problematic in that it can lead to collusion by absolving men of accepting responsibility for their current abusive actions through focusing on past experiences as excuses. This is not to say that issues from the past might not need to be addressed, but that this needs to be done separately from the focus on their violence.

Some of the earlier perpetrator interventions in the UK also relied on more individualistic or couple therapy-oriented approaches. Malloch and Webb (1993) identified these interventions as largely 'non-focused' statutory-sector provision,[1] consisting of social workers or probation officers who worked with male offenders as part of their generic caseload but whose interventions were not designed to deal exclusively with domestic violence. Malloch and Webb found that the 'non-focused' workers tended to view domestic violence as a result of individual inadequacies and/or problems within the relationship itself. This 'curing and caring' (p.140) approach was aimed at changing individual psychological processes, even possibly leading to reconciliation: '...the focus of work tends to be directed at improving the functioning of the male abuser or altering the functional dynamics of the relationship through marital therapy' (p.125).

Research in the UK into violent men's 'help-seeking' strategies (Hester *et al.* 2006) indicates that perpetrators who seek help from their general practitioners may be referred for individual counselling or therapy, which is likely to be inappropriate in such circumstances. The perpetrators interviewed as part of the study also indicated they had not found the individual counselling sessions very useful in tackling their abusive behaviour. Rather than disclosing their violent behaviour, some perpetrators attempted to position themselves as 'sad' (depressed) or 'mad' (in need of psychological or psychiatric care), with a resultant focus on 'poor me' rather than on their unacceptable behaviour.

10.3 Coordinated community approach to domestic violence and violent men

Because men's denial and minimization of violence are so entrenched and widespread (Cavanagh *et al.* 2001; Hearn 1996a; Henning, Jones and Holdford 2005; Ptacek 1988), and because so many see violence as a legitimate way of dealing with their female partners, it is vital that any interventions aimed at changing their behaviour are challenging and do not allow men to avoid any of the responsibility for their actions. This is the philosophy underpinning the pro-feminist model of work with violent men, which, in addition, combines empowering work for women. This approach was first developed in 1977 in Boston, Massachusetts, by EMERGE, established in close cooperation with the local women's shelter. This led to the establishment of other pro-feminist men's programmes, such as RAVEN. Both EMERGE and RAVEN have had projects across the USA.

One of the most well-known examples of a coordinated approach to domestic violence is the Domestic Abuse Prevention Project in Duluth, Minnesota, which combines empowering support services for women with programmes for violent men. It also coordinates the work of the police, courts, social services and women's shelters and attempts to inform practice and policy initiatives on domestic violence issues (Dobash and Dobash 1992; Paymar 2000; Pence and Paymar 1993). Some programmes include parenting groups for violent men as part of their domestic abuse programmes (see Mathews (1995) for a more detailed account of one such group). Thus, these programmes have far-ranging aims, including attempting to educate and inform the wider public, ensuring the safety of women and challenging individual men. Similar coordinated approaches, based on the Duluth model, have been established in other parts of the world: see Busch and Robertson (1994) for an example in New Zealand and Frances (1995) for an overview of community programmes in Australia. The Duluth Model, based on the Domestic Abuse Intervention Project (DAIP) in Duluth, Minnesota, is a community-based program for intervention in domestic abuse cases. The model sets out to be comprehensive in focusing on victim safety, incorporating and co-ordinating the responses of the many agencies and practitioners involved in responding to domestic violence within a locality. 'The project involves community organizing and advocacy that examines training programs, policies, procedures and texts – intake forms, report formats, assessments, evaluations, checklists and other materials' (Pence undated). It looks at how each practice, procedure, form or brochure is geared to either enhance or to compromise victim's safety.

At the heart of the approach is the safety of women and children, and the work with perpetrators is geared to this end.

The coordinated approach, and especially the Duluth model, has also underpinned most of the developments in the UK, as outlined below, although the model has rarely been implemented in its entirety (see also Scourfield and Dobash 1999).

10.4 UK programmes for violent men

In Britain, specific projects to work with violent men have, since the early 1990s, developed in a variety of ways and adopted a range of models of approaches (Humphreys et al. 2000; Malloch and Webb 1993; Radford, Blacklock and Iwi 2006; Scourfield 1995). Some of the earlier examples developed as part of wider and generic social work and probation work, such as AGENDA in Nottingham and the Domestic Violence Intervention Project (DVIP) in London, have drawn on the ideas of the Duluth project. The DVIP was the first to provide two linked services for supporting women and for challenging men. There have also been several Men Overcoming Violence (MOVE) groups throughout the country as well as other interagency and independent schemes, such as the Everyman Centre in Plymouth. The latter project (now called AHIMSA) was financed jointly by the local health authority and social services department, with some central government funding from the Department of Health, rather than from probation partnership funding. It also ran a parallel support service for women. It worked mostly with men who self-referred. Some initiatives have stemmed from interagency projects. These include the IMPACT project in Derby, run directly by the interagency forum and again based on the Duluth model. Similarly, Cleveland's domestic violence forum has run groups for male perpetrators and set up a women's support group to run in tandem with the men's programme (Hague, Malos and Dear 1996).

The UK mapping survey by Humphreys et al. (2000) found that of the 19 active programmes that responded, all but one referred to the Duluth model as a major influence, and nine respondents had gleaned their detailed knowledge from the

Scottish CHANGE manual (Morran and Wilson 1997), itself influenced by the Duluth model. All 19 respondents had direct links with support services for women, 15 running their own linked partner support and all providing information about relevant services for women and children. The most common self-description by projects was 'educational', with 16 projects giving this as a total or combined description. Fifteen groups said their main aim was increasing the safety of women and children, 13 that they existed to challenge or change men's attitudes to violence, and 11 that they aimed to reduce the risk of reoffending.

Over the years projects have varied in structure and approach in terms of the source of referrals (self-referral or court mandated, or both), the amount of involvement of and accountability to women survivors, and the philosophy that informs the work. More recently, some projects have added work with children, such as counselling support or raising awareness in schools, with examples being Safer Families in Gateshead, the NSPCC Domestic Violence Prevention Service in Cardiff (Rees and Rivett 2005) and the Preston Road Domestic Violence Project in Hull (Ellis *et al.* 2006). The DVIP in London has also developed work in conjunction with social care services in order to provide risk assessment in child protection cases (Radford *et al.* 2006).

As indicated earlier, the largest growth in programmes has been led in the past few years by the probation service. Again borrowing some aspects from the Duluth model, a so-called 'pathfinder' programme, the Integrated Domestic Abuse Programme (IDAP), was accredited in 2003 by the Correctional Services Accreditation Panel. This programme has been rolled out across the UK and is expected to operate within a multi-agency risk-management infrastructure. The programme is tightly organized, with set exercises and activities provided in a programme manual. The aim of the programme is to 'challenge the attitudes and beliefs of perpetrators…and require offenders to take responsibility for their actions and the effects on others by addressing offence minimisation and victim blaming' (Bilby and Hatcher 2004, p.2).

The development of the IDAP recognizes the importance of interventions with perpetrators of domestic violence and provides a welcome increase in such interventions. An evaluation of the pilot projects for the IDAP by Bilby and Hatcher (2004) expressed concerns, however, that the women's support services are not adequately staffed or may not be provided at all. Other authors have been concerned that the staffing levels required to run the programme may have been underestimated (RESPECT 2004). Rees and Rivett (2005), moreover, criticize the standardization of programmes that result from the IDAP, arguing that there are different types of abuser, who need different approaches, and that services for perpetrators thus need to be 'broad and inclusive' rather than the more narrowly defined 'criminal justice centred and highly prescribed' (p.278) approach of the new court mandated probation programme.

10.5 Running programmes for violent men in the UK: a pro-feminist approach

Mullender (1996a) and Adams (1988) outline the pro-feminist model as using cognitive-behavioural techniques in order to achieve individual change and the acceptance of individual responsibility. This is coupled with an educational element that places the violence in a social/structural context in order to challenge assumptions about men and women, while maintaining the centrality of power and control issues (see also Bowen, Brown and Gilchrist 2002). The emphasis is working in a group, as this allows the men's behaviours and responses to be challenged more effectively. Similar approaches have also been developed by therapists working individually with violent men where it is required that men take full responsibility for their actions (e.g. Jenkins 1990).

Adams (1988) provides a detailed account of how a group work programme based on these premises may develop. This involves a very directive approach from the workers, including the following:

- Initial counselling groups concentrate on the safety of the woman, with men being asked to devise 'safety plans' in order to minimize the possibility of further violence.

- Separate contact is made with the woman and she is offered support.

- Men are confronted about their minimization or denial of responsibility for the violence, including examining their excuses and reasons for violence.

- Men's other controlling and abusive behaviour patterns are identified.

- Men are asked to keep 'control logs' to make them more accountable for their behaviour.

- Video-taped exercises are used to show the controlling behaviour.

The RESPECT guidelines, providing a current national standard for work with perpetrators, states that the focus of perpetrator programmes should involve:

- an understanding of what constitutes violent behaviour
- that the perpetrator is 100% responsible for his behaviour
- that violent behaviour is a choice
- that violent behaviour is functional and intentional
- to challenge tactics which seek to deny minimise and/or blame
- to challenge and change the attitudes and beliefs which support his violence
- to acknowledge and question the social and gendered context of domestic violence
- to challenge men's expectations of power and control over partners

- to develop men's capacity to understand the impact of his violence on his partner and children both in the long and short term
- to learn and adopt positive, respectful and egalitarian ways of being
- the focus of intervention should be on men as perpetrators and not as victims
- projects should avoid collusion with the perpetrator's rationale.

(RESPECT 2004, reproduced with permission)

RESPECT suggests that the duration of programmes should be at least 75 hours over a minimum of 30 weeks and argues that less than this is 'potentially harmful'. Group work must be delivered by at least two facilitators, one male and one female.

10.6 Effectiveness of programmes for violent men

There are many questions still to be answered about the effectiveness of men's programmes, both in terms of whether they promote the safety of women and children and whether, and in what ways, they can achieve change in the behaviour of violent men. Few services have any systematic means of monitoring their efficacy, and there are difficulties in determining what constitutes 'success' and by whom this should be decided (Gondolf 2002; Humphreys *et al.* 2000; Mullender 1996a; Scourfield 1995). For instance, using criminal justice records to measure the impact of programmes by looking at patterns of reoffending will cover only activities and behaviours that are arrestable and relies on incidents being reported. Asking partners whether there have been further incidents is probably the most accurate measure of whether violence or abuse has re-occurred, but it is difficult (and may be unethical) to elicit such information over a longer period. There is also the concern that regardless of whether attendance in such programmes is court mandated or voluntary, the men attending programmes represent only a very small fraction of perpetrators of domestic violence. Any claims of success or otherwise need to be viewed, therefore, with some caution. None the less, the evaluation research indicates that the violent behaviour of some men can be changed through interventions with perpetrators and, in particular, through the use of programmes. As Dobash and colleagues conclude from a consideration of 30 perpetrator programme evaluations:

> On the basis of arrest records and the self-reports of offenders, many researchers and professionals conclude that most men do not use violence while participating on these treatment programmes and 50–80 per cent remain violence free for up to one year or more after programme completion.

(Dobash et al. 1999, p.109)

EVALUATIONS OF PROGRAMMES FOR VIOLENT MEN

Since the mid-1990s, there have been a small number of in-depth independent evaluations of UK programmes for violent men. Dobash *et al.* (1996, 1999) evaluated two such programmes in Scotland – CHANGE, established in the former Central Region of Scotland in 1989, and the Lothian Domestic Violence Probation Project (LDVPP), established in Edinburgh in 1990. In England, Burton *et al.* (1998) carried out an evaluation of the DVIP, based in West London, and the associated Women's Support Service (WSS) and Violence Prevention Programme (VPP). Skyner and Waters (1999) evaluated the Cheshire probation programme, involving a very small sample, and Bowen (2004) evaluated a probation programme in the Midlands as part of her doctoral work. More recently, Bilby and Hatcher (2004) evaluated the process of implementing the pilots for the probation IDAP programme, and Bell and Stanley (2005) carried out a partial evaluation of the perpetrator project attached to the Preston Road Domestic Violence Project in Hull.[2] In the USA, there have also been a number of evaluations of perpetrator programmes, the most significant being the multi-site evaluation by Gondolf and colleagues (see Dobash *et al.* 1999).

In this section, the evaluations by Dobash *et al.* (1996, 1999), Burton *et al.* (1998) and Gondolf (2000) are considered further, as these provide more detailed knowledge about the effectiveness of, and what works with regard to, perpetrator programmes.

The programmes evaluated by Dobash and colleagues were both based within the criminal justice system: men attended the programmes on a mandatory basis as a condition of their probation orders, following convictions for violent offences against their female partners. In order to assess the effectiveness of the programmes, the outcomes of the programmes were compared with those for offenders given traditional sanctions, such as fines, probation and prison sentences. Parallel information was obtained from some of the partners and ex-partners of the offenders. In all cases, data were collected at three stages: at the point of imposition of the criminal justice sanction, at three months and at 12 months. Attendance at the programmes occurred every week for a period of six to seven months and consisted of a structured, challenging cognitive-behavioural group work approach.

Dobash and colleagues found overall that all criminal justice sanctions had some positive effects in terms of the reduction of further violence. However, in comparison with those men given traditional sanctions, the programmes for violent men were most successful in changing men's behaviour. According to their partners, this applied in relation to a reduction in the violent behaviour, in the frequency of violent episodes and to overall improvements in their controlling and intimidating behaviour, all of which led to an enhanced quality of life for the women involved. In the longer term, although there had been a reduction in violence, a third of the men (33%) in the programme had committed at least one further violent act against their partners by the end of the 12-month follow-up period. Although men may benefit from talking explicitly about their violence, and can learn to accept some responsibility for their behaviour, it is clear that women and children cannot be guaranteed their safety during the process of such programmes or, indeed, afterwards.

The aspects of the group work that men found most helpful were:

- group discussions focusing on minimization and denial
- group discussions to identify 'triggers' to violence
- video work to show well-known scenes
- learning to take 'timeout' to prevent a violent episode.

The DVIP programme in West London, evaluated by Burton and colleagues, was different in that men could be accepted on to the VPP on either a court mandated or voluntary basis. Unlike the Scottish projects, the DVIP also ran, from separate premises, a linked WSS offering empowering support work for women in order to maximize their safety. Both the projects were evaluated by the research team by means of a multistage approach using questionnaires and in-depth interviews with violent men, the men's female partners, probation officers and staff from both projects. This was supplemented by analysis of group sessions and group reports.

The proactive support offered to women through the WSS was seen to be a crucial part of the overall programme aims of the DVIP, the aims being both to stop men's use of violence and to increase the safety of women. The work provided includes one-to-one work, group work and advocacy and explores issues such as self-esteem and the impact of violence on children. An important area of development in the DVIP was to integrate children's issues into all areas of its work (see also Radford *et al.* 2006).

Burton and colleagues found that for some women, involvement with the WSS had been 'successful' in a variety of ways, including:

- providing women with the opportunity to end the relationship safely
- providing women with the opportunity to renegotiate their relationships
- providing women with 'breathing space'
- enabling women to build stronger support networks.

The VPP aspect of the project consisted of a two-stage programme of group work over a 32-week period. The first 12 weeks of the programme focused on men's physical violence, and the following 20 weeks explored other aspects of men's abusive and violent behaviours, with the possibility of continued work after this.

Again, there was tentative evidence of the programme achieving some 'success', as some women reported that the violence stopped. For other women, there was a decrease in physical violence but not in other forms of abuse. This was a complex issue, as it is unclear whether other forms of violence increased, or whether they were more obvious once the physical violence was less, or whether attendance at the WSS had enabled women to define more of their partner's behaviour as 'abusive'. Other women benefited from the freedom and space provided them by their partner's attendance at the programme.

The evaluation of the men's programme raised a number of concerns, including the following:

- The attrition rate for both voluntary and court mandated attendance was extremely high, with only a minority of men completing the programme.

- Court mandated men who dropped out of the programme were dealt with leniently, by the imposition of fines, often paid by their female partners (as is the case when men break injunctions – see Chapter Six).

- Men were often motivated to attend the programme by hopes of reconciliation or to prevent the woman from leaving, rather than to change their behaviour.

- The programme provided no certainty that violence would not recur in the future.

- Men were selected for the programme only if they accepted their violent behaviour and took some responsibility for it. It is, therefore, not possible to generalize from the findings.

On the basis of their evaluation, Burton and colleagues make some suggestions about work with violent men, including the following:

- The safety of women and children must be central to any programme for violent men.

- Separate parallel support programmes for women are vital.

- Men's motivation needs to be explored and moved forward early in the programme.

- 'Voluntary' referrals to programmes are important, as these men may be the most motivated and the best investment and may have a positive influence on other men in the group.

The study by Gondolf (2000, 2001) in the USA is probably the most comprehensive evaluation to date, involving comparisons across four sites and over time, following perpetrators for up to four years. The study looked at the location of perpetrator or 'batterer' programmes within a wider 'intervention system' comprising criminal justice (arrests, court actions, probation supervision), involvement of victim services and other community services. The study concluded that the 'system' is particularly important – that is, the quality of the links between, and ability to respond by, agencies: 'Batterer programme outcome is, for instance, likely to be improved with swift and certain court referral, periodic court review or specialized probation surveillance, and ongoing risk management' (Gondolf 2001, p.199).

There were no major differences in outcomes between longer, more comprehensive programmes, and shorter, more streamlined programmes. Using gender-based cognitive-behavioural approaches was still deemed most effective, even if there was little information on which particular aspects of the counselling interventions work.

Overall, the study found that the majority of men enrolled in perpetrator programmes were affected positively by the intervention and stopped their violence for a sustained period of time. Focusing on physical assault as the measurement, nearly half the men re-assaulted their partners during the four-year follow-up period, but most did so within nine months of starting the programme. Two and half years after the programme, more than 80 per cent of the men had not re-assaulted in the previous year, and after four years more than 90 per cent of the men had not re-assaulted in the previous year. Thus, a majority of men appeared to have stopped their physical violence.

There were, however, about 20 per cent of men who repeatedly re-assaulted their partners during the follow-up period. Repeat assaulters were difficult to distinguish from those who were not: past violence, alcoholism and psychopathology were significant risk factors but have weak predictive powers. This was the group where the 'system' was most important, with the evaluation indicating that swifter, more intensive intervention by the system as a whole might deal better with this group:[3] 'Swifter and more certain court action, more sessions per week after intake, ongoing risk management, and other containment options might contribute to stopping repeat reassault and the danger it carries' (Gondolf 2001, p.213).

On the basis of his research, Gondolf (2000) recommends that perpetrator programmes include:

- funding to support coordination of system linkages and cooperation

- use of ethical decision-making (going beyond immediate effectives) in funding decisions

- continued use of gender-based cognitive-behavioural counselling

- emphasis on intensity rather than length of programmes, especially with regard to repeat assaulters

- effective screening of participants, especially with regard to severe alcohol and psychological problems.

Overall, the evaluations of perpetrator programmes suggest that the programmes, whatever their limitations, can have a positive impact. Moreover, although there is still much to learn about how and if violent men's behaviour can change, there are indications that this might best be achieved in coordinated, multifaceted responses to domestic violence.

10.7 Help-seeking by and intervention with perpetrators of domestic violence

Usually, it is the help-seeking strategies of victims/survivors of domestic violence and abuse that are the focus of research and policy (Hester and Westmarland 2005). This is not surprising, and is also correct, given that any attempt at ensuring the safety of women and children from violent men has to build on an understanding of the different strategies that victims/survivors adopt. It has become apparent, however, that looking at the help-seeking that perpetrators of domestic violence may adopt can also be useful in ensuring more effective, and possibly earlier, intervention to stop their violent behaviour.

Interviews with 62 male perpetrators of domestic violence, carried out to examine help-seeking pathways and potential opportunities for early intervention and prevention, were carried out as part of research by the University of Bristol and the Home Office (Hester *et al.* 2006). Most of the men interviewed were or had been on a perpetrator programme, and a small group were in prison. On average, each man had been in contact with three agencies, and some with up to nine different agencies, before they took part in a perpetrator programme. Specifically, of the 45 men interviewed by the Home Office team (in addition to the 26 men who had had contact with the police in relation to domestic violence):

- 32 men stated that they had been to their general practitioner before beginning the domestic violence programme

- 13 men had had contact with Relate, 11 with social services, six with the Samaritans, five with hospitals, five with alcohol services and four with drugs services

- some men had also been in contact with services such as counselling, legal aid or solicitors, and welfare services at work.

This indicates the importance of agencies being aware that men who seek or are referred to them for help may be perpetrators of domestic violence, even if this is not immediately apparent. However, of the 72 agencies interviewed as part of the research, many said that they did not refer perpetrators on because they were not aware of services or there were no local services to refer them on to.

Some men had contacted agencies directly due to their violent behaviour and appeared to have been explicit about this and that they wanted some help:

> I actually punched the wife...we have our arguments but after doing that it was something I never want to do again, so she went to her sister's and I went to the doctor and asked where I could go for help.
>
> *(Wade, quoted in Hester et al. 2006, p.12)*

These men appeared in general to have located the relevant service more easily. There were cases, however, where violence appeared to have been mentioned (taking into consideration the difficulties with men's accounts of their actions, in that they often minimize or deny their actions – see also Chapter One) but the agencies involved were unable to refer to an existing programme for perpetrators of domestic violence. The issue of timeliness was important, particularly for men whose help-seeking was tentative and commitment to change questionable. For example, a delay in getting on to a perpetrator programme was a concern for men who felt ready to engage immediately.

A number of men came into contact with agencies reactively. This was often contact with the police but in some cases was related to child contact issues (e.g. social services or CAFCASS). Contact with the police gave rise to potential conflict between enforcement and holding perpetrators to account or providing advice and referral. None the less, some men did suggest that a sanction, or the threat or consequence of sanction, gave them the incentive to initiate help-seeking:

> I was having problems at home, I would be violent and abusive and I decided that I needed to change. I was arrested by the police and banned from my own pub, so I decided that I needed to change.

> *(Noel, quoted in Hester et al. 2006, p.13)*

Where it was not apparent to agencies that the men were violent, the agencies would have needed to actively elicit disclosure of the behaviour in order for the behaviour to be brought into the open.

Some men contacted agencies with which they were familiar but without being explicit about their violence. This was the case in relation to general practitioners, to whom some men said they had reported problems with anger or other ailments, most commonly depression or 'feeling low' or 'down'. As indicated in Section 10.2, some men indicated that their general practitioners simply prescribed antidepressants or referred the men to inappropriate counselling services. Health practitioners surveyed tended not to feel that they had an obvious response to perpetrators of domestic violence. They recognized that it was inevitable that some of their clients were domestic abusers, but they did not see themselves as doing any focused work with such perpetrators or did not know how to identify them.

Methods to identify domestic violence as an issue, to facilitate readiness to change and to increase awareness of relevant other agencies for referral, and the capacity for this to be done without substantial delay, are highly relevant to enabling violent men to move towards points of change. Practitioners who may come into contact with perpetrators need the skills to ask about violent and abusive behaviour and to know how and where to make appropriate referrals. Moreover, there appear to be certain moments, or 'triggers to change', when there is a greater possibility that the men might be prepared to change their behaviour and where intervention is likely to be more effective. Research has found that these moments tended to be when the partner threatened to leave, or actually left. Child contact issues were also given as a reason for help-seeking. Sometimes, involvement by the police following an incident might have the same effect. As one man stated: 'My wife just said, "I have had enough. You either sort it out or we are going to have to go our separate ways." I did not want to lose my wife and children' (Noel, quoted in Hester *et al.* 2006, p.10).

It has to be recognized, however, that the period when a woman leaves or threatens to leave a violent partner has been identified as especially dangerous and the man is more likely to use or increase his violence (see Chapter One). Using such crisis moments to intervene with domestically abusive men, therefore, needs especially careful approaches and safety planning with or in relation to the women concerned (Hester *et al.* 2006).

10.8 Summary

- Programmes to challenge and change the behaviour of men who have been violent to female partners are still developing in the UK. As yet, many programmes do not appear to specifically address the impact of men's behaviour on children.

- The safety of women and children needs to be central to any programmes and other interventions for violent men, and programmes should offer separate parallel support for women.

- Programmes alone may be ineffective in achieving change in the behaviour of violent men and must be accompanied by effective legal sanctions and wider agency links.

- Men's denial and minimization of violence are entrenched, as is the notion that violence is a legitimate way for men to deal with their female partners.

- Approaches based on cognitive-behavioural approaches that also take into account gender are more likely to be effective.

- Regardless of the approach adopted, work with violent men requires specific skills. A central feature of this work must be the message that violence is not acceptable and must aim to challenge, stop and prevent further violence.

- Independent evaluations in the UK and USA of programmes for violent men have shown that the programmes have some success in changing men's behaviour and in increasing women's safety in a variety of ways.

- A wide range of agencies may have perpetrators of domestic violence as their clients, and practitioners in health, social care and other services need to develop the skills to ask perpetrators about violent and abusive behaviour as well as knowing where to refer them.

Notes

1   This was in contrast to the 'focused' approach of specialist projects that required interventions with high levels of 'challenging and confronting' of male attitudes about women (Malloch and Webb 1993, p.140).

2   A seven-year evaluation is currently under way in the UK involving perpetrator programmes in Gateshead and Cumbria. The evaluation will be completed in 2012, although interim findings will be available. (See www.nr-foundation.org.uk)

3   Research in the UK by Hester *et al.* (2006) found that criminal justice intervention with groups of male perpetrators who are serious repeat assaulters was often limited (with only one in ten being convicted of a criminal offence, and often resulting only in conditional discharge or a fine) and a general lack of a coordinated, let alone intensive, approach. About a fifth of those convicted (relating to 2% of incidents) were given community rehabilitation sentences, including attendance at a perpetrator programme.

CHAPTER ELEVEN

MULTI-AGENCY INVOLVEMENT AND COOPERATION IN RELATION TO DOMESTIC VIOLENCE

Women and children who are experiencing domestic violence, and the perpetrators who abuse them, may be in contact with a wide range of service providers. Research has shown consistently the importance of all services providing a coordinated approach to domestic violence in order to ensure that women and children are protected and supported (Diamond, Charles and Allen 2004; Hague, Malos and Dear 1996; Hester and Westmarland 2005). There have also been clear indications from child protection inquiries and Part 8 reviews (e.g. the report concerning Sukina Hammond, discussed in Chapter Two) of the dangers of the failure of agencies to work together in practice, particularly in relation to children living with domestic violence.

As discussed in Chapter Eight, historically the abuse of women and the abuse of children in the family (but by the same man) have been viewed as separate issues. This separation has tended to be replicated in the multi-agency initiatives that have developed in Britain since the 1990s. Multi-agency domestic violence forums have developed with an emphasis on the experiences of women victims/survivors, while multi-agency area child protection committees (ACPCs) have focused on children and their protection. Until recently, the issue of children and domestic violence has been mostly absent from multi- or interagency policies at a national level, in relation to both ACPCs and domestic violence forums, although a series of policy-related initiatives and reports have highlighted the need for a shared agenda regarding children and families living with domestic violence (Department for Education and Skills 2005; HMSO 1998; Home Office 2004; Stanley and Humphreys 2006). In particular, the new 'safeguarding' agenda in relation to children (Department for Education and Skills 2005; see Section 4.7 of this book), which supersedes ACPCs by safeguarding boards, is underpinned by a recognition that multi-agency links are crucial in order for children to be adequately protected against harm.

This chapter examines three areas of multi-agency working on domestic violence: the development of ACPCs into safeguarding boards, multi-agency domestic violence forums, and community safety or crime and disorder reduction partnerships.

11.1 From multi-agency ACPCs to local children's safeguarding boards

In the field of child protection, multi- or interagency cooperation has been operating since 1974 but was established in a more consistent and coordinated way in the wake of the Department of Health's *Working Together Under the Children Act* guidance (Home Office, Department of Health, Department for Education and Skills and Welsh Office 1991) (see also Atkinson 1996). By the late 1990s, there were approximately 150 ACPCs, covering every local authority in England, but they varied considerably in structure, funding and effectiveness (Hester *et al.* 2000).

In ACPC annual reports from 1992 onwards, there is evidence of an increasing awareness of domestic violence as an issue of concern for children, although there is less evidence concerning effective intervention (Atkinson 1996; Mullender 1998). There was also recognition by the Department of Health of the importance of interagency cooperation involving both ACPCs and domestic violence forums: 'In view of our increased understanding of the links between domestic violence and child protection, we need to think further about how ACPCs and Domestic Violence Fora can work together more effectively' (Department of Health 1998, p.11).

Mullender (1998) has argued that ACPCs were quite late in recognizing the needs of children who have lived in circumstances of domestic violence, and needed to develop more child-centred coordinated responses along the lines of those already in existence in Canada and the USA (see Chapter Nine). By the late 1990s, some ACPCs were beginning to develop initiatives to address this issue, including multi-agency training events, which have drawn on the expertise of children's workers in refuges as well as on a range of other professional and academic sources. The UK-wide mapping survey by Humphreys *et al.* (2000) found that in half the local authorities in England and Wales, and in 70 per cent in Northern Ireland, the local ACPC had representation from the domestic violence forum. The evaluations of the Crime Reduction Programme for domestic violence projects (Hester and Westmarland 2005) also indicated that ACPCs were increasingly incorporating work on domestic violence in order to produce safer and better outcomes for children.

Since April 2006, local safeguarding children boards (LSCBs) have been established to replace ACPCs. The Children Act 2004 requires that LSCBs are set up within each local authority to ensure greater coordination between agencies and, therefore, greater effectiveness in child protection and harm prevention. The lead responsibility for children experiencing domestic violence is now centred on the

Director and Lead Member for Children's Services and Local Safeguarding Children Boards (Local Government Association 2005).

The LSCBs were developed largely in response to the Laming Inquiry (2003), which criticized the lack of effective coordination between and intervention by agencies with regard to Victoria Climbie, murdered by her aunt and her aunt's partner. Although a number of local agencies had been involved with the family, including the police and social care services, Lord Laming identified a lack of coordinated response as well as a lack of executive authority. Laming concludes: 'More exhortation that services should work better together manifestly is not enough. Actual change is required if the safety and welfare of children is not to depend to an unacceptable degree on the personal working relationships of individual professionals' (Laming Inquiry 2003, p.1; see also Victoria Climbie Inquiry (Laming 2003), paragraphs 17.92 and 17.93).

Identifying the need for the establishment of new committees with greater authority, dedicated resources and more effective representation than the existing ACPCs, Lord Laming laid the foundations for the new LSCBs by recommending:

> At a local level every local authority with social services responsibilities should appoint a member committee for children and families and members should be drawn from each of the key services of Education, Police, Probation, Health, Primary Care, Social Services etc. Reporting to this committee must be a local board of management for services for children and families, chaired by the chief executive and with senior managers from each of the key services. The management board must identify the needs in their area, the resources available to meet those needs and to be accountable for the quality of the outcomes for children.
>
> *(Laming Inquiry 2003, p.1)*

Unlike the previous ACPCs, the LSCBs are statutory and have a wider remit that includes prevention of harm to children as well as protection of children. Statutory agencies from the criminal justice, health, education and family proceedings sectors are required to take part in addition to other children's services. As the guidance for commissioners of children's services points out, 'The list of local partnerships and services which need to collaborate effectively to address domestic violence is impressive' (Local Government Association 2005). The structural context is also defined clearly:

> The Local Strategic Partnership is the overarching partnership in each local authority area. Within this sits the Community Safety or Crime and Disorder Reduction Partnership, the Supporting People Commissioning Board, the Local Safeguarding Children Board and Children's Strategic Partnership. The Local Criminal Justice Board, the Local Family Justice Council,

multi-agency public protection arrangements (MAPPA) and arrangements to protect vulnerable adults (POVA) all have a part to play.

(Local Government Association 2005, executive summary)

The establishment of more extensive and comprehensive multi-agency working through the safeguarding agenda should mean that we are about to see a new direction in social care and other responses, which includes a more 'holistic' framework, involving work with children, adult victims/survivors and perpetrators, and where children's services plans include this wider perspective.

11.2 Development of multi-agency domestic violence forums

Hague and Malos (1993, 2005) and Hague, Malos and Dear (1996) have charted the relatively long history of multi- and interagency responses to domestic violence in Britain, showing that from the 1970s, Women's Aid groups attempted to work with the support of the statutory agencies. More coordinated and formal approaches to multi-agency developments began in the 1980s, mostly at local authority level. By the end of the 1980s, local innovative multi- or interagency projects had been established in several areas, notably Leeds, Nottingham, Wolverhampton and Hammersmith and Fulham. These have since become model examples for others to follow (see Hague and Malos 2005).

Developments at a national level in multi-agency domestic violence work date from the mid-1980s and in the 1990s were particularly influenced and promoted by several important policy documents and reports, including:

- the National Inter-Agency Working Party Report on Domestic Violence (Victim Support 1992)

- a Home Office (1990) circular encouraging an improved police response to domestic violence and the establishment of local domestic violence forums

- the Home Affairs Select Committee (1993) inquiry into domestic violence

- a Home Office (1995b) circular on interagency work and domestic violence

- a Department of Health (1997) circular on the responsibilities of local authorities in relation to the Family Law Act 1996, which noted the importance of interagency cooperation with regard to domestic violence and child protection, and recommended the setting up of domestic violence forums where these did not already exist.

All of this activity led to the establishment of many local multi-agency initiatives, many of which were developed further by means of criminal justice agendas, such as the Crime Prevention and Safer Cities projects and, more recently, the Crime Reduction Programme (Hester and Westmarland 2005) and crime and disorder reduction partnerships (CDRPs) (Home Office 2005). Multi-agency initiatives have also underpinned the development of specialist domestic violence courts (Cook *et al.*2004).

As outlined in Chapter Nine, in some localities, services for children who have lived with domestic violence have developed directly from the multi- or interagency forums. These include violence prevention programmes in schools and support groups for children. Both Hague, Malos and Dear (1996), in their study of multi-agency working, and Humphreys *et al.* (2000), in their mapping of UK provision for families experiencing domestic violence, found that some domestic violence forums had children's needs subgroups engaging in joint work, usually with social services and local children's charities. Cleveland's multi-agency domestic violence forum had such a subgroup, which worked with local children's charities, refuge workers, social services and education departments in order to develop innovative work with and for children. This included the production of policies on children and domestic violence and interagency procedures and practice guidance for the local ACPC. The group also worked to improve the funding and provision of children's workers in refuges. Similar initiatives on domestic violence and child protection have been and continue to be apparent elsewhere in the country. With the development of LSCBs, it may be that such work decreases within domestic violence forums, although the links continue to be crucial.

Below, we provide some evidence of what constitutes good practice in relation to multi-agency working and also some of the pitfalls. For further discussion of the history and development of multi-agency domestic violence forums, see Hague and Malos (2005).

11.3 Work of multi-agency domestic violence forums

Hague, Malos and Dear (1996) carried out some of the only UK-wide research on multi-agency responses to domestic violence. The research focused on the structure of the agencies, the work done and issues of power and equality. The research also assessed the role of Women's Aid refuges and examined the involvement of survivors of domestic violence. Children were not the main focus of the study, but there were some findings in relation to their welfare, which are discussed here.

The study identified the existence, by the mid-1990s, of around 200 multi-agency domestic violence initiatives, which varied considerably in structure and in the extent and nature of their activities. A few initiatives had funding to employ coordinators, but others had no funding at all, leading to difficulties with continuity and effective development work. There were also differences in the range of agencies represented. Aspects of multi-agency forums that were found to be important included the following:

- liaison, networking and the sharing of information, including each agency educating the other agencies on its work in relation to domestic violence

- coordinating local services, including the production of good practice guidelines and resource directories and carrying out monitoring exercises across agencies of responses to domestic violence

- improving local service practice and delivery of services

- initiating and developing training with regard to domestic violence

- involvement in public education and awareness work, such as the production of leaflets and posters and the use of plays, exhibitions and zero-tolerance campaigns

- establishing direct services for women and children, including telephone information and helplines, self-help groups and drop-in sessions for women and children.

Although it did not set out specifically to examine multi-agency working, the UK mapping survey by Humphreys *et al.* (2000) generally echoed the findings of Hague, Malos and Dear (1996). The study of Humphreys *et al.* also concludes that multi-agency coordination is in itself an indicator of good practice. This does not mean that solely establishing multi-agency forums is enough, however, as this requires the development of a coordinated and consistent approach by all the agencies concerned:

> …we refer to the co-ordination, or even, in some cases, integration of service provision and policy development so that agencies work to the same brief and adopt a consistent approach. The setting up of inter-agency forums is a tool with which to work towards this 'end', rather than being the 'end' in itself.
>
> *(Humphreys* et al. *2000, p.38)*

Humphreys *et al.* (2000) recommend that multi-agency strategies include the following features of good practice:

- consistency of services and policies across and within agencies

- attention to issues of confidentiality and permission

- full and active involvement of women's refuge, outreach and support

- attention to equality issues and effective mechanisms for consultation with service users

- clarity about decisions, actions and accountability

- monitoring the effectiveness and evaluation of interagency coordination

- measurable improvements in resourcing.

CONSULTATION WITH SERVICE USERS

An area that has been especially difficult to attain is that of including and consulting with users of domestic violence services. Hague, Mullender and Aris (2002), from a national survey of survivor involvement, found that very few of the survivors they interviewed had heard of their local domestic violence forum, and extremely few were represented directly on the forums. The research found that the most successful approach was not to invite survivors to the forum meetings but to establish specific advisory or monitoring groups consisting of survivors, with the function of overseeing the interagency work being carried out. Such groups were also found to provide support and to be fulfilling for the women concerned. Successful groups included Voice for Change in Liverpool and the Phoenix Group in Westminster.

INVOLVEMENT BY WOMEN'S AID

Women's Aid has for a long time played a central role in providing support and safety for women and children experiencing domestic violence. Maintaining this centrality within domestic violence forums, especially in relation to more powerful statutory agencies, can be difficult, however (Hague, Malos and Dear 1996). This is compounded by the fact that refuge participation is not always possible due to small staffing ratios and underfunding. This can lead to statutory agencies taking over the interagency work and to refuges and other women's support services being marginalized. This may be even more so in relation to specialist refuges for black and Asian women, which tend to be more underfunded than most (Hague and Malos 2005; Mama 1996).

Some interagency projects, such as those in Sheffield, Greenwich, Derby and Cleveland, have in the past adopted various methods to overcome the marginalization of women-centred organizations. Among these methods have been:

- agreed principles that refuges take a leading role

- refuges always take the chair of the forum

- a reserved place for a refuge delegate on the steering committee.

The mapping survey by Humphreys *et al.* (2000) showed that 80 per cent of Women's Aid refuges participated in domestic violence forums, with a large degree of involvement in forum subgroups. A large number of publications with Women's Aid involvement also resulted.

11.4 Community safety and crime reduction partnerships

As part of the increasing trend to criminalize domestic violence (Hester 2006a) (see also Chapter Five), the Crime and Disorder Act 1998 requires that local community safety or crime and disorder reduction partnerships are established in order to provide a strategic lead in combating a range of 'criminal' or 'disorderly' activities, including domestic violence. A survey of partnerships in 2003 (Diamond *et al.* 2004) found that 95 per cent of partnerships included domestic violence in their strategy, with 73 per cent saying that it was deemed a high priority.

Partnerships are required to have representation from a range of 'responsible authorities' and, in particular, the police and police authorities, local authorities, probation services, fire authorities and primary care trusts. The emphasis is thus on criminal justice agencies, although the inclusion of primary care trusts acknowledges the increasingly important role identified for the health sector in both the prevention and the provision of services in relation to domestic violence. The survey of partnerships found that the police were most likely to be engaged with the work of the partnership (81%), with between 61 and 65 per cent saying that local Women's Aid groups and refuges were highly engaged; however, only 35 per cent mentioned involvement by primary care trusts (Diamond *et al.* 2004).

Partnerships with a shared definition of domestic violence were more likely to have data-sharing protocols. The existence of, and links with, a local domestic violence forum was also found to be important in driving the work forwards and in attaining targets (Diamond *et al.* 2004).

With regard to children, the guide for partnerships produced by the Home Office (2004) focuses on the importance of partnerships having links with organizations such as Sure Start, which enable domestic violence prevention with pre-school children. The guide identifies work on domestic violence with primary and secondary school children in schools and colleges as important in the wider safeguarding and promotion of safety for children. It is unclear, however, to what extent either Sure Start or local education authorities are represented within partnerships.

11.5 General forum and partnership issues

Mullender (1996a) concludes that:

> Where they work well [interagency forums] are a constructive way of improving the services abused women receive, by pressing each member agency to be more rigorous in its response to the issue and by co-ordinating overall responses to women, children and men. At their best they can…highlight practice that needs to improve and points at which responses fall down between agencies…

> *(Mullender 1996a, p.250)*

This has been borne out by the studies undertaken since the 1990s, which indicate that well-coordinated multi-agency collaboration has the potential to improve services to women and children experiencing domestic violence and to maximize their continuous safety and wellbeing. It is also clear that working in partnership with a range of agencies with different remits and roles presents a number of difficulties and challenges. There are issues concerning the relative power positions of agencies both within and between the voluntary and statutory sectors. There is a need to address issues concerning 'ownership' and accountability of the interagency work carried out and a need to ensure that partnership policies and decisions can be translated into effective practice. Such work also faces major challenges from reorganizations in local authorities, health and education and the continuing purchaser/provider split, which can be seen to undermine the ethos of cooperation between agencies.

11.6 Summary

- Women and children who are experiencing domestic violence may be in contact with a variety of service providers, which need to provide a coordinated approach in order to maximize the continual safety and wellbeing of these women and children.

- In the past, the abuse of women and the abuse of children in the family (usually by the same man) were viewed as separate issues. This has led to the development of separate services and policies to address the needs of each group, as replicated in the development of domestic violence forums focusing mostly on the experiences of women, and ACPCs with an explicit focus on children and their protection.

- The development of a safeguarding children approach involving LSCBs may, if domestic violence is integrated in the work of the boards, provide a more wide-ranging approach that incorporates work with children, adult victims/survivors and perpetrators of domestic violence.

- Domestic violence forums, and, increasingly, also community safety and crime reduction and disorder partnerships, have played an important role in developing multi-agency links and approaches.

- The work of domestic violence forums, LSCBs and other partnerships needs to include recognition of the relative power positions of the different agencies involved and active involvement of Women's Aid and other community-based groups, including those from minority ethnic communities.

CHAPTER TWELVE

WORKING WITH AND SUPPORTING WOMEN EXPERIENCING DOMESTIC VIOLENCE

Some of the earliest responses in the UK to women experiencing domestic violence developed in the 1970s from the self-organized women's groups and centres within the women's liberation movement. In the absence of legal or statutory provision at that time, the first refuges were set up to meet the need of women and children for safe accommodation where their violent partners could not reach them (Harwin 1997; Rose 1985; Sutton 1978). Since then, the refuge movement, led by the Women's Aid Federations of England, Wales, Scotland and Northern Ireland and a range of women's services and projects, has been at the forefront of developing work with and supporting women. During the past couple of decades, support for women experiencing domestic violence has also developed within specialist advocacy projects and as part of the work of children's and other organizations (Hester and Westmarland 2005; Humphreys *et al.* 2000). This chapter looks at some of the approaches to supporting women that have developed from these areas, as well as the wider implications for agencies more generally.

Practitioners in a wide variety of settings are likely to come into contact with women who are living with or have experienced domestic violence. This may include, among others, the following:

- doctors and other health professionals, such as health visitors, midwives and nurses
- social workers
- family support teams
- housing advisory officers and housing support officers
- refuge and hostel workers
- solicitors

- teachers

- members of the police forces.

Women in contact with agencies may themselves make it clear that domestic violence is an issue, or this may become obvious from the nature of the situation, such as a request for rehousing as a consequence of domestic violence. Alternatively, the domestic violence may emerge or be disclosed through a process involving routine questioning about domestic violence, as detailed in Chapter Eight. As indicated in Chapter One, many women who contact agencies have been discouraged from seeking further help by the reaction they receive to their initial approach. An effective and sensitive response to women by all those who may be involved, both at this stage and subsequently, is likely to facilitate further support and help-seeking and may play an invaluable role in developing confidence and building trust. This chapter brings together from other chapters key features in this process and provides an overview of practice issues relevant to supporting women where domestic violence is involved. This chapter covers:

- facilitating effective support

- the implications of loss

- work with women in refuges

- work in the community – outreach, resettlement and floating support

- practice interventions – individual and group work approaches

- support for women with complex needs.

12.1 What constitutes effective support?

An awareness of the effects of domestic violence is essential in understanding the support needs of women while they are in a situation involving domestic violence and subsequent to the termination of a relationship. The impact of domestic violence will be different for each woman, necessitating a flexible approach to practical problems. At the same time, there will always be a parallel need for emotional support to be available, even if this may not be apparent from the initial contact.

> You look alright, you look like you're alright and you're really a strong person but inside of yourself, you're not. You know?
>
> *(Hayley, quoted in Abrahams 2004, p.194)*

Although less obvious than the marks of physical violence, the effects of emotional and psychological abuse can be more difficult to overcome and have a long-lasting impact (Abrahams 2004; Lodge, Goodwin and Pearson 2001; Mullender 1996a). The unpredictability of the abusive behaviour, coupled with feelings of isolation and the coercive control exercised by the abuser, result in feelings of fear and worthlessness and loss of self in terms of identity, respect, esteem and confidence. Effective support needs to take these issues into account. The following factors are generally seen as those that characterize effective support giving and facilitate positive outcomes:

- attention to safety and confidentiality
- being treated with respect
- taking a non-judgemental approach and believing what is said
- taking time to listen and understand
- the availability of mutual support.

12.2 Attention to safety and confidentiality

Ensuring personal safety for themselves and their children is of paramount importance for women who experience domestic violence (Charles and Jones 1993; Kirkwood 1993; Radford and Hester 2006). This concern is likely to be a long term preoccupation, even if the ultimate decision is to leave the relationship. Figures from the British Crime Survey show that, for a significant minority of women, physical and emotional abuse may well continue for many years after leaving the abusive partner or may change to other forms of abusive behaviour, such as harassment or stalking (Walby and Allen 2004) (see also Chapter One). Arrangements for child contact can be occasions for abuse to take place and continue (Hester and Pearson 1998; Radford and Hester 2006).

SAFETY PLANNING

Safety planning with women is an essential practical strategy, which will vary according to individual needs. Planning should respect the fact that women themselves know best what is safe and what is not a useful course of action. Planning may include some or all of the following (Hamby 1998; Humphreys et al. 2000):

- identifying a safe place in case of further violence
- awareness of safe personal contacts
- procedures for contacting helpline and emergency services
- security measures for the home, e.g. locks, panic buttons and alarms
- keeping important documents in a safe and secure place
- maintaining a cache of spare keys, money and emergency clothing.

CONFIDENTIALITY

The importance of interviewing partners separately, where both are involved with an organization, was discussed in Chapter Eight. Concerns about personal safety and confidentiality should also inform decisions about the location and setting of interviews and meetings. For example, as Davis (2003) indicates, the use of interview rooms with clear glass windows adjacent to a public reception area or fronting a roadway respects staff safety but offers women little protection or privacy, since they can be seen, even if not heard, by other members of the public, who may include partners, ex-partners and friends.

Protecting the identities and addresses of women who have moved to separate accommodation as a result of violence should be an essential protocol for all organizations. Any breach of confidentiality can lead to the woman concerned being traced, potentially with fatal consequences, or force her to move on from an area where she had hoped to settle:

> They [the agency] sent a letter to my home address…and it had their address on it. Which was…dead impressive. So he knew where I was. So I've got to move on…again.
>
> *(Amalie, quoted in interview data from Abrahams 2004, unpublished PhD thesis)*

If it is necessary to disclose information to other organizations, then the woman should be asked for her consent. If confidentiality has to be limited, for instance in relation to child protection issues, then this should be made clear to the woman.

12.3 Being treated with respect

Morris (2001) has pointed out that being treated with respect is a key element in the growth of self-esteem. Respect has also been identified as central in empowering individuals to take action for themselves (Croft and Beresford 1989). A study of the support needs of women escaping domestic violence, however, found that women experienced difficulty in coming to terms with being treated as individuals worthy of respect, since this was not an attitude they had encountered previously (Abrahams 2004):

> People treating you as though you're a worthy person, that's really been something I found very, very difficult to get my head around. That's a shock. And the fact that you're actually a worthy person and that your ideas and ideals matter and are important. You know, the respect.
>
> *(Barbara, quoted in Abrahams 2004, p.186)*

Once women could believe that the respect was genuine, they saw respect as having been crucial in the rebuilding of their confidence, self-esteem and self-respect. They also commented that respect included being honest and 'up front' with them about what was happening and giving support to them to define their problems, in making choices and in taking their own actions, rather than imposing solutions.

12.4 Taking a non-judgemental approach and believing what is said

Fear of not being believed, or of being blamed in some way, may deter women from disclosing abuse fully. They may need to test out attitudes and develop a feeling of mental safety and trust over a period of time before they feel able to talk about their experiences of abuse and discuss their support needs. The response to any disclosure is, therefore, of great importance in developing a woman's confidence and building trust. The response needs to be consistent and positive, demonstrate a belief in what has been said, and be supportive and non-judgemental in order to reassure the woman that she is being taken seriously and to encourage further discussion of her needs.

12.5 Taking time to listen and understand

Isolation can be a significant element in domestic violence, denying a woman the opportunity for her voice to be heard and emphasizing feelings of powerlessness and low self-esteem. In these circumstances, providing the time to listen and understanding can, in itself, be a validating and healing process. Humphreys and Thiara (2002), in their study of women accessing outreach and resettlement services, found that this was an aspect of service provision that was highly valued and an important factor in giving women the confidence to cope with their difficulties:

> Just having someone who understands and that is willing to give you time and listen to your problems. I feel that they have given me the confidence to deal with a domestic violence problem and not to hide away and cope with this on my own.
>
> *(Nola, quoted in Humphreys and Thiara 2002, p.27)*

12.6 Availability of mutual support

Research has commented consistently on the strength that women may draw from each other and from their shared experiences (Charles 1994; Giles-Sims 1998). Mutual support has also been a cornerstone of the Women's Aid approach to domestic violence since its inception. The availability of support from women who share similar experiences breaks the silence and isolation that has been imposed on them and enables women to make the discovery that they are not, as they may have believed, alone in what they are going through and that they are not abnormal:

> It was like a sigh of relief…there was other people in the same boat as me that I could talk to.
>
> *(Val, quoted in Abrahams 2004, p.199)*

> To know that I wasn't the only one and, you know, that I wasn't…as dull and stupid as he made out. Because we've all, basically, been through the same type of thing. The emotional abuse is terrible. To be told, for nearly eight years, that I was stupid and I was thick and…you know, you believe it. And, together, talking to women in the similar type of situation, when you've made friends, you know you're not.
>
> *(Stacey, quoted in Abrahams 2004, p.199)*

Women who took part in a Parliamentary Internet consultation confirmed the importance of mutual support in building self-esteem, bringing normality into their lives and creating new friendships (Bossy and Coleman 2000). Although mutual support is a major feature of most refuges, many self-help and support groups have also been started by women who have experienced domestic violence or by service providers, and a similar function can be served by drop-in centres. These aspects of mutual support are discussed in more detail later in this chapter.

12.7 Implications of loss for support work

Research has shown that women who experience domestic violence suffer immense social, economic, emotional and psychological losses. These may include the loss of safety and security, loss of physical health and emotional wellbeing, and loss of self, love, faith in the possibility of change and confidence in the future (Giles-Sims 1998; Laing 2001; Rai and Thiara 1997). For women who leave abusive relationships, there may be the loss of a home that they have spent many years trying to build up and keep together, often in the face of the recurrent destruction of furniture and fabric by their abuser. There may also be the loss of older children, family, friends, pets, a job, economic security and a familiar environment and community. Finally, there is the loss of the relationship, where feelings may be confused, ambivalent and painful. The cumulative effect of these losses can be hard to bear:

> I cried all the way till when I got here… I knew I wasn't going back there and it was…I don't know, I don't know how I felt, I just knew I were upset anyway. I were devastated because I was coming so far away from home and I wasn't going back and the kids weren't going back.
>
> *(Val, quoted in Abrahams 2004, p.174)*

Given the significant and lasting consequences of the losses that may be involved, making the decision to end the relationship can be extremely difficult. For those women who do so, the process of recovery has been shown to be similar to that experienced following bereavement (Abrahams 2004) and to comprise three fluid, interlinked phases:

1   An initial impact, with feelings of shock, numbness, confusion, unreality and grief.

2   A transition period of oscillating emotions, uncertainty and adaptation.

3   A period of adjusting to the changes and building a new way of life.

As in bereavement, recovery takes time and progress is not linear. Women are likely to experience periods when they return to their earlier feelings of confusion and sadness before being able to move forwards again. Moving through these phases is made more difficult by the effects that domestic violence has had on their emotional wellbeing, confidence and self-esteem. Support at a personal and emotional level is, therefore, equally necessary to that required in dealing with the different practical problems encountered at each phase of recovery. Although these findings come from a study of current and former refuge residents, the experience of loss is likely to have a significant influence on the lives of all women who experience domestic violence and on the choices and decisions that they make. An understanding of this process and its implications is, therefore, likely to add to the effectiveness of support giving.

12.8 Work with women in refuges

Throughout the UK, there is now a network of Women's Aid refuges providing safe accommodation and support for women and children. In recognition of the specific cultural and practical needs of some women, there is some specialist provision for women from minority communities, including a network of Asian refuges. Some of these groups provide the only community-specific refuge in the UK; for instance, that for Jewish women is unique in Europe. Although general refuges are open to all women, specialist refuges offer women from particular minority communities or special groups a choice of which provision to use. Factors that may influence this decision include perceived racism in mainstream refuges, lack of trust in their own community, specific cultural or language needs and the approach that the women have towards integration (Batsleer *et al.* 2002; Rai and Thiara 1997). A limited number of other specialist refuges exist, for example for women without children, for women who have been sexually abused and for women who have learning difficulties. Provision in refuges for women with limited mobility or other physical problems is, in general, very limited (Humphreys *et al.* 2000). Although a member of Women's Aid, Refuge operates its own provision, and there are also specialist refuges for black and Asian women that operate outside the Women's Aid network. Additionally, there are a growing number of refuges provided directly by housing associations.[1]

Services provided by refuge groups are rated consistently highly by service users (Hague, Mullender and Aris 2002; Johnson 1995; Morley and Mullender 1994; Rai and Thiara 1997). This is despite the fact that, in general, funding of refuges is inadequate, inconsistent and insecure (Ball 1994; Humphreys *et al.* 2000). There are still insufficient refuge spaces to meet demand, and provision is located unevenly throughout the country (Harwin 1997).

The Women's Aid approach to support for women is based on a statement of key values that derive from its roots in the women's movement:

- to believe women and children and to make their safety a priority
- to support and empower women to take control of their own lives
- to recognise and care for the needs of children affected by domestic violence
- to promote equal opportunities and anti-discriminatory practice.

(Humphreys et al. *2000, p.6)*

Within these values, local groups have the flexibility to develop services and ways of working that are responsive to the needs of the women who approach them and the availability of financial and other resources. A survey of Women's Aid service provision in 1999 showed that over 90 per cent of refuges provided the following services (Women's Aid Federation of England 2000):

- safe and secure accommodation for women and children
- referral to safer or more appropriate accommodation if necessary
- confidential help and support: information is not disclosed to other agencies without the woman's knowledge and consent. If confidentiality has to be limited or breached, for example in issues such as child abuse, then this is made clear to the woman
- one-to-one support: helping women to regain confidence and self-esteem and supporting them in obtaining the necessary material, financial and emotional resources to control their own lives
- provision of information and advice on matters such as housing and benefits and basic legal advice
- support and advocacy with statutory agencies such as the Child Support Agency, housing and benefits offices and legal services (although support is aimed at enabling women to self-advocate in the long term, advocacy from workers may be necessary initially in order to overcome the problems associated with dealing with statutory and other institutions and the lack of confidence and self-esteem created by the abuse).

Additional services most commonly provided for women included support groups, formal counselling, educational and vocational activities, provision of clothing and help in removing and reclaiming possessions. As the authors of the report comment, the wide diversity of service users and their needs can be met only by a flexible and imaginative approach and the sharing of information and ideas across the refuge network and in multi-agency working within the wider community.

12.9 Outreach, resettlement and floating support

In addition to working with women who enter refuges, Women's Aid projects have always offered some form of support to residents who are rehoused in the local area and have recognized the need to provide support and advice on a wider basis to women in the community who may be experiencing, or have experienced, domestic abuse. These services are regarded by service users as an important source of support in their efforts to turn around their lives, although they are consistently underfunded and underresourced (Humphreys and Thiara 2002; Lodge *et al.* 2001). Humphreys and Thiara (2002), in their detailed study of these projects, reported frequent comments such as 'essential' and 'literally lifesaving'. Similar remarks were noted by Hester and Westmarland (2005) in a meta-evaluation of domestic violence crime reduction projects for the Home Office. Support work of this nature may be referred to as outreach, resettlement or aftercare, or floating support.

Outreach and resettlement have been identified as key elements in helping families to access support and information, recover from the trauma of domestic abuse, build new lives and sustain independent tenancies (Charles 1994; McGee 2000; Rai and Thiara 1997).

Women who are living in abusive relationships have complex and difficult situations to deal with. It is important to provide time and space for them to talk about what is happening and to come to their own decisions about staying or leaving, without pressurizing them. This may take considerable time and involve exploring a number of options, which may include leaving and then returning to the relationship. It is important, therefore, that support continues to be available during this time (Batsleer *et al.* 2002; Bossy and Coleman 2000).

For women who terminate an abusive relationship, the study by Humphreys and Thiara (2002) found that intensive support was most needed in the first six months after establishing a separate household, although many women needed to access support services over longer periods of time – some for more than two years. Similar findings were reported from the evaluation of a project supporting rehoused families run by the homelessness organization Shelter (Jones, Pleace and Quilgars 2002), where 40 per cent of the service users had been made homeless as a result of domestic violence and practical and emotional support had been a major factor in assisting them to resettle and remain in a tenancy. This support was needed for an average of 261 days for each family. Although some services are now building time limits into service provision, there would appear to be a need for some degree of continuing support to be available over an extended period of time.

OUTREACH

The term 'outreach' is commonly used to refer to support work with women and children who are not resident in a refuge. They may be living with an abusive partner or parent or may be in the complex process of ending the relationship. Women who are living independently for the first time may be encountering continued harassment, while other women may need support when matters connected with a previous violent relationship (such as child contact) suddenly emerge and cause a crisis.

Outreach work is of particular significance in rural areas, where domestic violence is as much a feature of life as it is in urban areas. Greater physical isolation, combined with additional external factors such as limited public transport, remote statutory agencies and issues of confidentiality within small communities, can adversely affect a woman's ability to seek help and make it difficult to access appropriate services (Hester and Westmarland 2005; Lodge *et al.* 2001). A flexible, mobile outreach service, where staff members are able to meet a woman at a safe location, can overcome these problems and provide a lifeline for this group of women.

Outreach can also be used to describe projects beyond the scope of this chapter that aim to make services for women and children more visible and accessible (e.g. education, information campaigns, training of other agencies – see also Chapter Nine). Some projects also use the term 'outreach' to refer to the support given to ex-residents as they re-establish themselves in the community. More often, this is referred to as 'resettlement' or 'aftercare', although the latter term has been criticized for carrying negative medical and benevolent connotations (Kelly and Humphreys 2001).

RESETTLEMENT

Women who are rehoused from a refuge will, in general, have to build up a home for themselves and their children, starting with very few resources. They will need to adjust to living on their own, build bridges to the local community and form an appropriate network with agencies, organizations and formal and informal support systems. Barriers to achieving this include financial hardship, feelings of isolation and lack of support, the behaviour and emotional responses of their children and post-separation violence (Humphreys and Thiara 2002). As noted earlier, such barriers are experienced by a substantial minority of women. Women from minority ethnic communities, and, in particular, women whose legal status in this country is uncertain, are most likely to suffer financial hardship and are more likely to report feelings of isolation and lack of support. These problems are also evident in the service user consultation by Bossy and Coleman (2000). Batsleer *et al.* (2002), in their study of minority women, similarly point out the difficulties and isolation faced by women who are trying to build new lives in areas where they are not known and where they are unable to meet their deep needs for cultural and religious identification. Specific support services for these groups of women are, therefore, important.

FLOATING SUPPORT

'Floating support' is used increasingly to describe both outreach and resettlement support. It has been defined under the Supporting People programme as 'a support service not dependent on residency in a particular property or type of property' (Department of the Environment, Transport and the Regions 2001, p.99). The aim is to provide a flexible service to people living in their own homes and is attached to a person rather than a tenancy for a period of time before 'floating on' to another individual in need of support.

TYPES OF OUTREACH AND RESETTLEMENT SUPPORT

Outreach and resettlement projects offer flexible support responsive to the particular circumstances of each woman and her family. Over time, women will access different aspects of these services to meet their needs. The Women's Aid Federation of England (2000) survey shows that the services most frequently accessed by women are:

- telephone support and information
- support and advocacy with organizations and agencies
- one-to-one support
- drop-in sessions.

Local projects are able to provide advice and information by telephone, and many have dedicated helplines. Some projects have been able to set up advice centres, and these may also run advice sessions with solicitors, housing agencies and other specialists (Humphreys *et al.* 2000). Underpinning these services is the freephone 24-hour National Domestic Violence Helpline (0808 2000 247) run in partnership between Women's Aid and Refuge. There is still, however, a need for these services to be better publicized, since women have commented consistently that they were unaware that any help was available to them and have emphasized the importance of advice and information being readily accessible and advertised (Bossy and Coleman 2000; Lodge *et al.* 2001; McGee 2000): 'Women are going through hell out there and they need to be told that there is somewhere they can get help' (Charmian, quoted in Abrahams 2004, p.181).

Women contacting outreach and resettlement projects have needs and entitlements from a wide range of statutory agencies and other organizations, such as health services, housing, benefits and access to the legal system. For reasons including the complexity of the systems, the number of agencies involved and the loss of self-esteem engendered by domestic abuse, women may, initially, lack the knowledge, expertise and confidence to act alone in getting these needs met satisfactorily. This is where advocacy – that is, helping women to get their needs met by other agencies – is important to support women in accessing these resources and, if necessary, to advocate on their behalf to achieve a fair and acceptable outcome. The ultimate aim is always to encourage self-advocacy and independent action (Hester and Westmarland 2005; Kelly and Humphreys 2001).

A number of Women's Aid groups facilitate regular meetings run on a drop-in basis and have been found to provide opportunities for mutual support and an environment where women do not have to explain where they are coming from (Abrahams 2004; Bossy and Coleman 2000; Humphreys and Thiara 2002):

> It's nice to know that you can still, just, sort of, drop in a chair or whatever and have a chat with somebody you know knows your circumstances. Because maybe you don't want to let other people know. Whereas here, you know, they know your circumstances.
>
> *(Barbara, quoted in Abrahams 2004, p.245)*

The meetings may be limited to former residents, may be a mix of residents and ex-residents or may be open to any woman who has experienced or is experiencing domestic violence. A crèche is usually provided, and activities and discussions are likely to be arranged by the women themselves. Other support on offer may include support groups and counselling, which we discuss below.

12.10 Practice interventions: individual and group work approaches

Providing personal and emotional support to women who are experiencing or have experienced domestic violence plays a key role in assisting the women to recover from the abuse and rebuild their lives. Highly specialized therapeutic interventions can be helpful to some women in this respect, but some researchers and practitioners in this field have pointed out that not all women want or need this type of support and that most women are able to rebuild their lives using their own individual strengths and the emotionally supportive relationships around them, including that of other individuals with similar experiences (Dutton 1992; Herman 2001; Laing 2001). Support that assists this process, using an approach that respects the woman and her autonomy and that is sensitive to her needs, can be provided by a wide range of services, individuals and organizations, including the wider social community. Laing (2001), in a comprehensive overview of working with women, suggests that using the terms 'practice' and 'interventions' rather than 'counselling' and 'therapy' to describe support of this nature provides a better understanding of the broad range of interventions that can offer effective support.

Support needs vary with each woman, reflecting the woman's social and individual circumstances. Women access the services that they feel are appropriate for them at any particular moment (Laing 2001). Abrahams' (2004) study of support work found that, in general, women knew what their needs for personal support were and when they were ready to move from one level to another, from low-level support that validated their experiences to individual counselling or group work, and, equally, when this was not appropriate for them.

COUPLE COUNSELLING AND FAMILY THERAPY

The use of couple counselling and family therapy where domestic abuse is involved is seen as inappropriate because it may jeopardize the woman's safety and prevent her from speaking freely for fear of subsequent retaliation (RESPECT 2004) (see also Chapter Ten).[2] Both forms of intervention may shift the central focus away from the male violence, placing responsibility either on the couple jointly or on the family and expecting the woman to change or adjust to the situation (Dobash et al. 2000; Hamby 1998; Hester et al.1997; Mullender 1996a). It has been argued that this type of intervention should be considered only if the violence has ceased. None the less, some therapists suggest that these approaches may be drawn on where practitioners have an understanding of the complexities of domestic violence and frame their interventions to take account of gender-based issues related to risk and safety, power and control and wider social issues (Haddock 2002; Rivett 2001; Vetare and Cooper 2001).

12.11 Practice interventions: working with individuals

LOW-KEY INTERVENTIONS

Low-key interventions may take place in a variety of situations and need to incorporate the factors identified in Part One as being supportive, respecting the woman and her choices, believing the woman's experiences, providing the necessary space for the woman to talk and be heard, and taking time to listen to and understand the woman. This type of support involves the use of counselling skills (active listening, empathy, a non-judgemental attitude) to create a supportive environment in which information and encouragement can be offered, options debated and strategies for moving on (mentally and physically) discussed. Interventions using these skills may also be appropriate in helping a woman to prepare for specific events such as court appearances and in working with her in an advocacy situation. The use of counselling skills to assist a working relationship in this way is related closely to other ways of offering support, such as befriending, but needs to be differentiated from counselling practice, which adopts a more structured approach (Bond 2000; Feltham 2000).

COUNSELLING AND PSYCHOTHERAPY

Although for many women 'a listening ear may be all that is required' (Mullender 1996a, p.132), research has shown that there is a high level of demand from women for counselling to be available if they wish to take advantage of this service (Abrahams 2004; Lodge et al. 2001; Rai and Thiara 1997). It is important that counselling is an independent service, delivered by women who have both a holistic understanding of domestic violence and its effects and training in counselling theory and practice.

As with family therapy, traditional models of counselling and psychotherapy can be seen as contentious, because they may focus on perceived personal inadequacy and victim-blaming (Whalen 1996) without considering issues of power and control within the relationship and society as a whole (Bondi and Burman 2001). Work by feminist researchers and practitioners has, however, introduced new concepts and ways of working that locate the violence within wider social, political and historical contexts (Dutton 1992; Herman 2001). In particular, approaches that consider the traumatic effects of domestic violence on a woman's mental health and emotional wellbeing have been developed, focusing on the restoration of feelings of physical and mental safety and enabling the woman to deal with the experience of loss, rebuild her identity and regain control over her life, in order to make her own choices and reconnect to the community at large (Coleman and Guildford 2001; Dutton 1992; Herman 2001; Whalen 1996).

There are many different theoretical approaches to counselling and psychotherapy, and it is difficult to evaluate their effectiveness, since outcomes depend on whose perspective is sought (client, therapist, administrator) and the method of assessment adopted. Outcomes can also be influenced by events in the surrounding social environment and other uncontrollable factors, such as the quality of the relationship with the therapist (McLeod 2000). Two systematic reviews, of workplace (McLeod 2001) and primary care (Mellor-Clark 2000) counselling, and covering a wide range of problematic issues, including relationships, showed a high level of client satisfaction, positive outcomes and alleviation of distress.

Counselling and psychotherapy can be provided by a variety of individuals and organizations, including primary care trusts. Entry into formal mental health services of this nature, however, can be seen as problematic by women who have issues around domestic violence, since this may be seen as stigmatizing by the woman herself and to others around her, and she may fear that treatment, including medication, may be used as negative testimony in areas such as child contact or child protection (Humphreys and Thiara 2003; Stark and Flitcraft 1996).

12.12 Practice interventions: group work

As noted earlier, mutual support has been a longstanding tradition in women's services, and working in groups has been recognized as one of the most effective ways of facilitating this: 'Women brought together can offer each other support, validation and strength, and a growing sense of personal awareness, in a way that is difficult to achieve otherwise' (Butler and Wintram 1991, p.1).

Support groups are an important element in the Duluth model, facilitating reflection and awareness and providing a space for mutual support and self-help (Shepard 1999). This is in addition to the support groups provided in conjunction with perpetrator groups (see Chapter Ten). For women who are experiencing or have experienced domestic violence, the groups offer opportunities to talk openly and to make sense of their experiences. Such groups have been shown to reduce feelings of isolation by building social networks with other women, enabling them to understand, as a group, that the violence was not their fault, and providing an environment where they can rebuild their emotional strength and gain confidence and self-esteem (Batsleer *et al.* 2002; Laing 2001; Mullender 1996a; Mullender and Ward 1991). Groups may also create opportunities for joint activities, such as workshops on a variety of topics and group trips, thus providing further opportunities for personal growth and the handling of new situations (Butler and Wintram 1991).

Self-help or support groups may be closed (i.e. limited to a set number of original participants) or open, where participants may enter or leave at any time; they may be run by the women themselves, with or without support from an external facilitator; and they can operate in a wide variety of environments. Support groups may be mainstream (open to all women) or culturally specific. Batsleer *et al.* (2002), in their study of women from minority communities, which included Jewish and Irish women, found that women moved from one type of group to another, according to their perceived needs and that, although there were challenges to be overcome in facilitating mixed groups, these sessions had proved valuable for all those involved. The study clearly indicated the value of having both sorts of provision available.

Women who take part in support groups rate the groups highly, seeing them as empowering and an important part of their support network (Abrahams 2004; Batsleer *et al.* 2002; Bossy and Coleman 2000; Humphreys and Thiara 2002):

> The group was excellent. You could spark off each other, work together. It gave me confidence to try practical ways to change things.

> *(Charmian, quoted in Abrahams 2004, p.210)*

> It's given me a perspective through which I can see my own situation…a very important part of the healing process.

> *(Batsleer et al. 2002, p.186)*

Evaluation of two supported self-help groups (Hester with Scott 2000; Hester and Westmarland 2005) showed that women regarded the groups as having been sources of knowledge, sharing, support and strength and felt that there had been positive growth during the time they had attended, with increases in confidence, self-esteem and hope for the future:

> I am able to face tomorrow with a lot of eagerness.

> *(Hester and Westmarland 2005, p.89)*

Groups are, however, resource-intensive and demanding to run (Batsleer *et al.* 2002; Humphreys and Thiara 2002), and issues such as childcare facilities, availability of transport, language support and accessible premises need to be taken into account. Groups are not suited to everyone, and women may not feel comfortable in, or be suited to working in, a group:

> It's a bit too personal to be discussed in front of other people.
>
> *(Barbara, quoted in Abrahams 2004, p.212)*

Although all of these self-help and support groups can be regarded as therapeutic or healing in their own right, directly therapeutic groups are also available in some areas. These differ from self-help and support groups in the depth at which they work and are intended to assist individuals who have shared similar problems to explore together the difficult experiences in their lives, such as domestic violence or sexual abuse, and deal with their feelings in a safe and supportive environment (Arnold and Magill 2000). These groups are normally closed, often with some assessment of the participants as to their potential to benefit from the group, and are facilitated by one or more individuals with training and experience in this work and with a background in counselling or psychotherapy. This is necessary because of the sensitivity of the topic, the in-depth nature of the work and the damage that could be caused to participants without skilled support.

12.13 Practice interventions: support for women with complex needs

As indicated in Chapter One, research has indicated that there are clear links between domestic violence and the development of mental health problems, including a high level of depression, suicide and self-harm and a range of symptoms associated with a diagnosis of post-traumatic stress disorder (Coleman and Guildford 2001; Humphreys and Thiara 2003; Stark and Flitcraft 1996). That women living with domestic violence are a high-risk group for mental health problems was recognized in the *National Service Framework on Mental Health* (Department of Health 1999). There has been less research on the links between domestic violence and substance (drugs, alcohol) misuse, with most of the available material focusing on substance use/misuse by the violent partner (Barron 2004). Stark and Flitcraft (1996), however, found that women experiencing domestic violence were six times more likely to abuse drugs and 15 times more likely to misuse alcohol than the general female population. Most authors suggest that women turn to drugs and alcohol only after the violence has begun, using them as self-medication to alleviate the pain and distress of the situation (Ettore 1997; Stark and Flitcraft 1996; Stephens and McDonald 2000) (see also Chapter One). The interconnection between domestic violence, mental health problems and substance misuse has been shown to exist cross-culturally (Batsleer *et al.* 2002), with suicide and self-harm having been recognized as particularly prevalent among young Asian women (Chantler *et al.* 2001; Newham Asian Women's Project 1998).

For women with these complex problems, it can be difficult to acknowledge both the violence and the associated problems. This is especially true of women from minority communities, who may face additional barriers and taboos in seeking help (Batsleer *et al.* 2002). Information and advice is not readily available for these women, making it difficult for them to access appropriate services where these exist. Women's needs for support with domestic violence, mental health issues and substance misuse overlap, but services themselves tend to be compartmentalized around a single focus issue, and service provision in general is uneven and inadequate (Barron 2004; Humphreys and Thiara 2003).

A comprehensive survey of service provision and attitudes across professional and voluntary organizations working in the fields of mental health, substance misuse and domestic violence concluded that the limited services that were available were not meeting the needs of women with complex problems (Barron 2004). There was a generally low awareness of domestic violence issues and their relationship with mental health and substance misuse by workers in these fields: most did not look for indications that domestic violence might be an issue, and routine enquiries about abuse were not usually undertaken. This lack of awareness meant that the focus remained on the presenting problem, without consideration of the wider implications of the situation that had led to the needs for services.

Services were not responsive to the social needs of women who contacted or were referred to them with problems of mental health or substance misuse. Access and transport to day centres was problematic, childcare was seldom provided and there was a lack of women-only services, although Barron (2004) found that substance misuse services were sometimes more responsive to these needs. Women referred for residential treatment were commonly accommodated in mixed-sex units, which could be traumatic for women who had been abused by male perpetrators. Admission to residential units was particularly problematic for women with children, since leaving the children with the perpetrator or arranging for the children to be taken into care opened up the possibility of losing them completely.

For women who need to leave home because of domestic violence, Barron (2004) found that there was a shortage of refuge provision that could offer support to women with complex problems. Mainstream refuges needed to consider the nature and severity of the woman's needs, the needs of other residents and children, and the availability of resources within the refuge and from other agencies before accommodation could be offered. All refuges, of necessity, have rules that ban the possession or use of illegal drugs on the premises. Refuges reported a lack of specialized training for staff and that problems were often experienced in accessing support from other agencies.

Barron (2004) found, none the less, that major efforts were being made to take a proactive approach to these difficulties. In some areas, including Nottinghamshire, the Stella project in London, in Tower Hamlets, in Northampton and other places, good practice guidelines were being developed, networking and information-sharing were being encouraged, and mutual training for workers in the fields of

domestic violence, mental health and substance misuse was leading to greater awareness and understanding. Barron points out, however, that there is a need for additional resources to be made available in order to provide safe responsive services for
women. Among her recommendations are:

- the development of policies, protocols and good practice guidelines for
  all organizations where domestic violence can be an issue

- the involvement of mental health and substance misuse workers in
  domestic violence forums and crime and disorder reduction programmes

- cross-training of workers in these fields in order to raise awareness and
  understanding of domestic violence and of those who work with issues
  of domestic violence in recognizing and understanding the needs of
  service users with complex problems, leading to greater confidence in
  asking about and responding to issues around domestic violence, mental
  health and substance misuse

- greater interagency collaboration, networking and support between
  agencies and a holistic approach to service provision

- provision of woman-friendly services, with consideration being given to
  accessibility, childcare provision, residential units where women can be
  accommodated with their children, and women-only services

- some specialist refuge provision, with support provided over longer
  periods of the day. Although sometimes sufficient support can be given
  in mainstream refuges to women with complex needs, many refuges offer
  shared facilities, which are not always suitable for the needs of these
  groups of women and are not able to offer the higher degree of support
  required.

12.14 Summary

- An awareness of the pervasive nature of domestic violence, and an
  understanding of its effects on women, will enable individuals in a wide
  range of settings to offer more effective support to women who are living
  with or have experienced domestic violence.

- Women are likely to experience loss of self-esteem, confidence and
  self-respect as a result of abuse. Emotional support is, therefore, as
  important as practical assistance in helping to rebuild confidence and
  generate positive outcomes.

- There are certain factors that characterize effective support giving,
  including attention to safety and confidentiality, being treated with

respect, taking a non-judgemental approach, being believed, taking time to listen and understand, and the availability of mutual support.

- Women who experience domestic violence suffer immense social, economic, emotional and psychological losses. The potential and actual consequences of these losses will have a significant impact on their lives and on the choices and decisions that they make.

- Recovery from these losses is made more complex by the traumatic effects that domestic violence has had on their emotional wellbeing, confidence and self-worth. Recovery involves a process similar to that which takes place following bereavement: an intense initial impact, followed by a period of transition and adjustment, before a new way of living can be adopted. This process takes time to complete, and women are likely to move back and forth between phases.

- A network of refuges exists across the UK, offering safe accommodation, advice and support to women who have left abusive relationships. There is some provision for women with specific needs and for women from minority ethnic communities. Refuges also offer assistance in resettlement into the local area.

- Support and advice are also offered on a wider basis to women who are experiencing or have experienced domestic violence. A freephone National Domestic Violence Helpline (0808 2000 247) run in partnership between Women's Aid and Refuge operates on a 24-hour basis. There are many local helplines, advice centres and outreach projects.

- Outreach services are particularly important for women in rural areas, where the isolation imposed by the abuser is compounded by inadequate public transport, the remoteness of relevant agencies and the scattered nature of the communities.

- Support needs to be available within the community on a long-term basis, so that women can take time to make decisions appropriate to their needs and feel confident that there will be someone to turn to if necessary. Availability of long-term support has been shown to be vital in enabling women to successfully live independently.

- Many women will be able to rebuild their lives using their own strengths and drawing on emotional support from those around them. This support is likely to involve the use of counselling skills to enhance working relationships.

- Formal counselling that takes into account the traumatic effects of abuse on emotional wellbeing and sets it in the wider social context is also

welcomed by service users and is regarded very positively by the
majority of those who access this service.

• Although not everyone is suited to working in this way, support groups
have been shown to be an effective way of facilitating mutual support
between women. These groups provide opportunities for women to make
sense of their experiences, reduce feelings of isolation by creating new
social networks and begin the process of regaining confidence and
self-esteem.

• Service provision for women who, in addition to domestic violence
issues, have mental health problems or misuse drugs or alcohol, often as a
result of the violence, are extremely limited. Although action is being
taken to remedy the deficit in some areas, awareness of the ways in
which these complex needs interact is, at present, very limited.

Notes

1   A freephone 24-hour National Domestic Violence Helpline (0808 2000 247) run in partnership between Women's Aid and Refuge provides a link to the refuge network and offers
help and support to women experiencing domestic violence.

2   The same applies to the use of mediation (Hester *et al.* 1997).

REFERENCES

Abrahams, C. (1994) *The Hidden Victims: Children and Domestic Violence.* London: NCH Action for Children. www.nch.org.uk.

Abrahams, H. (2004) 'A Long, Hard Road to Go By: A Study of the Support Work Carried Out in Women's Aid Refuges', unpublished PhD thesis. Bristol: University of Bristol. Shortly to be published as *Supporting Women after Domestic Violence: Loss, Trauma and Recovery* (2007). London: Jessica Kingsley Publishers.

Adams, D. (1988) 'Treatment Models of Men who Batter: A Profeminist Analysis.' In K. Yllo and M. Bograd (eds) *Feminist Perspectives on Wife Abuse.* Newbury Park, CA: Sage.

Ahluwalia, K. and Gupta, R. (1997) *Circle of Light.* London: HarperCollins.

Alessi, J.J. and Hearn, K. (1984) 'Group Treatment of Children in Shelters for Battered Women.' In A.R. Roberts (ed.) *Battered Women and their Families.* New York: Springer.

Anderson, L. (1997) *Contact Between Children and Violent Fathers: In Whose Best Interests?* London: Rights of Women.

Andrews, B. and Brown, G.W. (1988) 'Marital violence in the community: a biographical approach.' *British Journal of Psychiatry 153,* 305–312.

Armstrong, H. (1994) *ACPC: National Conference: Discussion Report: Annual Reports ACPCs 1992–93.* London: Department of Health.

Arnold, L. and Magill, A. (2000) *Making Sense of Self-Harm.* Abergavenny: The Basement Project.

Atkinson, C. (1996) 'Partnership working – supporting those who work with the children of domestic violence.' Paper given at the Behind Closed Doors Seminar – The Effects of Domestic Violence on Children and Vulnerable Young People, Thames Valley.

Ball, M. (1990) *Children's Workers in Women's Aid Refuges.* London: National Council of Voluntary Childcare Organisations.

Ball, M. (1994) *Funding Refuge Services: A Study of Refuge Support Services for Women and Children Experiencing Domestic Violence.* Bristol: Women's Aid Federation of England.

Ball, M. (1995) *Domestic Violence and Social Care: A Report on Two Conferences Held by the Social Services Inspectorate.* London: Department of Health.

Barnardo's, NSPCC and University of Bristol (2003) *Making an Impact: Children and Domestic Violence: Update 2003.* Barkingside: Barnardo's. Available from NSPCC Training, 3 Gilmour Close, Beaumont Leys, Leicester LE4 1EX.

Barnish, M. (2004) *Domestic Violence: A Literature Review – Summary.* London: Home Office.

Barron, J. (1990) *Not Worth the Paper...? The Effectiveness of Legal Protection for Women and Children Experiencing Domestic Violence.* Bristol: Women's Aid Federation of England.

Barron, J. (2004) *Struggle to Survive: Challenges for Delivering Services on Mental Health, Substance Misuse and Domestic Violence.* Bristol: Women's Aid Federation of England.

Barron, J., Harwin, N. and Singh, T. (1992) *Women's Aid Federation of England Written Evidence to House of Commons Home Affairs Committee Inquiry into Domestic Violence.* Bristol: Women's Aid Federation of England.

Batsleer, J., Burman, E., Chantler, K., McIntosh, H., *et al.* (2002) *Domestic Violence and Minoritisation: Supporting Women to Independence.* Manchester: Manchester Metropolitan University.

Bell, J. and Stanley, N. (2005) 'Tackling domestic violence at a local level: an evaluation of the Preston Road Domestic Violence project.' Hull: University of Hull.

Bhatti-Sinclair, K. (1994) 'Asian Women and Violence from Male Partners.' In C. Lupton and T. Gillespie (eds) *Working with Violence.* Basingstoke: Macmillan.

Bilby, C. and Hatcher, R. (2004) *Early Stages in the Development of the Integrated Domestic Abuse Programme (IDAP): Implementing the Duluth Domestic Violence Pathfinder.* Home Office online report 29/04. London: Home Office.

Binney, V., Harkell, G. and Nixon, J. ([1981] 1988) *Leaving Violent Men: A Study of Refuges and Housing for Battered Women.* Bristol: Women's Aid Federation of England.

Bond, T. (2000) *Standards and Ethics for Counselling in Action,* 2nd edn. London: Sage.

Bondi, L. and Burman, E. (2001) 'Women and mental health: a feminist review.' *Feminist Review 68,* 6–33.

Borkowski, M., Murch, M. and Walker, V. (1983) *Marital Violence: The Community Response.* London: Tavistock.

Bossy, J. and Coleman, S. (2000) *Womanspeak: Parliamentary Domestic Violence Internet Consultation.* Bristol: Women's Aid Federation of England.

Bourlet, A. (1990) *Police Intervention in Marital Violence.* London: Open University Press.

Bowen, E. (2004) 'Evaluation of a community based domestic violence offender rehabilitation programme.' Birmingham: University of Birmingham.

Bowen, E., Brown, L. and Gilchrist, E. (2002) 'Evaluating probation based offender programmes for domestic violence perpetrators: a pro-feminist approach.' *Howard Journal of Criminal Justice 41*, 3, 221–236.

Bowker, L.H., Arbitell, M. and McFerron, J.R. (1988) 'On the Relationship Between Wife Beating and Child Abuse.' In K. Yllo and M. Bograd (eds) *Feminist Perspectives on Wife Abuse.* Newbury Park, CA: Sage.

Bowstead, J., Lall, D. and Rashid, S. (1995) *Asian Women and Domestic Violence: Information for Advisers.* London: London Borough of Greenwich Women's Equality Unit.

Brandon, M. and Lewis, A. (1996) 'Significant harm and children's experiences of domestic violence.' *Child and Family Social Work 1*, 1, 33–42.

Bridge Child Care Consultancy Service (1991) *Sukina: An Evaluation of the Circumstances Leading to her Death.* London: Bridge Child Care Consultancy Service.

Browning, D.H. and Boatman, B. (1977) 'Incest: children at risk.' *American Journal of Psychiatry 134*, 1, 69–72.

Bull, J. (1993) *Housing Consequences of Relationship Breakdown.* London: HMSO.

Burge, S. (1989) 'Violence against women as a health care issue.' *Family Medicine 21*, 368–373.

Burton, S., Regan, L. and Kelly, L. (1998) *Supporting Women and Challenging Men: Lessons from the Domestic Violence Intervention Project.* Bristol: Policy Press.

Busch, R. and Robertson, N. (1994) '"Ain't No Mountain High Enough (to Keep Me from Getting to You)": An Analysis of the Hamilton Abuse Intervention Pilot Project.' In J. Stubbs (ed.) *Women, Male Violence and the Law.* Sydney: University of Sydney Law School.

Butler, S. and Wintram, C. (1991) *Feminist Groupwork.* London: Sage.

Carlson, B.E. (1990) 'Adolescent observers of marital violence.' *Journal of Family Violence 5*, 285–299.

Carroll, J. (1994) 'The protection of children exposed to marital violence.' *Child Abuse Review 3*, 6–14.

Catchpole, A. (1997) 'Working with Children who have Been Abused.' In M. John (ed.) *A Charge Against Society: The Child's Right to Protection.* London: Jessica Kingsley Publishers.

Cavanagh, K., Dobash, R.E., Dobash, R.P. and Lewis, R. (2001) '"Remedial work": men's strategic responses to their violence against intimate female partners.' *Sociology 35*, 3, 695–714.

Cawson, P. (2002) *Child Maltreatment in the Family.* London: NSPCC.

Chantler, K., Burman, E., Bashir, J. and Bashir, C. (2001) *Attempted Suicide and Self Harm: South Asian Women.* Manchester: Women's Studies Research Centre, Manchester Metropolitan University.

Charles, N. (1994) 'The housing needs of women and children escaping domestic violence.' *Journal of Social Policy 23*, 4, 465–487.

Charles, N. and Jones, A. (1993) *The Housing Needs of Women and Children Escaping Domestic Violence.* Cardiff: Tai Cymru.

Children Act Sub-Committee of the Lord Chancellor's Advisory Board on Family Law (2002) *Guidelines for Good Practice on Parental Contact in Cases Where There Is Domestic Violence.* London: HMSO.

Children's Subcommittee of the London Coordinating Committee to End Woman Abuse (1994) 'Make a Difference: How to Respond to Child Witnesses of Woman Abuse.' In A. Mullender and R. Morley (eds) *Children Living with Domestic Violence: Putting Men's Abuse of Women on the Child Care Agenda.* London, Ontario: Whiting and Birch.

Christensen, L. (1990) 'Children's living conditions: an investigation into disregard of care in relation to children and teenagers in families of wife mal-treatment.' *Nordisk Psychology 42*, 161–232.

Christopoulos, C., Cohn, A.D., Shaw, D.S., Joyce, S., *et al.* (1987) 'Children of abused women: 1. Adjustment at time of shelter residence.' *Journal of Marriage and the Family 49*, 611–619.

Cleaver, H. and Freeman, P. (1995) *Parental Perspectives in Cases of Suspected Child Abuse.* London: HMSO.

Cleaver, H., Unell, L. and Aldgate, J. (1999) *Children's Needs: Parenting Capacity: The Impact of Parental Mental Illness, Problem Alcohol and Drug Use and Domestic Violence on Children's Development.* London: HMSO.

Cockett, M. and Tripp, J. (1994) *The Exeter Family Study: Family Breakdown and its Impact on Children.* Exeter: University of Exeter Press.

Coleman, G. and Guildford, A. (2001) 'Threshold Women's Mental Health Initiative: striving to keep women's mental health issues on the agenda.' *Feminist Review 68*, 173–180.

Cook, D., Burton, M., Robinson, A. and Vallely, C. (2004) 'Evaluation of Specialist Domestic Violence Courts/Fast Track Systems.' CPS/DCA/Criminal Justice System Race Unit: London.

Croft, S. and Beresford, P. (1989) 'User-involvement, citizenship and social policy.' *Critical Social Policy 9*, 2, 5–18.

Cummings, E.M., Zahn-Waxler, C. and Radke-Yarrow, M. (1984) 'Developmental changes in children's reactions to anger in the home.' *Child Psychology and Child Psychiatry 25*, 63–74.

Daro, D., Edleson, J.L. and Pinderhughes, H. (2004) 'Finding common ground in the study of child maltreatment, youth violence, and adult domestic violence.' *Journal of Interpersonal Violence 19*, 3, 282–298.

Davis, C. (2003) *Housing Associations: Re-housing Women Leaving Domestic Violence – New Challenges and Good Practice*. Bristol: Policy Press.

Davis, L.V. and Carlson, B.E. (1987) 'Observations of spouse abuse: what happens to the children?' *Journal of Interpersonal Violence 2*, 3, 278–291.

Debbonaire, T. (1994) 'Work with Children in Women's Aid Refuges and After.' In A. Mullender and R. Morley (eds) *Children Living with Domestic Violence*. London: Whiting and Birch.

Debbonaire, T. (1995) 'Children in Refuges: The Picture Now.' In A. Saunders, C. Epstein, G. Keep and T. Debbonaire (eds) *It Hurts Me Too: Children's Experiences of Domestic Violence and Refuge Life*. Bristol: Women's Aid Federation of England, Childline and National Institute for Social Work.

Debbonaire, T. (1997) *Briefing Paper on Child Contact*. Bristol: Women's Aid Federation of England.

Debbonaire, T. (1999) 'Domestic Violence and Inter-agency Child Protection Work: An Overview of Recent Developments.' In N. Harwin, G. Hague and E. Malos (eds) *Domestic Violence and Multi-Agency Working: New Opportunities, Old Challenges?* London: Whiting and Birch.

Debbonaire, T. and Westminster Domestic Violence Forum (2002) *Domestic Violence Prevention Pack for Schools*. London: Westminster Domestic Violence Forum.

Department for Communities and Local Government (2006) *Homelessness Code of Guidance for Local Authorities*. London: DCLG in association with DH and DfES.

Department for Education and Skills (2003) *Every Child Matters*. Nottingham: DfES publications.

Department for Education and Skills (2005) *Every Child Matters: Change for Children – An Overview of Cross Government Guidance*. London: HMSO.

Department of the Environment, Transport and the Regions (2001) *Supporting People: Policy into Practice*. London: Department of the Environment, Transport and the Regions.

Department of Health (1995) *Child Protection: Messages from Research*. London: HMSO.

Department of Health (1997) *Family Law Act 1996: Part IV Family Homes and Domestic Violence*, Local Authority Circular LAC(97) 15. London: Department of Health.

Department of Health (1998) *Working Together to Safeguard Children. New Government Proposals for Inter-Agency Co-operation*, consultation paper. London: Department of Health.

Department of Health (1999) *National Service Framework on Mental Health*. London: Department of Health

Department of Health (2000) *Domestic Violence: A Resource Manual for Health Care Professionals*. London: Department of Health.

Department of Health (2003a) *What to Do if You Are Worried about a Child Being Abused*. London: Department of Health.

Department of Health (2003b) *Guidance on Accommodating Children in Need and their Families*. Local Authority Circular LAC(2003) 13. London: Department of Health.

Department of Health (2004) *National Service Framework for Children, Young People and Maternity Services*. London: Department of Health.

Diamond, A., Charles, C. and Allen, T. (2004) *Domestic Violence and Crime and Disorder Reduction Partnerships: Findings from a Self-completion Questionnaire*. Home Office Online Report 56/04. London: Home Office. www.homeoffice.gov.uk/rds.

Dobash, R.E. and Dobash, R.P. (1980) *Violence Against Wives: A Case Against the Patriarchy*. London: Open Books.

Dobash, R.E. and Dobash, R.P. (1984) 'The nature and antecedent of violent events.' *British Journal of Criminology 24*, 3, 269–288.

Dobash, R.E. and Dobash, R.P. (1992) *Women, Violence and Social Change*. London: Routledge.

Dobash, R. and Dobash, R. (2000) 'The Politics and Policies of Responding to Violence Against Women.' In J. Hanmer, C. Itzin, S. Quaid and D. Wigglesworth (eds) *Home Truths about Domestic Violence*. London: Routledge.

Dobash, R. and Dobash, R. (2001) 'Risk, danger and safety.' *SAFE: The Domestic Violence Quarterly December*, 7–9.

Dobash, R.E., Dobash, R.P. and Cavanagh, K. (1985) 'The Contact Between Battered Women and Social and Medical Agencies.' In J. Pahl (ed.) *Private Violence and Public Policy*. London: Routledge.

Dobash, R.P., Dobash, R.E., Cavanagh, K. and Lewis, R. (1996) *Research Evaluation of Programmes for Violent Men*. Edinburgh: HMSO.

Dobash, R.P., Dobash, R.E., Cavanagh, K. and Lewis, R. (1999) 'A research evaluation of British programmes for violent men.' *Journal of Social Policy 28*, 2, 205–233.

Dobash, R., Dobash, R., Cavanagh, K. and Lewis, R. (2000) *Changing Violent Men*. London: Sage.

Dodd, T., Nicholas, S., Povey, D. and Walker, A. (2004) 'Crime in England and Wales 2003–4.' *Home Office Statistical Bulletin October*.

Dominy, N. and Radford, L. (1996) *Domestic Violence in Surrey: Towards an Effective Inter-Agency Response*. London: Roehampton Institute and Surrey Social Services.

Ducharme, J., Atkinson, L. and Poulton, L. (2000) 'Success-based, noncoercive treatment for oppositional behaviour in children from violent homes.' *Journal of the American Academy of Child and Adolescent Psychiatry 39*, 995–1003.

Dutton, M. (1992) *Empowering and Healing the Battered Woman: A Model for Assessment and Intervention.* New York: Springer Publishing Co.

Edleson, J.L. (1995) 'Mothers and Children: Understanding the Links between Woman Battering and Child Abuse.' Paper presented at the Strategic Planning Workshop on Violence against Women, 31 March. Washington, DC: National Institute of Justice.

Edleson, J.L. (1999) 'The overlap between child maltreatment and woman battering.' *Violence Against Women 5*, 5, 134–154.

Edwards, S. (1989) *Policing Domestic Violence.* London: Sage.

Ellis, J., Stanley, N. and Bell, J. (2006) 'Prevention Programmes for Children and Young People.' In C. Humphreys and N. Stanley (eds) *Domestic Violence and Child Protection.* London: Jessica Kingsley Publishers.

Epstein, C. and Keep, G. (1995) 'What Children Tell Childline about Domestic Violence.' In A. Saunders, C. Epstein, G. Keep and T. Debbonaire (eds) *It Hurts Me Too: Children's Experiences of Domestic Violence and Refuge Life.* Bristol: Women's Aid Federation of England, Childline and National Institute for Social Work.

Ettore, E. (1997) *Women and Alcohol: A Private Pleasure or a Public Problem?* London: Women's Press.

Evans, A. (1991) *Alternatives to Bed and Breakfast: Temporary Housing Solutions for Homeless People.* London: National Housing and Town Planning Council.

Evans, A. and Duncan, S. (1988) *Responding to Homelessness: Local Authority Policy and Practice.* London: HMSO.

Evason, E. (1982) *Hidden Violence: A Study of Battered Women in Northern Ireland.* Belfast: Farset Press.

Fantuzzo, J.W. and Lindquist, C.U. (1989) 'The effects of observing conjugal violence on children: a review and analysis of research methodology.' *Journal of Family Violence 4*, 1, 77–94.

Fantuzzo, J.W., DePaola, L.M., Lamber, L., Mariono, T., *et al.* (1991) 'Effects of interpersonal violence on the psychological adjustment and competencies of young children.' *Journal of Consulting and Clinical Psychology 59*, 258–265.

Farmer, E. (2006) 'Using Research to Develop Child Protection and Child Care Practice.' In C. Humphreys and N. Stanley (eds) *Domestic Violence and Child Protection.* London: Jessica Kingsley Publishers.

Farmer, E. and Moyers, S. (2005) *Children Placed with Family and Friends: Placement Patterns and Outcomes – A Report for the Department for Education and Skills.* Bristol: Bristol University, School for Policy Studies.

Farmer, E. and Owen, M. (1995) *Child Protection Practice: Private Risks and Public Remedies.* London: HMSO.

Farmer, E. and Pollock, S. (1998) *Substitute Care for Sexually Abused and Abusing Children.* Chichester: John Wiley & Sons.

Feltham, C. (2000) 'An Introduction to Counselling and Psychotherapy.' In S. Palmer (ed.) *Introduction to Counselling and Psychotherapy.* London: Sage.

Finkelhor, D. (1996) 'Long-term Effects of Sexual Abuse.' Paper presented to Child Abuse and Neglect Conference, Dublin, Ireland, 2 April.

Fonagy, P., Steele, M., Steele, H., Higgitt, A. and Mayer, L.S. (1994) 'The Emmanuel Miller Memorial Lecture 1992: the theory and practice of resilience.' *Journal of Child Psychology and Psychiatry 35*, 2, 231–258.

Forman, J. (1995) *Is There a Correlation between Child Sexual Abuse and Domestic Violence? An Exploratory Study of the Links between Child Sexual Abuse and Domestic Violence in a Sample of Intrafamilial Child Sexual Abuse Cases.* Glasgow: Women's Support Project.

Frances, R. (1995) 'An Overview of Community-Based Intervention Programmes for Men who are Violent or Abusive in the Home.' In R.E. Dobash, R.P. Dobash and L. Noaks (eds) *Gender and Crime.* Cardiff: University of Wales Press.

Gamache, D. and Snapp, S. (1995) 'Teach Your Children Well: Elementary Schools and Violence Prevention.' In E. Peled, P. Jaffe and J.L. Edleson (eds) *Ending the Cycle of Violence: Community Responses to Children of Battered Women.* Thousand Oaks, CA: Sage.

Garmezy, N. (1985) 'Stress-Resistant Children: In Search of Protective Factors.' In J. Stevenson (ed.) *Recent Research in Development Psychopathology.* Oxford: Pergamon.

Gelles, R.J. and Loseke, D. (eds) (1993) *Current Controversies in Family Violence.* London: Sage.

Gibbons, J., Conroy, S. and Bell, C. (1995) *Operating the Child Protection System: A Study of Child Protection Practices in English Local Authorities.* London: HMSO.

Giles-Sims, J. (1998) 'The Aftermath of Partner Violence.' In J. Jasinski and L. Williams (eds) *Partner Violence: A Comprehensive Review of Twenty Years of Research.* London: Sage.

Glaser, D. and Prior, V. (1997) 'Is the term child protection applicable to emotional abuse?' *Child Abuse Review 6*, 315–329.

Goddard, C.R. and Carew, R. (1988) 'Protecting the child: hostages to fortune?' *Social Work Today 20*, 16, 12–14.

Goddard, C. and Hiller, P. (1993) 'Child sexual abuse: assault in a violent context.' *Australian Journal of Social Issues* 28, 1, 20–33.

Goldblatt, H. (2003) 'Strategies of coping among adolescents experiencing interparental violence.' *Journal of Interpersonal Violence 18*, 2, 532–552.

Gondolf, E.W. (2000) '30-month follow-up of court-referred batterers in four cities.' *International Journal of Offender Therapy and Comparative Criminology 44*, 1, 41–61.

Gondolf, E.W. (2001) 'Limitations of experimental evaluation of batterer programs.' *Trauma, Violence, and Abuse 2*, 79–88.

Gondolf, E.W. (2002) *Batterer Intervention Systems: Issues, Outcomes and Recommendations.* Thousand Oaks, CA: Sage.

Graham, P., Rawlings, E. and Rimini, W. (1988) 'Survivors of Terror: Battered Women, Hostages and the Stockholm Syndrome.' In K. Yllo and M. Bograd (eds) *Feminist Perspectives on Wife Abuse.* London: Sage.

Graham-Bermann, S.A. (1998) 'The Impact of Woman Abuse on Children's Social Development: Research and Theoretical Perspectives.' In G.W. Holden, R. Geffner and E.N. Jouriles (eds) *Children Exposed to Marital Violence: Theory Research and Applied Issues.* Washington, DC: American Psychological Association.

Graham-Bermann, S.A. and Levendosky, A.A. (1998) 'Traumatic stress symptoms in children of battered women.' *Journal of Interpersonal Violence 14*, 111–128.

Grotberg, E. (1997) 'The International Resilience Project.' In M. John (ed.) *A Charge Against Society: The Child's Right to Protection.* London: Jessica Kingsley Publishers.

Grusz02nski, R.J., Brink, J.C. and Edleson, J.L. (1988) 'Support and education groups for children of battered women.' *Child Welfare 67*, 5, 431–444.

Haddock, S. (2002) 'Training family therapists to assess for and intervene in partner abuse: a curriculum for graduate courses, professional workshops and self-study.' *Journal of Marital and Family Therapy 28*, 2, 193–202.

Hague, G. and Malos, E. (1993) *Domestic Violence: Action for Change.* Cheltenham: New Clarion Press.

Hague, G. and Malos, E. (2005) *Domestic Violence: Action for Change*, 3rd edn. Cheltenham: New Clarion Press.

Hague, G., Kelly, L., Malos, E., Mullender, A. and Debbonaire, T. (1996) *Children, Domestic Violence and Refuges. A Study of Needs and Responses.* Bristol: Women's Aid Federation of England.

Hague, G., Malos, E. and Dear, W. (1996) *Multi-Agency Work and Domestic Violence.* Bristol: Policy Press.

Hague, G., Mullender, A., Kelly, L., Malos, E. and Debbonaire, T. (2000) 'Unsung Innovation: The History of Work with Children in UK Domestic Violence Refuges.' In J. Hanmer, C. Itzin, S. Quaid and D. Wigglesworth (eds) *Home Truths About Domestic Violence: Feminist Influences on Policy and Practice – A Reader.* London: Routledge.

Hague, G., Mullender, A. and Kelly, L. (2001) *Canadian Innovations and Violence against Women.* Bristol: Policy Press.

Hague, G., Mullender, A. and Aris, R. (2002) *Professionals by Experience: A Guide to Service User Participation and Consultation for Domestic Violence Services.* Bristol: Women's Aid Federation of England.

Hague, G., Mullender, A., Aris, R. and Dear, W. (2002) *Abused Women's Perspectives: Responsiveness and Accountability of Domestic Violence and Inter-Agency Initiatives.* Bristol: School for Policy Studies, University of Bristol.

Hallett, C. (1995) 'Child Abuse: An Academic Overview.' In P. Kingston and B. Penhale (eds) *Family Violence and the Caring Professions.* Basingstoke: Macmillan.

Hamby, S. (1998) 'Partner Violence: Prevention and Intervention.' In J. Jasinski and L. Williams (eds) *Partner Violence: A Comprehensive Review of Twenty Years of Research.* London: Sage.

Hampshire Inspection and Advisory Service (undated) 'What is a Healthy School?' Hampshire: Hampshire County Council. www3.hants.gov.uk/education/hias/healthyschools/whatisahealthyschool.htm (accessed September 2006).

Hanmer, J. (1989) 'Women and Policing in Britain.' In J. Hanmer, J. Radford and E. Stanko (eds) *Women, Policing and Male Violence.* London: Routledge.

Hanmer, J. and Saunders, S. (1984) *Well-Founded Fear: A Community Study of Violence to Women.* London: Hutchinson.

Hanmer, J. and Saunders, S. (1993) *Women, Violence and Crime Prevention.* Aldershot: Avebury.

Harne, L. (2004) 'Childcare, Violence and Fathering: Are Violent Fathers Who Look After Their Children Likely to be Less Abusive?' In R. Klein and B. Wallner (eds) *Gender, Conflict, and Violence.* Vienna: Studien-Verlag.

Harne, L. and Rights of Women (1997) *Valued Families: The Lesbian Mother's Legal Handbook.* London: Women's Press.

Harris Hendriks, J., Black, D. and Kaplan, T. (1993) *When Father Kills Mother: Guiding Children Through Trauma and Grief.* London: Routledge.

Harwin, N. (1997) 'The Role of Women's Aid and Refuge Support Services for Women and Children.' In S. Bewley, J. Friend and G. Mezey (eds) *Violence Against Women.* London: Royal College of Obstetricians and Gynaecologists.

Hearn, J. (1996a) 'Men's Violence to Known Women: Historical, Everyday and Theoretical Constructions by Men.' In B. Fawcett, B. Featherstone, J. Hearn and C. Toft (eds) *Violence and Gender Relations.* London: Sage.

Hearn, J. (1996b) 'Men's Violence to Known Women: Men's Accounts and Men's Policy Developments.' In B. Fawcett, B. Featherstone, J. Hearn and C. Toft (eds) *Violence and Gender Relations*. London: Sage.

Henning, K., Jones, A.R. and Holdford, R. (2005) '"I didn't do it, but if I did I had a good reason": minimization, denial and attributions of blame among male and female domestic violence offenders.' *Journal of Family Violence 20*, 3, 131–139.

Herman, J. (2001) *Trauma and Recovery*, 2nd edn. London: Pandora.

Hershorn, M. and Rosenbaum, A. (1985) 'Children of marital violence: a closer look at unintended victims.' *American Journal of Orthopsychiatry 55*, 260–266.

Hester, M. (2000) 'Child Protection and Domestic Violence: Findings from a Rowntree NSPCC Study.' In J. Hanmer, C. Itzin, S. Quaid and D. Wigglesworth (eds) *Home Truths About Domestic Violence: Feminist Influences on Policy and Practice – A Reader*. London: Routledge.

Hester, M. (2004) 'Future trends and developments: violence against women in Europe and East Asia.' *Violence Against Women 10*, 12, 1431–1448.

Hester, M. (2006a) 'Making it through the criminal justice system: attrition and domestic violence.' *Social Policy and Society 4*, 1, 79–90.

Hester, M. (2006b) 'Asking About Domestic Violence.' In C. Humphreys and N. Stanley (eds) *Domestic Violence and Child Protection*. London: Jessica Kingsley Publishers.

Hester, M. and Pearson, C. (1997a) 'Domestic Violence and Parental Contact: Children's Right to Safety.' In M. John (ed.) *A Charge against Society: The Child's Right to Protection*. London: Jessica Kingsley Publishers.

Hester, M. and Pearson, C. (1997b) 'Domestic violence and children: the practice of family court welfare officers.' *Child and Family Law Quarterly 9*, 3, 281–290.

Hester, M. and Pearson, C. (1998) *From Periphery to Centre: Domestic Violence in Work with Abused Children*. Bristol: Policy Press.

Hester, M. and Radford, L. (1992) 'Domestic violence and access arrangements for children in Denmark and Britain.' *Journal of Social Welfare and Family Law 1*, 57–70.

Hester, M. and Radford, L. (1996) *Domestic Violence and Child Contact Arrangements in England and Denmark*. Bristol: Policy Press.

Hester, M. with Scott, J. (2000) *Women in Abusive Relationships: Group Work and Agency Support*. Sunderland: University of Sunderland in association with Barnardo's.

Hester, M. and Westmarland, N. (2005) *Tackling Domestic Violence: Effective Interventions and Approaches*, Home Office research study 290. London: Home Office.

Hester, M., Kelly, L. and Radford, J. (eds) (1996) *Women, Violence and Male Power*. Buckingham: Open University Press.

Hester, M., Pearson, C. and Radford, L. (1997) *Domestic Violence: A National Survey of Court Welfare and Voluntary Sector Mediation Practice*. Bristol: Policy Press.

Hester, M., Pearson, C. and Harwin, N. (2000) *Making an Impact: Children and Domestic Violence – A Reader*. London: Jessica Kingsley Publishers.

Hester, M., Westmarland, N., Gangoli, G., Wilkinson, M., *et al.* (2006) *Domestic Violence Perpetrators: Identifying Needs to Inform Early Intervention*. Newcastle: Northern Rock Foundation and University of Bristol.

Higgins, G. (1994) 'Hammersmith Women's Aid Childhood Development Project.' In A. Mullender and R. Morley (eds) *Children Living with Domestic Violence*. London: Whiting and Birch.

Hilberman, E. and Munson, K. (1977) 'Sixty battered women.' *Victimology 2*, 460–470.

Hilton, N.Z. (1992) 'Battered women's concerns about their children witnessing wife assault.' *Journal of Interpersonal Violence 7*, 1, 77–86.

HM Government (2006) *Working Together to Safeguard Children: A Guide to Inter-Agency Working to Safeguard and Promote the Welfare of Children*. London: The Stationery Office.

HM Inspectorate of Court Administration (2005) *Domestic Violence, Safety and Family Proceedings: Thematic Review of the Handling of Domestic Violence Issues by the Children and Family Court Advisory and Support Service (CAFCASS) and the Administration of Family Courts in Her Majesty's Courts Service (HMCS)*. London: HMICA.

HMSO (1998) Crime and Disorder Act 1998. London: HMSO.

Hoff, L. (1990) *Battered Women as Survivors*. London: Routledge.

Holden, G.W. and Ritchie, K.L. (1991) 'Linking extreme marital discord, child rearing, and child behaviour problems: evidence from battered women.' *Child Development 62*, 311–327.

Holder, R., Kelly, L. and Singh, T. (1994) *Suffering in Silence: Children and Young People who Witness Domestic Violence*. London: Hammersmith and Fulham Domestic Violence Forum.

Home Affairs Select Committee (1993) *Report of Inquiry into Domestic Violence*. London: HMSO.

Home Office (1990) *Domestic Violence*, Home Office circular 60/90. London: Home Office.

Home Office (1994) *National Standards for Probation Service Family Court Welfare Work*. London: Home Office.

Home Office (1995a) *Child Protection: Messages from Research*. London: Home Office.

Home Office (1995b) *Inter-Agency Circular Work: Inter-Agency Co-Ordination to Tackle Domestic Violence*. London: Home Office.

Home Office (1998) *Living without Fear: An Integrated Approach to Tackling Domestic Violence*. London: Home Office.

Home Office (2003) *Safety and Justice: The Government's Proposals on Domestic Violence*. Home Office Consultation Paper Cm 5847. London: Home Office.

Home Office (2004) *Developing Domestic Violence Strategies: A Guide for Partnerships*. London: Home Office Violent Crimes Unit.

Home Office (2005) *National Report on Domestic Violence*. London: Home Office.

Home Office (2006) Domestic Violence Mini-site. www.crimereduction.gov.uk/dv/dv01.htm (accessed November 2006).

Home Office, Department of Health, Department for Education and Skills and Welsh Office (1991) *Working Together Under the Children Act 1989: A Guide to Arrangements for Inter-Agency Co-operation for the Protection of Children from Abuse*. London: HMSO.

Homer, M., Leonard, A. and Taylor, P. (1984) *Private Violence, Public Shame: A Report on the Circumstances of Women Leaving Domestic Violence in Cleveland*. Cleveland: Cleveland Refuge and Aid for Women and Children.

Hooper, C.-A. (1987) 'Getting him off the hook: the theory and practice of mother blaming in child sexual abuse.' *Trouble and Strife 12*, 20–25.

Hooper, C.-A. (1992) *Mothers Surviving Child Sexual Abuse*. London: Routledge.

Hooper, C.-A. (1995) 'Women's and their children's experiences of domestic violence: rethinking the links.' *Women's Studies International Forum 18*, 3, 349–360.

Housing Act (1996) London: HMSO.

Hughes, H.M. (1988) 'Psychological and behavioural correlates of family violence in child witnesses and victims.' *American Journal of Orthopsychiatry 58*, 1, 77–90.

Hughes, H. (1992) 'Impact of spouse abuse on children of battered women.' *Violence Update 1*, 9–11.

Hughes, H. and Barad, S. (1983) 'Psychological functioning of children in a battered women's shelter.' *American Journal of Orthopsychiatry 53*, 3, 525–531.

Hughes, H.M., Parkinson, D. and Vargo, M. (1989) 'Witnessing spouse abuse and experiencing physical abuse: a "double whammy"?' *Journal of Family Violence 4*, 2, 197–209.

Humphreys, C. (1997a) *Case Planning Issues Where Domestic Violence Occurs in the Context of Child Protection*. Coventry: University of Warwick.

Humphreys, C. (1997b) 'Child sexual abuse allegations in the context of divorce: issues for mothers.' *British Journal of Social Work 27*, 529–544.

Humphreys, C. (2000) *Starting Over: Women and Children's Experiences of Domestic Violence Outreach*. Bristol: Women's Aid.

Humphreys, C. and Thiara, R. (2002) *Routes to Safety: Protection Issues Facing Abused Women and Children and the Role of Outreach Services*. Bristol: Women's Aid Federation of England.

Humphreys, C. and Thiara, R. (2003) 'Mental health and domestic violence: "I call it symptoms of abuse."' *British Journal of Social Work 33*, 209–226.

Humphreys, C., Hester, M., Hague, G., Mullender, A., *et al.* (2000) *From Good Intentions to Good Practice: Mapping Services Working with Families where there is Domestic Violence*. Bristol: Policy Press.

Hurley, D.J. and Jaffe, P. (1990) 'Children's observations of violence: II. Clinical implications for children's mental health professionals.' *Canadian Journal of Psychiatry 35*, 6, 471–476.

Hyden, M. (1994) *Woman Battering as Marital Act: The Construction of a Violent Marriage*. Oxford: Oxford University Press.

Hyman, C.A. (1978) 'Some characteristics of abusing families referred to the NSPCC.' *British Journal of Social Work 8*, 2, 171–179.

Imam, U.F. (1994) 'Asian Children and Domestic Violence.' In A. Mullender and R. Morley (eds) *Children Living with Domestic Violence*. London: Whiting and Birch.

Inter-Ministerial Group (2005) *Domestic Violence: A National Report*. London: Home Office.

Jaffe, P. (1996) 'Children of domestic violence: special challenges in custody and visitation dispute resolution.' *Special Challenges in Custody and Visitation 24*, 19–30.

Jaffe, P., Wolfe, D.A., Wilson, S.K. and Zak, L. (1985) 'Critical issues in the assessment of children's adjustment to witnessing family violence.' *Canada's Mental Health 33*, 4, 14–19.

Jaffe, P., Wilson, S. and Wolfe, D. (1986) 'Promoting changes in attitude and understanding of conflict among child witnesses of family violence.' *Canadian Journal of Behavioural Science 18*, 356–380.

Jaffe, P., Wolfe, D.A., Wilson, S.K. and Zak, L. (1986a) 'Similarities in behavioural and social maladjustment among child victims and witnesses to family violence.' *American Journal of Orthopsychiatry 56*, 1, 142–146.

Jaffe, P., Wolfe, D.A., Wilson, S.K. and Zak, L. (1986b) 'Family violence and child adjustment: a comparative analysis of girls' and boys' behavioural symptoms.' *American Journal of Psychiatry 14*, 1, 74–77.

Jaffe, P., Wolfe, D.A., Wilson, S.K. and Zak, L. (1986c) 'Emotional and physical health problems of battered women.' *Canadian Journal of Psychiatry 31*, 625–629.

Jaffe, P., Hurley, D. and Wolfe, D. (1990) 'Children's observations of violence: 1. Critical issues in child development and intervention planning.' *Canadian Journal of Psychiatry 35*, 6, 466–469.

Jaffe, P., Wolfe, D.A. and Wilson, S.K. (1990) *Children of Battered Women*. Newbury Park, CA: Sage.

James, G. (1994) *Study of Working Together: Part 8 Reports*. London: Department of Health.

Jenkins, A. (1990) *Invitations to Responsibility: The Therapeutic Engagement of Men who are Violent and Abusive*. Adelaide: Dulwich Centre Publications.

Johnson, N. (1995) 'Domestic Violence: An Overview.' In P. Kingston and B. Penhale (eds) *Family Violence and the Caring Professions*. London: Macmillan.

Johnston, J. (1992) *High Conflict and Violent Divorcing Families: Findings on Children's Adjustment and Proposed Guidelines for the Resolution of Disputed Custody and Visitation – Report of the Project*. Corte Madera, CA: Center for the Family in Transition.

Jones, A. (1991) *Women Who Kill*. London: Victor Gollancz.

Jones, A., Pleace, N. and Quilgars, D. (2002) *Firm Foundations: An Evaluation of the Shelter 'Homeless to Home' Service*. London: Shelter.

Jouriles, E.N., Barling, J. and O'Leary, K.D. (1987) 'Predicting child behaviour problems in maritally violent families.' *Journal of Abnormal Child Psychology 15*, 165–173.

Jouriles, E.N., Murphy, C.M. and O'Leary, K.D. (1989) 'Interspousal aggression, marital discord, and child problems.' *Journal of Consulting and Clinical Psychology 57*, 453–455.

Jouriles, E.N., McDonald, R., Norwood, W.D. and Ezell, E. (2001) 'Issues and Controversies in Documenting the Prevalence of Children's Exposure to Domestic Violence.' In S.A. Graham-Bermann and J.L. Eddleson (eds) *Domestic Violence in the Lives of Children, the Future of Research, Intervention and Social Policy*. Washington: American Psychological Association.

Kaye, M. (1996) 'Domestic violence, residence and contact.' *Child and Family Law Quarterly 8*, 4, 285–296.

Kelly, L. (1988) *Surviving Sexual Violence*. Cambridge: Polity Press.

Kelly, L. (1992) 'Disability and child abuse: a research review of the connections.' *Child Abuse Review 1*, 157–167.

Kelly, L. (1994) 'The Interconnectedness of Domestic Violence and Child Abuse: Challenges for Research, Policy and Practice.' In A. Mullender and R. Morley (eds) *Children Living with Domestic Violence*. London: Whiting and Birch.

Kelly, L. (1996) 'When woman protection is the best kind of child protection: children, domestic violence and child abuse.' *Administration 44*, 2, 118–135.

Kelly, L. and Humphreys, C. (2001) 'Supporting Women and Children in their Communities.' In J. Taylor-Browne (ed.) *What Works in Reducing Domestic Violence: A Comprehensive Guide for Professionals*. London: Whiting and Birch.

Kelly, L. and Radford, J. (1996) 'Nothing Really Happened: The Invalidation of Women's Experiences of Sexual Violence.' In M. Hester, L. Kelly and J. Radford (eds) *Women, Violence and Male Power*. Buckingham: Open University Press.

Kelly, L., Regan, L. and Burton, S. (1991) *An Exploratory Study of the Prevalence of Sexual Abuse in a Sample of 1200 16 to 21 Year Olds: Final Report to the ESRC*. London: Child Abuse Studies Unit, University of North London.

Kilpatrick, K.L. and Williams, L.M. (1997) 'Post-traumatic stress disorder in child witnesses to domestic violence.' *American Journal of Orthopsychiatry 67*, 639–644.

Kirkwood, C. (1993) *Leaving Abusive Partners*. London: Sage.

Kitzmann, K.M., Gaylord, N.K., Holt, A.R. and Kenny, E.D. (2003) 'Child witnesses to domestic violence: a meta-analytic review.' *Journal of Consulting and Clinical Psychology 71*, 2, 339–352.

Kolbo, J., Blakely, E.H. and Engleman, D. (1996) 'Children who witness domestic violence: a review of empirical literature.' *Journal of Interpersonal Violence 11*, 2, 281–293.

Laing, L. (2001) 'Working with women: exploring individual and group work approaches.' www.austdvclearinghouse.unsw.edu.au (accessed 20 February 2004).

Laming, L. (2003) 'The Victoria Climbie Inquiry – Report of an Inquiry.' www.victoria-climbie-inquiry.org.uk/keydocuments/lordstate.htm (accessed 11 September 2006).

Laming Inquiry (2003) Speech by Lord Laming 25 January 2003. www.victoria-climbie-inquiry.org.uk/keydocuments/lordstate.htm (accessed 11 September 2006).

Law Commission (1992) *Domestic Violence and the Occupation of the Matrimonial Home* (HC1; Law Commission number 207). London: Law Commission.

Lehmann, P. (1997) 'The development of post-traumatic stress disorder (PTSD) in a sample of child witnesses to mother assault.' *Journal of Family Violence 12*, 3, 241–257.

Levendosky, A.A., Huth-Bocks, A.C., Semel, M.A. and Shapiro, D.L. (2002) 'Trauma symptoms in preschool-age children exposed to domestic violence.' *Journal of Interpersonal Violence 17*, 2, 150–164.

Levine, M.B. (1975) 'Interparental violence and its effect on the children: a study of 50 families in general practice.' *Medicine, Science and the Law 15*, 3, 172–176.

Lobel, K. (ed.) (1986) *Naming the Violence: Speaking Out About Lesbian Battering.* Emeryville, CA: Seal Press.

Local Government Association (2005) *Vision for Services for Children and Young People Affected by Domestic Violence – Guidance to Local Commissioners of Children's Services.* London: Local Government Association.

Lodge, S., Goodwin, J. and Pearson, C. (2001) *Domestic Violence in Devon: A Mapping Exercise.* Exeter: Devon County Council & Devon and Cornwall Constabulary.

London Borough of Greenwich (1987) *A Child in Mind: Protection of Children in a Responsible Society – Report of the Commission of Inquiry into the Circumstances Surrounding the Death of Kimberley Carlile.* London: London Borough of Greenwich.

London Borough of Hackney (1993) *The Links Between Domestic Violence and Child Abuse: Developing Services.* London: Hackney Council Press and Publicity Team.

London Borough of Hackney (1994) *Good Practice Guidelines: Responding to Domestic Violence.* London: London Borough of Hackney Women's Unit.

London Borough of Islington (1995) *S.T.O.P Domestic Violence.* London: Islington Council.

Loosley, S. (1994) 'Women's Community House Children's Programme: A Model in Perspective.' In A. Mullender and R. Morley (eds) *Children Living with Domestic Violence.* London: Whiting and Birch.

Malloch, M.S. and Webb, S.A. (1993) 'Intervening with male batterers: a study of social workers' perceptions of domestic violence.' *Social Work and Social Sciences Review 4*, 2, 119–147.

Malos, E. and Hague, G. (1993a) *Domestic Violence and Housing: Local Authority Responses to Women and Children Escaping from Domestic Violence.* Bristol: Women's Aid Federation and University of Bristol.

Malos, E. and Hague, G. (1993b) 'Homelessness and domestic violence: the effect on children and young people.' *Childright 99*, 15–19.

Mama, A. (1996) *The Hidden Struggle: Statutory and Voluntary Sector Responses to Violence Against Black Women in the Home.* London: Whiting and Birch.

Mathews, D.J. (1995) 'Parenting Groups for Men Who Batter.' In E. Peled, P.G. Jaffe and J.L. Edleson (eds) *Ending the Cycle of Violence.* Thousand Oaks, CA: Sage.

Maynard, M. (1985) 'The Response of Social Workers to Domestic Violence.' In J. Pahl (ed.) *Private Violence and Public Policy.* London: Routledge.

McCarry, M. (2003) 'The Connections Between Masculinity and Domestic Violence: What Young People Think', unpublished PhD thesis. Bristol: Universtiy of Bristol.

McGee, C. (1996) 'Children's and Mother's Experiences of Child Protection Following Domestic Violence.' Paper presented at Violence, Abuse and Women's Citizenship International Conference, Brighton, June 20.

McGee, C. (2000) *Childhood Experiences of Domestic Violence.* London: Jessica Kingsley Publishers.

McGibbon, A., Cooper, L. and Kelly, L. (1989) *What Support?* Hammersmith and Fulham Council Community Police Committee Domestic Violence Project. London: Polytechnic of North London.

McKay, M.M. (1994) 'The link between domestic violence and child abuse: assessment and treatment consider-ations.' *Child Welfare 73*, 1, 29–39.

McLeod, J. (2000) 'Research Issues in Counselling and Psychotherapy.' In S. Palmer (ed.) *Introduction to Counselling and Psychotherapy.* London: Sage.

McLeod, J. (2001) *Counselling in the Workplace: The Facts.* Rugby: BACP.

McWilliams, M. and McKiernan, J. (1993) *Bringing it All Out into the Open: Domestic Violence in Northern Ireland.* Belfast: HMSO.

Mellor-Clark, J. (2000) *Counselling in Primary Care in the Context of the NHS Quality Agenda: The Facts.* Rugby: BACP.

Mezey, G.C. and Bewley, S. (1997) 'Domestic violence and pregnancy.' *British Medical Journal 314*, 1295.

Milner, J. (1996) 'Men's Resistance to Social Workers.' In B. Fawcett, B. Featherstone, J. Hearn and C. Toft (eds) *Violence and Gender Relations.* London: Sage.

Mirrlees-Black, C. (1999) *Domestic Violence: Findings from a New British Crime Survey Self-completion Questionnaire.* Home Office Research Study 191. London: Home Office.

Mirrlees-Black, C., Mayhew, P. and Percy, A. (1996) *The British Crime Survey – Engalnd and Wales.* London: Govern-ment Statistical Service.

Mooney, J. (1994) *The Hidden Figure: Domestic Violence in North London.* London: Islington Police and Crime Prevention Unit.

Mooney, J. (2000) 'Revealing the Hidden Figure of Domestic Violence.' In J. Hanmer, C. Itzin, S. Quaid and D. Wigglesworth (eds) *Home Truths about Domestic Violence.* London: Routledge.

Moore, J.G. (1975) 'Yo-yo children: victims of matrimonial violence.' *Child Welfare 54,* 8, 557–566.

Moore, T., Pepler, D., Weinberg, B., Hammond, L., *et al.* (1990) 'Research on children from violent families.' *Canada's Mental Health 38,* 19–23.

Morley, R. (1993) 'Recent responses to "domestic violence" against women: a feminist critique.' *Social Policy Review 5,* 175–206.

Morley, R. and Mullender, A. (1994) *Preventing Domestic Violence to Women.* Crime Prevention Unit series, paper 48. London: Home Office Police Department.

Morran, D. and Wilson, M. (1997) *Men Who Are Violent to Women: A Groupwork Practice Manual.* Lyme Regis: Russell House Publishing.

Morris, L. (2001) 'Emotional literacy for kids.' *Counselling and Psychotherapy Journal 12,* 8, 15–18.

Mullender, A. (1994) 'School-based Work: Education for Prevention.' In A. Mullender and R. Morley (eds) *Children Living with Domestic Violence: Putting Men's Abuse of Women on the Child Care Agenda.* London: Whiting and Birch.

Mullender, A. (1996a) *Rethinking Domestic Violence: The Social Work and Probation Response.* London: Routledge.

Mullender, A. (1996b) 'Children living with domestic violence.' *Adoption and Fostering 20,* 1, 8–15.

Mullender, A. (1997) 'Domestic violence and social work: the challenge to change.' *Critical Social Policy 50,* 53–78.

Mullender, A. (1998) 'Social Service Responses to Domestic Violence: The Inter-Agency Challenge.' In N. Harwin, G. Hague and E. Malos (eds) *Domestic Violence and Multi-Agency Working: New Opportunities, Old Challenges?* London: Whiting and Birch.

Mullender, A. (2001) 'Meeting the Needs of Children.' In J. Taylor-Browne (ed.) *What Works in Reducing Domestic Violence: A Comprehensive Guide for Professionals.* London: Whiting and Birch.

Mullender, A. (2004) *Tackling Domestic Violence: Providing Support for Children who have Witnessed Domestic Violence.* Home Office development and practice report. London: Home Office.

Mullender, A. and Debbonaire, T. (2000) *Child Protection and Domestic Violence: A Practitioner's Guide.* Birmingham: Venture Press.

Mullender, A. and Morley, R. (eds) (1994) *Children Living with Domestic Violence: Putting Men's Abuse of Women on the Child Care Agenda.* London: Whiting and Birch.

Mullender, A. and Ward, D. (1991) *Self-directed Groupwork: Users Take Action for Empowerment.* London: Whiting and Birch.

Mullender, A., Hague, G., Imam, U., Kelly, L. and Malos, E. (2000) *Children's Needs, Coping Strategies and Understandings of Woman Abuse.* Coventry: University of Warwick.

Mullender, A., Hague, G., Imam, U., Kelly, L. *et al.* (2002) *Children's Perspectives on Domestic Violence.* London: Sage.

National Children's Bureau (1993) *Investigation into Inter-Agency Practice Following the Cleveland Area Child Protection Committee's Report Concerning the Death of Toni Dales.* London: National Children's Bureau.

National Inter-Agency Working Party (1992) *Domestic Violence.* London: Victim Support.

Nazroo, J. (1995) 'Uncovering gender differences in the use of marital violence: the effect of methodology.' *Sociology 29,* 3, 475–494.

Newham Asian Women's Project (1998) *Young Asian Women and Self Harm: A Mental Health Needs Assessment of Young Asian Women in East London.* London: Newham Inner City Multifund and Newham Asian Women's Project.

O'Hagan, K. and Dillenburger, K. (1995) *Abuse of Women Within Childcare Work.* Buckingham: Open University Press.

O'Hara, M. (1994) 'Child Deaths in the Context of Domestic Violence: Implications for Professional Practice.' In A. Mullender and R. Morley (eds) *Children Living with Domestic Violence: Putting Men's Abuse of Women on the Child Care Agenda.* London: Whiting and Birch.

Pagelow, M.D. (1982) 'Children in Violent Families: Direct and Indirect Victims.' In S. Hill and B.J. Barnes (eds) *Young Children and Their Families.* Lexington, MA: Lexington Books.

Pahl, J. (ed.) (1985) *Private Violence and Public Policy.* London: Routledge.

Parton, N. (1990) 'Taking Child Abuse Seriously.' In The Violence Against Children Study Group (ed.) *Taking Child Abuse Seriously.* London: Unwin Hyman.

Paymar, M. (2000) *Violent No More: Helping Men End Domestic Abuse* (1st and 2nd rev. eds). Alameda, CA: Hunter House.

Peake, A. and Fletcher, M. (1997) *Strong Mothers: A Resource for Mothers and Carers of Children who have been Sexually Assaulted.* Lyme Regis: Russell House.

Peled, E. (1997) 'Intervention with children of battered women: a review of current literature.' *Children and Youth Services Review 19,* 4, 277–299.

Peled, E. and Davis, D. (1995) *Groupwork with Children of Battered Women: A Practitioner's Manual.* Thousand Oaks, CA: Sage.

Peled, E. and Edleson, J.L. (1992) 'Breaking the secret: multiple perspectives on groupwork with children of battered women.' *Violence and Victims 7,* 4, 327–346.

Pence, E. (undated) *Community-Based Intervention: Overview.* Duluth, MN: Domestic Abuse Intervention Project. www.duluth-model.org/daipoverview.html.

Pence, E. and Paymar, M. (1993) *Education Groups for Men who Batter: The Duluth Model.* New York: Springer.

Pfouts, J.H., Schopler, J.H. and Henley, H.C. (1982) 'Forgotten victims of family violence.' *Adolescent Psychiatry 41,* 1095–1103.

Porter, B.K. and O'Leary, K.D. (1980) 'Marital discord and childhood behaviour problems.' *Journal of Abnormal Child Psychology 8,* 287–295.

Povey, D. (ed.) (2004) *Crime in England and Wales 2002/2003: Supplementary Volume 1 – Homicide and Gun Crime.* London: Home Office.

Pringle, K. (1995) *Men, Masculinities and Social Welfare.* London: UCL Press.

Protective Behaviours (undated) www.protectivebehaviours.co.uk (accessed November 2006).

Ptacek, J. (1988) 'Why Do Men Batter Their Wives?' In K. Yllo and M. Bograd (eds) *Feminist Perspectives on Wife Abuse.* Newbury Park, CA: Sage.

Quaid, S. and Itzin, C. (2000) 'The Criminal Justice Response to Women Who Kill: An Interview with Helena Kennedy.' In C. Itzin and J. Hanmer (eds) *Home Truths about Domestic Violence: Feminist Influences on Policy and Practice.* London: Routledge.

Radford, L. and Hester, M. (2006) *Mothering through Domestic Violence.* London: Jessica Kingsley Publishers.

Radford, J., Kelly, L. and Hester, M. (1996) 'Introduction.' In M. Hester, L. Kelly and J. Radford (eds) *Women, Violence and Male Power.* Buckingham: Open University Press.

Radford, L., Blacklock, N. and Iwi, K. (2006) 'Domestic Risk Assessment and Safety Planning in Child Protection – Assessing Perpetrators.' In C. Humphreys and N. Stanley (eds) *Domestic Violence and Child Protection.* London: Jessica Kingsley Publishers.

Rai, D. and Thiara, R. (1997) *Re-defining Spaces: The Needs of Black Women and Children in Refuge Support Services and Black Workers in Women's Aid.* Bristol: Women's Aid Federation of England.

Rees, A. and Rivett, M. (2005) '"Let a hundred flowers bloom, let a hundred schools of thought contend": towards a variety in programmes for perpetrators of domestic violence.' *Probation Journal: The Journal of Community and Criminal Justice 52,* 3, 277–288.

RESPECT (2004) *Statement of Principles and Minimum Standards of Practice for Domestic Violence Perpetrator Programmes and Associated Women's Services.* London: RESPECT. www.respect.uk.net/pages/Principles_and_Standards.

Rivett, M. (2001) 'Working systematically with family violence: controversy, context and accountability' *Journal of Family Therapy 23,* 4, 397–404.

Rivett, M.J., Howarth, E. and Harold, G. (2006) '"Watching from the stairs": towards an evidence-based practice in work with child witnesses of domestic violence.' *Clinical Child Psychology and Psychiatry 11,* 1, 103–125.

Rose, H. (1985) 'Women's Refuges: Creating New Forms of Welfare?' In C. Ungerson (ed.) *Women and Social Policy.* London: Macmillan.

Rosenbaum, A. and O'Leary, K. (1981) 'Children: the unintended victims of marital violence.' *American Journal of Orthopsychiatry 51,* 4, 692–699.

Rosenberg, M.S. (1984) 'Inter-generational Family Violence: A Critique and Implications for Witnessing Children.' Paper presented at the 92nd Annual Convention of the American Psychological Association, Toronto, October.

Rosenberg, M. and Simmons, R. (1971) *Black and White Self-Esteem: The Urban School Child.* Washington, DC: American Sociological Association.

Ross, S.M. (1996) 'Risk of physical abuse to children of spouse abusing parents.' *Child Abuse and Neglect 20,* 7, 589–598.

Rossman, B.B.R. (1998) 'Descartes' Error and Post-Traumatic Stress Disorder: Cognition and Emotion in Children who are Exposed to Parental Violence.' In G.W. Holden, R. Geffner and E.N. Jouriles (eds) *Children Exposed to Marital Violence: Theory, Research and Applied Issues.* Washington, DC: American Psychological Association.

Rutter, M. (1985) 'Resilience in the face of adversity: protective factors and resistance to psychiatric disorder.' *British Journal of Psychiatry 147,* 598–611.

Sandwell Against Domestic Violence Project (2000) *Violence Free Relationships: Asserting Rights – A Programme for Young People.* Sandwell: Sandwell Against Domestic Violence Project.

Saradjian, J. (1997) 'Typical and Atypical Female Perpetrators of Child Sexual Abuse.' Paper presented at BASPCAN conference, London, 9 December 1997.

Saunders, A., Epstein, C., Keep, G. and Debbonaire, T. (1995) *It Hurts Me Too: Children's Experiences of Domestic Violence and Refuge Life.* Bristol: Women's Aid Federation of England, Childline and National Institute for Social Work.

Saunders, B.E. (2003) 'Understanding children exposed to violence: toward an integration of overlapping fields.' *Journal of Interpersonal Violence 18,* 4, 356–376.

Saunders, B.E., Williams, L.M., Hanson, R.F., Smith, D.W. and Rheingold, A. (2002) 'Functioning of Children with Complex Victimization Histories.' Presented at the annual meeting of the International Society for Traumatic Stress Studies, Baltimore, MD, 7–10 November 2002.

Saunders, D.G. (1988) 'Wife Abuse, Husband Abuse, or Mutual Combat?' In K. Yllo and M. Bograd (eds) *Feminist Perspectives on Wife Abuse.* Newbury Park, CA: Sage.

Saunders, H. (2001) *Making Contact Worse? Report of a National Survey of Domestic Violence Refuge Services into the Enforcement of Contact Orders.* Bristol: Women's Aid Federation of England.

Saunders, H. (2004) *Twenty-Nine Child Homicides: Lessons Still to Be Learnt on Domestic Violence and Child Protection.* Bristol: Women's Aid.

Scourfield, J. (1995) *Changing Men.* Norwich: University of East Anglia.

Scourfield, J.B. and Dobash, R.P. (1999) 'Programmes for violent men: recent developments in the UK.' *Howard Journal of Criminal Justice 38,* 2, 128–143.

Shepard, M. (1999) 'Advocacy for Battered Women: Implications for a Co-ordinated Community Response.' In M. Shepard and E. Pence (eds) *Co-ordinating Community Responses to Domestic Violence: Lessons from Duluth and Beyond.* London: Sage.

Silvern, L. and Kaersvang, L. (1989) 'The traumatised children of violent marriages.' *Child Welfare 68,* 4, 421–436.

Silvern, L., Karyl, J. and Landis, T. (1995) 'Individual Psychotherapy for the Traumatized Children of Abused Women.' In E. Peled, P. Jaffe and J.L. Edleson (eds) *Ending the Cycle of Violence: Community Responses to Children of Battered Women.* Thousand Oaks, CA: Sage.

Sinclair, R. and Bullock, R. (2002) *Learning from Past Experience: A Review of Serious Case Reviews.* London: Department of Health.

Skyner, D.R. and Waters, J. (1999) 'Working with perpetrators of domestic violence to protect women and children: a partnership between Cheshire Probation Service and the NSPCC.' *Child Abuse Review 8,* 46–54.

Smart, C. (1995) 'Losing the struggle for another voice: the case of family law.' *Dalhousie Law Journal 18,* 2, 1–23.

Smith, G. (1997) 'Psychological Resilience.' In NSPCC (ed.) *Turning Points.* London: NSPCC.

Smith, L. (1989) *Domestic Violence: An Overview of the Literature.* Home Office research studies 107. London: HMSO.

Stagg, V., Wills, G.D. and Howell, M. (1989) 'Psychopathology in early childhood witnesses of family violence.' *Topics in Early Childhood Special Education 9,* 73–87.

Stanko, B. (2000) *The Day to Count: A Snapshot of the Impact of Domestic Abuse in the UK.* London: Royal Holloway, University of London.

Stanko, E.A., Crisp, D., Hale, C. and Lucraft, H. (1998) *Counting the Costs: Estimating the Impact of Domestic Violence in the London Borough of Hackney.* London: Crime Concern.

Stanley, J. and Goddard, C. (1993) 'The association between child abuse and other family violence.' *Australian Social Work 46,* 2, 3–8.

Stanley, N. and Humphreys, C. (2006) 'Multi-agency and Multi-disciplinary Work: Barriers and Opportunities.' In C. Humphreys and N. Stanley (eds) *Domestic Violence and Child Protection: Directions for Good Practice.* London: Jessica Kingsley Publishers.

Stanley, N. and Penhale, B. (1999) 'The mental health problems of mothers experiencing the child protection system: identifying the needs and appropriate responses.' *Child Abuse Review 8,* 1, 34–45.

Stark, E. and Flitcraft, A.H. (1988) 'Women and children at risk: a feminist perspective on child abuse.' *International Journal of Health Studies 18,* 1, 97–119.

Stark, E. and Flitcraft, A.H. (1996) *Women at Risk: Domestic Violence and Women's Health.* London: Sage.

Stephens, N. and McDonald, R. (2000) 'Assessment of Women Who Seek Shelter from Abusing Partners.' In J. Vincent and E. Jouriles (eds) *Domestic Violence: Guidelines for Research Informed Practice.* London: Jessica Kingsley Publishers.

Straus, M., Gelles, R.J. and Steinmetz, S.K. (1980) *Behind Closed Doors: Violence in the American Family.* Newbury Park, CA: Sage.

Sturge, C. and Glaser, D. (2000) 'Contact and domestic violence: the experts' court report.' *Family Law September,* 615–628.

Sudermann, M., Jaffe, P. and Hastings, E. (1995) 'Violence Prevention Programs in Secondary (High) Schools.' In E. Peled, P. Jaffe and J.L. Edleson (eds) *Ending the Cycle of Violence: Community Responses to Children of Battered Women.* Thousand Oaks, CA: Sage.

Sullivan, C. (2001) *Evaluating the Outcomes of Domestic Violence Service Programs: Some Practical Considerations and Strategies.* National Electronic Network on Violence against Women. www.vawnet.org/DomesticViolence/Research/VAWnetDocs/AR_evaldv.php.

Sutton, J. (1978) 'The growth of the British movement for battered women.' *Victimology* 2, 3/4, 576–584.

Taylor, J. and Chandler, T. (1995) *Lesbians Talk: Violent Relationships*. London: Scarlet Press.

Thoburn, J., Lewis, A. and Shemmings, D. (1995) *Paternalism or Partnership? Family Involvement in the Child Protection Process*. London: HMSO.

Thomas, A. and Niner, P. (1989) *Living in Temporary Accommodation: A Survey of Homeless People*. London: HMSO.

Thomas, A., Chess, S. and Birch, H. (1968) *Temperament and Behaviour Disorders in Children*. New York: New York University Press.

Thurston, R. and Beynon, J. (1995) 'Men's Own Stories, Lives and Violence: Research as Practice.' In R.E. Dobash, R.P. Dobash and L. Noaks (eds) *Gender and Crime*. Cardiff: University of Wales Press.

Tormes, Y. (1972) *Child Victims of Incest*. Denver, CO: American Humane Association.

Trinder, L., Connolly, J., Kellet, J., Notley, C. and Swift, L. (2006) *Making Contact Happen or Making Contact Work? The Process and Outcomes of In-Court Conciliation*. London: Department of Constitutional Affairs.

Truesdell, D.L., McNeil, J.S. and Deschner, J.P. (1986) 'Incidence of wife abuse in incestuous families.' *Social Work* 31, 138–140.

Tyler Johnson, J. (1992) *Mothers of Incest Survivors: Another Side of the Story*. Bloomington: Indiana University Press.

Vetare, A. and Cooper, J. (2001) 'Working systematically with family violence: risk, responsibility and collaboration.' *Journal of Family Therapy* 23, 4, 378–396.

Victim Support (1992) *Report of a National Inter-agency Working Party on Domestic Violence Convened by Victim Support*. London: Victim Support.

Violence Against Children Study Group (1990) *Taking Child Abuse Seriously*. London: Unwin Hyman.

Wade, A. and Smart, C. (2002) *Facing Family Change: Children's Circumstances, Strategies and Resources*. York: Joseph Rowntree Foundation.

Wagar, J.W. and Rodway, M.R. (1995) 'An evaluation of a group treatment approach for children who have witnessed wife abuse.' *Journal of Family Violence* 10, 295–306.

Walby, S. (2004) *The Cost of Domestic Violence*. London: Department of Trade and Industry.

Walby, S. and Allen, J. (2004) *Domestic Violence, Sexual Assault and Stalking: Findings from the British Crime Survey*. Home Office research study no. 276. London: Home Office.

Walker, L. (1984) *The Battered Woman Syndrome*. New York: Springer Press.

Wallis, M. (1996) 'Outlawing stalkers.' *Policing Today* 2, 4, 25–29.

Weinehall, K. (1997) 'To grow up in the vicinity of violence: young people's stories about domestic violence.' *Akademiska avhandlingar vid Pedagogiska institutionen, Umea universitet* 45, 328–342.

Weinehall, K. (2005) '"Take My Father Away from Home!" Children Growing Up in the Proximity of Violence.' In M. Eriksson, M. Hester, S. Keskinen and K. Pringle (eds) *Tackling Men's Violence in Families: Nordic Issues and Dilemmas*. Bristol: Policy Press.

Westmarland, N., Hester, M. and Reid, P. (2004) *Routine Enquiry about Domestic Violence in GP Practices: A Pilot Study*. Bristol: University of Bristol.

Westra, B.L. and Martin, H.P. (1981) 'Children of battered women.' *Maternal-Child Nursing Journal* 10, 41–51.

Whalen, M. (1996) *Counselling to End Violence against Women: A Subversive Model*. London: Sage.

Wilson, S.K., Cameron, S., Jaffe, P. and Wolfe, D. (1989) 'Children exposed to wife abuse: an intervention model.' *Social Casework* 70, 180–184.

Wolfe, D.A., Jaffe, P., Wilson, S. and Zak, L. (1985) 'Children of battered women: the relation of child behaviour to family violence and maternal stress.' *Journal of Consulting and Clinical Psychology* 53, 5, 657–665.

Wolfe, D.A., Zak, L., Wilson, S. and Jaffe, P. (1986) 'Child witnesses to violence between parents: critical issues in behavioural and social adjustment.' *Journal of Abnormal Child Psychology* 14, 1, 95–104.

Wolfe, D.A., Jaffe, P., Wilson, S. and Zak, L. (1988) 'A Multivariate Investigation of Children's Adjustment to Family Violence.' In G.T. Hotaling, D. Finkelhor, J.T. Kirkpatrick and M.A. Straus (eds) *Family Abuse and Its Consequences: New Directions in Research*. Newbury Park, CA: Sage.

Women's Aid Federation of England (1989) *Breaking Through: Women Surviving Male Violence*. Bristol: Women's Aid Federation of England.

Women's Aid Federation of England (1992) *A Women's Aid Approach to Working with Children*. Bristol: Women's Aid Federation of England.

Women's Aid Federation of England (2000) 'National Research Project on Refuge Support Services 1998–99', unpublished report.

Women's Aid Federation of England (2006) www.womensaid.org.uk (accessed November 2006). Bristol: Women's Aid Federation of England.

Women's Coalition Against Family Violence (1994) *Blood on Whose Hands? The Killing of Women and Children in Domestic Homicides*. Brunswick, Vic.: Women's Coalition Against Family Violence.

Yearnshaw, S. (1997) 'Analysis of Cohort.' In S. Bewley, J. Friend and G. Mezey (eds) *Violence Against Women*. London: Royal College of Obstetricians and Gynaecologists.

SUBJECT INDEX

Page numbers in *italic* indicate boxes or tables.

abuse of children 41–4
  by mothers 177
  'direct' abuse 66–8
  disclosure of 178–82, 192–3
  therapeutic interventions 206
  UK research 47–52
abusers *see* perpetrators
accommodation
  assessing need for 143–4
  priority need for 142–3
  provision of temporary 145–7
  resettlement support 256–7
ACPCs *see* area child protection
  committees
adolescents, effects of violence on
  70–2, 74
advocacy for women 117, 199,
  257–8
age of child, influencing factor
  69–72
alcohol abuse 50–1, 262
allocation schemes, social housing
  148–9
ancillary orders 128
anger management 222–3
anti-discriminatory policies in
  refuges 200
area child protection committees
  (ACPCs) 238–40
Asian children
  impact of violence on 75
  secrecy about violence 81–2
Asian women
  difficulties leaving violent men
  34
  mental health issues 50–1
assessment of need 177–8
assessment of risk 194–5
'associated persons' 124, 142,
  149–50

balance of harm test, occupation
  orders 128
'battered women's syndrome' 31–2
Best Value Performance Indicator
  (BVPI) 156–7
black children
  impact of violence on 74–6
  and resilience 83
black women
  access to services 36
  protection for children 59
  reporting of violence 110

CAFCASS 94–5
Canada
  children disclosing violence
  191–2
  perpetrator programmes 223–4
  primary prevention work
  210–12
  work with children 208
child abuse *see* abuse of children
child contact 24–5, 29, 31, 56–60,
  97, 116, 234–5
Child Protection: Messages from Research
  (DoH) 102
child protection studies 47–52,
  171–2
child protection vs. domestic
  violence, different histories
  168
children
  assessing needs of 177–8
  behavioural difficulties 202–3
  deaths linked to violence 46–7
  'direct' abuse of 42–4, 66–8
  disclosure of violence 189–93
  impact of violence on 63–6
    factors influencing 68–84
  implicated in violence 54–5
  individual work with 204–6
  legislation on safety of 91–105
  and negative fathering 30–1
  and post-separation violence
  56–60
  practice interventions for
  195–209
  preventive work with 209–16
  protecting mothers 192–3
  in refuges 197–200
  resilience of 82–4
  safety of during disclosure
  194–5
  services for 188–9
  survival strategies 79–82
  witnessing violence 44–6, 66–8,
  84–5
Children Act (1989)
  absence of domestic violence in
  91–2
  care and protection orders
  99–100
  case-law precedents 96–7
  and contact arrangements 95–6
  Every Child Matters 103–4
  finding of fact 97–9
  parental responsibility 93–4
  and removing abuser 100–2
  Section 8 guidance 97
  support for children in need
  102–3
  welfare checklist 92–3
Children Act (2004) 91, 104,
  238–9

Children and Families Court
  Advisory Support Service *see*
  CAFCASS
Circular to Chief Constables (1990)
  110
civil law
  advantages/disadvantages of
  using 137
  inadequacy of 121–2
  see also Family Law Act (1996)
  Part IV
Climbié, Victoria, death of 239
Code of Guidance, housing law
  149–53
community safety 112, 244
concealment of violence 81–2,
  182–4, 190
confidentiality issues 194, 250
Conflict Tactics Scale (CTS) 19, 43
contact orders 58, 94–9
coordinated community approaches
  224–5
coping strategies
  of children 79–82
  of women 33–7
counselling for women 259–60
couple counselling 259
court orders 122–3, 128–9
  child contact 58, 94–9
  emergency protection 100–1,
  129, 130
  interim care 100–1
  non-molestation 94–9, 125, 129
  see also occupation orders
Crime and Disorder Act (1997) 112
Crime and Disorder Act (1998) 244
crime reduction partnerships 244
criminal harassment offence 112–14
Criminal Justice Act (1988) 115
criminal law
  advantages/disadvantages of
  using 136
  harassment 112–14
  police powers 111–12
  prosecution process 115–17
Crown Prosecution Service (CPS)
  contact issues 60
  liaison with police 110–11
  procedures 115–17
CTS *see* Conflict Tactics Scale
'cycle of battering' 31–2

Dales, Toni, death of 46, 193
deaths of children, link to domestic
  violence 46–7
disability of children, influencing
  factor 77
disclosure of violence 35
  by children 189–90
    encouraging 190–2
    and fear of child abuse 193–4
    resistance to 81–2

281

AUTHOR INDEX